LAROUSSE

Dictionary of

NORTH
AMERICAN
HISTORY

LAROUSSE

Dictionary of

NORTH AMERICAN HISTORY

Editor
Min Lee

LAROUSSE

LAROUSSE
Larousse plc
43–45 Annandale Street, Edinburgh EH7 4AZ
Larousse Kingfisher Chambers Inc.
95 Madison Avenue, New York, New York 10016

First published by Larousse plc 1994

10 9 8 7 6 5 4 3

Copyright © Larousse plc 1994

British Library Cataloguing in Publication Data
for this book is available from the British Library

Library of Congress Cataloging in Publication Data
for this book is available from The Library of Congress

ISBN 0-7523-0005-9

Cover design: Paul Wilkinson, Larousse plc

Typeset from author-generated disks by BPC Digital Data Ltd
Printed in Great Britain by Clays Ltd, St Ives plc

Preface

This book provides a concise overview of the history of North America. It is based on the work compiled by the extensive team of contributors and consultants for the *Dictionary of World History*, and has been updated and added to where appropriate. Like that work, it concentrates on the main diplomatic, military and political, rather than the cultural and social, landmarks. The selection of events and people has been made on the basis of the influence which they have exerted on North American history; thus Santa Anna and Ho Chi Minh feature in these pages along with Washington and Kennedy.

Reference to the information contained here will be swift and easy, because all articles follow a strict alphabetical order. Within an article, the highlighting of a word or phrase in bold type indicates that a full reference to it can be found elsewhere in the book. The presence of additional information on any topic is indicated by the symbol ▷ at the end of each entry.

The strength of a small book such as this lies both in the accuracy and relevance of each short entry, and in its careful and accurate cross referencing. For the first stage I thank the contributors, and for the second the two editors, Angela Cran and Alison Jones, who have endlessly searched the editorial database.

Min Lee
June 1994

Acknowledgements

Grateful acknowledgements are due to all contributors and consultants to *Dictionary of World History* and especially to Bruce Lenman the Consultant Editor and Katharine Boyd the Managing Editor of that title.

A

Abernathy, Ralph (1926–90)
US civil rights leader. A Baptist minister, he became chief aide to Martin Luther **King**, Jr, and helped organize the boycott of buses by the black community in Montgomery in 1955. He assumed the presidency of the **SCLC** (Southern Christian Leadership Conference) after King was assassinated in 1968 and continued in that post until his resignation in 1977. ▷ **civil rights movement; Parks, Rosa Lee**

abolitionism
A 19c movement to end slavery in the US South, it was distinguished from earlier anti-slavery movements by its uncompromising attitude. It crystallized around the American Anti-Slavery Society, founded in 1833, and made slavery an issue that could not be ignored. Blacks as well as whites, and women as well as men, actively participated in the movement. ▷ **Douglass, Frederick; Garrison, William Lloyd; Howe, Julia Ward**

Abraham, Plains/Heights of, Battle of (1759)
The site of a battle in Quebec City, Canada, in which British forces under **James Wolfe** defeated a French/Canadian force under **Montcalm** and **Vaudreuil**, and gained control over Quebec. Wolfe and Montcalm were both killed in the battle.

Acadia
Part of France's American empire; what is today Prince Edward Island, Nova Scotia, New Brunswick, and the mainland coast from the Gulf of St Lawrence to Maine. The first settlement was established at Port Royal in 1605 by the sieur de Monts, and the area was exchanged between France and England until the Treaty of Utrecht (1713) handed most of Acadia to Britain. In 1755 10 000 Acadians were evicted from the territory for resolving to pursue a policy of neutrality in the conflicts between France and Britain. The last French stronghold, Louisbourg, fell in 1758. ▷ **New France**

Acheson, Dean Gooderham (1893–1971)
US lawyer and politician. Educated at Yale and Harvard, he was Under-Secretary (1945–7) and then Secretary of State (1949–53) in the Truman administration. He developed US policy for the containment of **communism**, helped to formulate the **Marshall Plan** (1947–8) and participated in the establishment of **NATO** (1949).

Adams, Charles Francis (1807–86)
US diplomat. The son of John Quincy **Adams**, he studied at Harvard, was admitted to the Bar (1828), and became a representative from Massachusetts (1858–61). As Minister to Britain (1861–8), he strove to maintain British neutrality during the **American Civil War**.

Adams, John (1735–1826)
US politician and 2nd President. Educated at Harvard, and admitted to the Bar in 1758, he emerged as a leader of US resistance to Britain's imposition of the **Stamp Act** (1765), and led the debate that resulted in the **Declaration of Independence**. He served in Congress until 1777, after which he had an extensive diplomatic career in Europe. He took part in negotiating a peace treaty with Great Britain, and served as Minister to Great Britain (1785–8). He became the first US Vice-President, under George **Washington** (1789), an office he found frustrating. Both were re-elected in 1792, and in 1796 Adams was elected President with Thomas **Jefferson** as Vice-President. Adams's presidency was marked by factionalism within his cabinet and his party, especially over the issue of war with France. Adams opposed a war, which made him an unpopular president, and he was defeated by Jefferson on seeking re-election in 1800. He retired to his home at Quincy, where he died. ▷ **Federalist Party**

Adams, John Quincy (1767–1848)
US politician and 6th President. The son of John **Adams**, he studied at Harvard, and was admitted to the Bar in 1790. He had an extensive and brilliant diplomatic career between 1794 and 1817, except when he served in the US Senate (1803–8). As Secretary of State under James **Monroe**, he negotiated with Spain the treaty for the acquisition of Florida, and played an important part in the formulation of the **Monroe Doctrine**. As President

(1825–9), he failed to establish a strong base of public and political support and was therefore frustrated by executive and congressional factionalism. After his defeat by Andrew **Jackson** in 1828, he was elected to the House of Representatives, where through the 1830s and 1840s he became a strong opponent of the extension of slavery.

Adams, Samuel (1722–1803)
American revolutionary political leader. Educated at Harvard, he became Lieutenant-Governor (1789–94) and Governor (1794–7) of Massachusetts. He was a strong supporter of revolution against Britain, and helped to plan the **Boston Tea Party**. Adams was a member of the **Continental Congress** (1774–81) and one of the signatories of the **Declaration of Independence**. ▷ **American Revolution**

Addams, Jane (1860–1935)
US social reformer. She founded the first US settlement house, Hull House in Chicago, dedicated to settlement work among the immigrant poor, where she made her home. Addams worked to secure social justice by sponsoring legislation relating to housing, factory inspection, female suffrage and the cause of pacifism. She also campaigned for the abolition of child labour and the recognition of labour unions. Many of these reforms were adopted by the Progressive Party as part of its platform in 1912; Addams seconded Theodore **Roosevelt**'s nomination for President and was an active campaigner on his behalf. In 1931 she shared the Nobel Peace Prize, awarded in recognition of her efforts to end hostilities in **World War I**. ▷ **progressivism**

affirmative action
The name given to US policies requiring businesses and other institutions to enact employment practices concerning minorities ranging from the employment and promotion of ethnic minorities and women, to the setting of employment quotas. Such policies were established in the early 1970s to counteract discrimination in the past, but have been challenged in recent times as 'reverse discrimination'.

AFL–CIO (American Federation of Labor and Congress of Industrial Organizations)
A federation of labour unions in the US, Canada, Mexico, Panama and US dependencies, formed in 1955 from the merger of

the AFL (mainly craft unions, founded in 1886) with the CIO (mainly industrial workers' unions, founded in 1935). Its aims include educational campaigns on behalf of the labour movement, the settlement of disputes among affiliates, and political support for beneficial legislation. ▷ **Lewis, John L; United Automobile Workers**

Agnew, Spiro Theodore (1918–)
US politician. The son of a Greek immigrant, after service in **World War II** he studied law at the University of Maryland. In 1966 he was elected Governor of Maryland on a liberal platform, supporting anti-discrimination and anti-poverty legislation, but by 1968 he had become considerably more conservative. As a compromise figure acceptable to many in the Republican party, he became Richard **Nixon**'s running mate in the 1968 election, and took office as Vice-President in 1969. He resigned in 1973 after charges of corruption during his years in Maryland politics were brought against him. ▷ **Republican Party**

Alabama Claims (1869–72)
A diplomatic dispute in which the USA held Britain accountable for damage inflicted to the Union during the **American Civil War** by Confederate naval vessels (the *Alabama*, *Florida* and *Shenandoah*) built in Britain. The dispute was resolved in 1872 when an international tribunal (Italy, Switzerland and Brazil), ruled that Britain should pay an indemnity to the USA of US$15 500 000. ▷ **Washington, Treaty of**

Alamán, Lucas (1792–1853)
Mexican politician and historian. The intellectual father of Mexican conservatism, his views were shaped by the wrecking of Guanajuato (his birthplace) in **Hidalgo (y Costilla)**'s revolt in 1810, and his training as a mining engineer. Repelled by the aftermath of the Riego Revolt in Spain (1820), he argued that monarchical rule would provide stability for an independent Mexico. After independence (1821), he negotiated with the Vatican and France to set up a Mexican royal house. Minister of State under **Iturbide**, and Foreign Minister and Minister of State for Anastasio Bustamante and **Santa Anna**, he was a friend of the Church and writer of the monumental, and still readable, *Historia de México*.

Alamo, The

A fortified mission in San Antonio, Texas, held in 1836 during the Texas War of Independence against Mexico. In a heroic act of resistance, some 180 Texans defended the Alamo for 12 days against several thousand Mexicans, until the last survivors were overwhelmed. ▷ **Mexican War**

Alaska, Sale of (1867)

Tsarist Russian interests in Alaska were sold to the USA for $7 million, a price which seemed so high at the time that the Tsarist government had to spend a large sum of money influencing both members of Congress and influential newspapers. Russian efforts to establish a position on both sides of the North Pacific had begun more than a century before. However, defeat in the Crimean War and the acquisition of the Amur Basin from China by the Treaty of **Beijing** (1860) made Alexander II decide to concentrate on the north-west Pacific. Once the **American Civil War** was over, Secretary of State William Seward was quick to realize the long-term strategic and economic value of Alaska both for the continental USA and for its expansion into the Pacific.

Albany Congress (1754)

A meeting in Albany, New York, of representatives from seven British colonies in North America at which Benjamin Franklin proposed his 'plan of union' to unite the separate American British colonies. The Albany Plan of Union was rejected by the Colonial governments and the Crown. However, the plan served as a model for the joint action of the mainland colonies in the **American Revolution**.

Albany Regency

A group of Democrats organized (c.1817) by Martin **Van Buren** to run New York while he served in the US Senate in Washington. Situated in Albany, New York, which he had established as his power base, the Regency was one of the first effective political machines using the **spoils system** to fill public office, and influenced the future development of US political parties.

Alden, John (?1599–1687)

English colonist. He sailed with the *Mayflower* in 1620, and settled initially in Plymouth. One of the founders of Duxbury in 1631, he served as assistant to the Governor of Massachusetts (1633–41, 1650–86), and was twice Deputy Governor (1664–5, 1677). He features in Henry Wadsworth Longfellow's poem 'The Courtship of Miles Standish'.

Alexander, William (1577–1640)

Scottish statesman, poet and scholar. Having gained the patronage of King James VI of Scotland and I of England through his poetry and his kinship to the Earl of Argyll, he gained the King's support for his aim of acquiring a colony for Scotland, along the lines of **New France** and New England. He was granted (1621) the proprietorship of Nova Scotia ('New Scotland'), the three Atlantic provinces and the Gaspé peninsula. The last was claimed also by the French, and the renewal of their claim eventually led to the failure of his ambitions. Alexander's major problem was to find Scots willing to settle in the colony, and James sought to help him by the promise of hereditary baronetcies and territory in the colony to Scots who would support a number of settlers. However, this measure failed under both James and his son, Charles I. In 1631 Alexander was commanded to yield Port-Royal to the French, after a challenge from Richelieu's Company of One **Hundred Associates**. He died with his dream unfulfilled, surrounded by creditors.

Alger, Horatio (1834–99)

US author and proponent of the 'rags to riches' myth. The son of a Unitarian minister, he also trained as a minister but resigned in 1866. His novels (eg *Ragged Dick* (1867), *Luck and Pluck* (1869) and *Tattered Tom* (1871)) about poor boys who made good, inspired thousands of rural poor to move to cities in search of opportunity. He helped prepare the presidential campaign literature for James A **Garfield**, portraying him as a poor boy born in a log cabin.

Algonquin

A small group of Native Americans speaking Algonquian languages and living along the Ottawa River in Canada. They were allied with the French during the **French and Indian War**, and most were killed by the Iroquois. The few remaining Algonquin live near Quebec and Ontario.

Alien and Sedition Acts (1798)
Four US laws passed by a Federalist-controlled Congress intended to restrain the political opposition, at a time of crisis in US relations with the warring powers of Europe. The Alien Acts delayed citizenship and gave the President great power over foreigners, while the Sedition Act authorized fining and imprisonment for public criticism of the government. ▷ **Kentucky and Virginia Resolutions**

Allan, Sir Hugh (1810–82)
Canadian entrepreneur. He emigrated to Montreal in 1826, became partner in an ocean-going shipping line and by 1859 was one of the wealthiest men in the province. His relationship with Conservative politicians enabled him to win back the contract to deepen the St Lawrence in 1854. In 1862 the British Secretary for War accused him of charging excessive fares, and causing the death of many immigrants. He was also charged with bribery in the Pacific Scandal of 1873 which brought down the Conservative government. In return for donating campaign funds to the party, he had hoped to receive the charter for building the **Canadian Pacific Railway**.

Allen, Ethan (1738–89)
American soldier, revolutionary leader and writer. Allen distinguished himself early in the Revolutionary War when he led Vermont's **Green Mountain Boys** in the capture of Fort Ticonderoga from the British (10 May 1775). He then assisted in an effort to capture Montreal, but was himself captured. He returned to Vermont and continued to campaign for its independence. ▷ **American Revolution**

Alliance for Progress
A 10-year programme (1961–71) of modernization and reform for 22 countries in Latin America, sponsored by the US government in reaction to the advent of Fidel **Castro**'s Cuba and Kubitschek (de Oliveira)'s abortive 'Operation Pan American' initiative. However, it fell foul of the Kennedy administration's **Cold War** impulse and its partiality for orthodox economic policies, and few of its aims were achieved. ▷ **Kennedy, John F**

America First Committee

Political organization (1940–41) opposing US involvement on behalf of the Allies in **World War II**. The committee attracted support from many conservatives fearing costly military commitment as well as pro-Nazi sympathizers, and the renowned aviator Charles **Lindbergh** was a chief spokesman. It campaigned unsuccessfully against the **Lend-Lease Agreement** and the repeal of the **Neutrality Acts**, but its propaganda was undoubtedly effective in the early years of the war. After the Japanese attack on **Pearl Harbor** (7 Dec 1941), however, the committee ended its activities, urging its members to support the war effort.

American Civil Liberties Union (ACLU)

US legal defence association founded to protect the constitutional rights of free speech, privacy and equal protection under the law. The ACLU board selects areas where **civil rights** and liberties are under threat and provides legal assistance and expenses for litigants in its test cases. In its early days the ACLU provided the defence counsel in the **Sacco and Vanzetti Affair** and the Scopes Monkey Trial. During **World War II** it protested against the internment of the **Nisei** and in the post-war years acted on behalf of many harassed by McCarthyism and subjected to blacklisting. Throughout its existence it has been associated with unpopular political causes and has won cases concerning academic freedom, labour/business relations and civil rights. ▷ **Darrow, Clarence; McCarthy, Joseph**

American Civil War (1861–5)

A conflict between Northern states (the Union) and Southern states that had seceded (the Confederacy). The causes of the war included disagreement over slavery (which by then existed only in the South) and conflict over how much control the federal government should exert over the states (states' rights). The election in 1860 of Abraham **Lincoln**, who was hostile to slavery and opposed its extension to new territories (although he did not believe at first that he could interfere with it where it already existed) precipitated the conflict. South Carolina seceded almost at once from the Union, followed within a short time by 10 other states. These 11 states formed the Confederacy early in 1861. War broke out on 12 Apr 1861, when Southern forces opened fire on **Fort Sumter**, South Carolina, and took possession of the fort. Most of the Civil War battles were fought in the South, and the

Confederacy won some early victories, particularly at **Bull Run** and **Fredericksburg** and in the **Peninsular Campaign**. But **Antietam** (1862) was a victory for the North. Shortly after Antietam, President Lincoln signed the **Emancipation Proclamation** freeing all slaves in the Confederacy. This further reduced the available manpower in the South and as the war continued, the Union, with its far greater manpower and industrial resources, gradually began to prevail. The Battle of **Vicksburg** in 1863 was a major victory, and the Battle of Gettysburg, followed by Lincoln's **Gettysburg Address**, marked a turning point in the war. By 1864, Union forces captured Atlanta and completed a march of destruction through Georgia to the sea. The war ended on 9 Apr 1865, when Confederate General Robert E **Lee** surrendered to Ulysses S **Grant** at **Appomattox Court House**. At enormous cost of life, the war had succeeded in keeping the Union together and in bringing an end to slavery in the USA.

American Colonization Society
A US group founded in 1816 whose goal was to resettle freed slaves in Africa. By 1860, 11 000 former slaves had been transported to Liberia. The society was attacked by abolitionists but supported by some slaveholders anxious to keep freed blacks separate from slaves. It was dissolved in 1912. ▷ **abolitionism**

American Legion
An association in the USA for former members of the armed forces (veterans) of **World War I** and **World War II**, the **Korean War** and the **Vietnam War**. It is the largest such organization in the world. Incorporated in 1919, its aims are to rehabilitate veterans, promote child welfare, ensure a strong national defence, and encourage patriotism.

American Revolution (1775–83)
The war that established the 13 American colonies as independent from Britain, often called the American War of Independence. In the years 1763 to 1775 relations between the North American colonies and Britain became increasingly strained as Britain began taking measures to tighten control over the colonies. Colonial resistance was especially high over the issue of whether the British parliament had the right to tax the colonies without their representation. Anti-British sentiment was more organized in the major port towns, with considerable support coming from the

elected assemblies. The tension during this period was reflected in the **Stamp Act** crisis (1765–6), resistance to the **Townshend Acts** (1767–70), the **Boston Massacre** (1770), the burning of the customs cruiser *Gaspée* (1772), and the **Boston Tea Party** (1773). The British Parliament's passage of the **Intolerable Acts** (1774) to punish Massachusetts for the Tea Party led to the calling of the First **Continental Congress** (1774). In Apr 1775 fighting broke out between British troops and the colonial militia known as the **Minutemen** at the Battles of **Lexington and Concord** in Massachusetts. Other military engagements followed, including the colonial capture of Fort Ticonderoga (May 1775), the Battle of **Bunker Hill**, and the unsuccessful colonial expedition in Quebec, Canada. In June 1775 the Second Continental Congress elected George **Washington** to command the Continental Army and in July adopted the **Declaration of Independence**. Following the British evacuation of Boston in May 1776, the main theatre shifted to New York, New Jersey and Pennsylvania. Washington's troops suffered a number of defeats in the New York area, including the Battle of Long Island (Aug 1776), but his surprise attacks at Trenton (25 Dec 1776) and Princeton (Jan 1777), New Jersey, though small victories, did much to reinvigorate the colonial cause. In the Battle of Brandywine (Sep 1777) in Pennsylvania, however, Washington's troops were once again defeated. In June 1777 British troops had begun to move down from Canada and at first seemed assured of victory, but shrewd American manoeuvring resulted in defeat of the British and the surrender of **Burgoyne** following the Battle of Saratoga in upstate New York. This American triumph convinced the French to enter the war officially, bringing to the colonists badly needed material support, troops, monetary credit and a fleet. During the winter of 1778 Washington's troops suffered great hardship while wintering in **Valley Forge**. By the spring the colonial forces had regathered their strength and Washington's men made a good showing at the Battle of **Monmouth** (June). Later that year fighting shifted southward, when Sir Henry Clinton commanded an invasion of South Carolina. Clinton's successor, Lord **Cornwallis**, led the army gradually north until Washington and the French Admiral de Grasse trapped him on the Yorktown Peninsula in Virginia, where he surrendered in 1781. The defeat resulted in the fall of the British Prime Minister, Lord North, who had prosecuted the war, and ended British will for further fighting. After almost two years of negotiating, the Treaty of Paris was signed in Sep 1783, recognizing the independence of the USA. The revolution had an impact felt far beyond the battlefield. Although support had not been universal — many loyalists fled at the war's end and became the core of English-speaking Canada — the various coalitions uniting entrepreneurs, professionals, planters, farmers and urban working people had given form to the most advanced political hopes of their time. The newly created republic was an institution that political thinkers of the day had doubted was capable of governing a large area or of even surviving at all. The new country, founded by a democratic movement and based on an ideology of 'equal rights', opened the way for the long-term decline of monarchy in the rest of the world. ▷ **Camden, Battle of; Charleston, Battles of; Committees of Correspondence; Connecticut Compromise; Constitutional Convention; Cowpens, Battle of; Gaspée; Green Mountain Boys; Sons of Liberty; Sugar Act; Yorktown Campaign**

Amish

US pietistic sect. Founded in Berne, Switzerland, around 1693 by Jacob Amman, a conservative Mennonite preacher, the Amish gained some adherents in the Palatinate and Alsace-Lorraine, and began to emigrate to America in 1727. Like earlier Mennonite emigrants attracted to Pennsylvania by the promise of toleration and the prospect of withdrawal from the secular world, a group of about 500 settled in Berks and Lancaster counties. From the 1740s larger numbers followed, settling in New York State, Ohio, Indiana and Illinois. Their perpetuation within US society has been secured by forbidding the use of modern technological developments especially in communication and transport. The Amish now number about 80 000, mostly dependent on non-mechanized farming for their livelihood and living in rural communities, where their horse-drawn buggies, characteristic clothing (still using hooks and eyes rather than buttons) and German dialect are the most obvious indications of their presence. Always resistant to institutionalization, they have consistently refused to establish churches or colleges, and they educate their own children, a practice supported by a 1972 Supreme Court decision. Together with the **Mennonites** they represent the last vestiges of Reformation anabaptism in the modern world.

Anabaptists (Rebaptizers)

The collective name given to various groups of believers on the radical wing of the 16c Reformation committed to the baptism of

11

believing adults only. They emphasized adherence to the word of scripture and strict Church discipline as ranking higher than the law of the state, which made them liable to much harassment and persecution, and the movement was all but stamped out. Some followers were able to regroup under the name of **Mennonites**, while modern-day Baptists can be considered a more distant off-shoot.

Annapolis Convention (1786)
In the **American Revolution**, a gathering at Annapolis, Maryland, of delegates from five states to discuss commercial problems. The main result was a call for a meeting the following year to consider changes in the **Articles of Confederation**. That meeting wrote the present Federal Constitution. ▷ **Constitutional Convention; US Constitution**

Annexation Manifesto (1849)
A Canadian proposal (produced chiefly by Montreal **Tories**, A T **Galt** among them, and some **Rouges**), which argued that annexation to the USA was preferable to the proposed union of the colonies. Since the ending of colonial preference, Canadian trading problems had become very severe, and with the repeal of the **Navigation Acts** it looked as if the colonies were being abandoned. Annexation would raise farm prices, lower import costs, and make US capital available for industrial development. The reaction to the proposal was disappointing for the signatories: not only were the French thoroughly opposed, but the USA showed little interest.

Anthony, Susan Brownell (1820–1906)
US reformer and champion of women's rights. After teaching and pursuing temperance work, she was instrumental in the passage of the Women's Property Rights Act (1860). From 1869 she was a leader of the National Woman Suffrage Association, becoming President of the US branch in 1892. ▷ **National American Woman Suffrage Association**

Antietam, Battle of (16–17 Sep 1862)
A battle of the **American Civil War** (also known as the Battle of Sharpsburg), fought in Maryland. In military terms the North won a technical victory, but both McClellan's and Robert E **Lee's**

troops suffered huge casualties. The Union cause gained enough credibility to allow President **Lincoln** to issue his preliminary **Emancipation Proclamation**. ▷ **Confederate States of America**

Anti-Masonic Party (1830–6)

US political party. Dedicated to driving Freemasons out of public life, it arose from the highly publicized disappearance (1826) of the author of a book revealing Masonic secrets. It was the first 'third party' in the USA, nominating a presidential candidate in 1832 at the first national party convention.

Anti-Saloon League

US organization. Established in 1893, its aim was to end the use of alcohol by state and local anti-alcohol laws and by amending the **US Constitution**. The League remained in existence during and after the **Prohibition** period, and became part of the National Temperance League in 1950.

Anti-Trust Acts

US legislation passed to control the development of monopoly capitalism. The Sherman Act (1890) forbade all combinations 'in restraint of trade'. Ambiguities in wording led to its use against labour unions instead of corporations, or trusts. The Clayton Act (1914) was intended to clear up the ambiguities and make enforcement easier.

Anzio Landing (22–3 Jan 1944)

Landing by 50 000 US and British troops during **World War II** at a small port 60 miles behind the German defences of the so-called Gustav Line. Although the Germans were taken by surprise, they were able to confine the Allied troops and prevent them from using Anzio as a bridgehead. In late May the forces at Anzio eventually made contact with the advancing troops of General Alexander who had overrun the Gustav Line.

ANZUS (1951)

An acronym for the treaty concluded between **A**ustralia, **N**ew **Z**ealand, and the **U**nited **S**tates for mutual security in the Pacific against armed attack. The treaty encompasses not only the metropolitan territories of the three, but also island territories under their jurisdiction, their armed forces, and their aircraft and shipping. New Zealand participation lapsed in 1985, following that country's refusal to admit US nuclear-powered warships to its waters.

Apache
A Native American people. Members of the Athapascan linguistic group, they originally migrated from Canada, and settled in the south-western USA. During the 19c their fierce warriors dominated the region, leading raids against both Native American and white settlements. They proved formidable opponents of the US army when from 1861, led by **Cochise** and **Geronimo**, they fought against federal troops in the Apache Wars. Following their defeat in 1886, they were assigned to reservations in Arizona and New Mexico. ▷ **Native Americans; Indian Wars**

Apollo-Soyuz Project
A landmark joint space mission conducted by the USA and USSR in July 1975, following an agreement signed by President Richard **Nixon** and Premier Alexei Kosygin in May 1972. A project of the period of US–Soviet **détente**, Apollo-Soyuz also demonstrated the capability for joint operations between the major space powers and, as such, the potential for on-orbit emergency rescue missions. The rendezvous (17 July 1975) lasted nearly two days. The crews (T Stafford, V Brand, D Slayton and A Leonov, V Kubasov) conducted a series of joint experiments. A special adaptor docking module was constructed for the mission.

Appomattox Court House
The site in Virginia, USA, of the surrender (9 Apr 1865) of the Confederate Army under Robert E **Lee** to Union forces under Ulysses S **Grant**. Although a few Confederates remained under arms, the surrender marked the effective end of the **American Civil War**.

Arnhem, Battle of (Sep 1944)
Major conflict in occupied Dutch territory towards the end of **World War II**, in which the German forces thwarted Allied attempts to break through. Operation 'Market Garden' was designed by Field Marshal **Montgomery**, and involved the largest airlift operation of the war, parachuting 10 000 troops on 17 Sep

1944 into the Dutch rivers area, to take key bridges over the Rhine, Maas and Waal. Allied forces advanced to Nijmegen, but at Arnhem met the 9th and 10th German Panzer divisions, which successfully resisted attack and eventually forced an Allied withdrawal on 25 Sep to behind the Rhine River.

Arnold, Benedict (1741–1801)

US general and turncoat. In the **American Revolution** he joined the colonial forces, and for his gallantry at the siege of Quebec (1775) was made a brigadier-general. He also fought with distinction at the Battles of Ridgefield and **Saratoga**, and in 1778 was placed in command of Philadelphia. His resentment at being passed over for promotion, followed by his marriage to a woman of loyalist sympathies, led him to conspire with John André to deliver West Point to the British. When the plan was detected and André was captured, Arnold fled behind British lines, and was given a command in the royal army. After the war he lived in obscurity in London, where he died.

Arthur, Chester Alan (1830–86)

US politician and 21st President. He qualified in law, and then became leader of the **Republican Party** in New York State. He was Vice-President when James A **Garfield** became President (1881), and succeeded him on his death, holding the presidency from 1881 until 1885. During his administration he supported civil service and vetoed a Chinese exclusion bill.

Articles of Confederation

The constitution of the USA from 1781 to 1788. Prepared by the **Continental Congress**, it established a single-house Congress, with one vote for each state and with no executive, courts, or independent revenue. Its weaknesses led to its replacement by the present **US Constitution** in 1788.

Astor, John Jacob (1763–1848)

German-born US millionaire. The son of a butcher, he emigrated to the USA in 1783 and eventually became the wealthiest man in America, worth more than US$20m at his death. His first fortune was made through the Western fur trade, the second in New York real estate. Astor used his friendship with **Jefferson** to advantage, in one instance gaining permission for one of his ships to sail to

Canton during the 1807 embargo. Astor helped the government finance the **War of 1812** by taking over and selling to the public the unsubscribed portion of a government loan. He also used his influence to ease through **Congress** the Act establishing the Second Bank of United States. His major philanthropy was the endowment of the Astor Library, now the New York Public Library.

Atlantic Charter (Aug 1941)
A declaration of principles to govern the national policies issued by US President Franklin D **Roosevelt** and British Prime Minister Winston Churchill after a secret meeting off the Newfoundland coast. Echoing Woodrow **Wilson**'s **Fourteen Points**, and the **Four Freedoms** of Roosevelt's Jan 1941 State of the Union Address, the charter called for the rights of self-determination, self-government and free speech for all peoples, promised a more equitable international economic system, and called for the abandonment of the use of force, pending the establishment of a system of general security. After the entry of the USA into the war, the charter was endorsed internationally by the inclusion of its provisions in the Declaration of the United Nations signed by the USA, Great Britain, the USSR and China, on 1 Jan 1942, and by 22 other states on the following day. It served as an ideological basis for Allied cooperation during the war. ▷ **World War II**

Attucks, Crispus (?1723–70)
American patriot, one of the leaders of the protestors in the **Boston Massacre**. He is thought to have been a runaway slave. He was one of the five victims killed by British soldiers on 5 Mar 1770.

Austin, Stephen Fuller (1793–1836)
American pioneer. He colonized Texas in 1822. He was imprisoned in 1833 for his attempts to encourage the separation of Texas from Mexico. After his release, he served for a short time as Secretary of State in the new Republic of Texas (1836).

Axis Powers
The name given to the cooperation of Nazi Germany and Fascist Italy (1936–45), first used by Mussolini. In May 1939 the two countries signed a formal treaty, the 'Pact of Steel'. In Sep 1940, Germany, Italy and Japan signed a tripartite agreement, after which all three were referred to as Axis Powers. ▷ **World War II**

Aztecs

The most powerful people of Mesoamerica during the 15–16c. Their main city, Tenochtitlán (present-day Mexico City), near Lake Texcoco, became the most densely populated city of the region. They built up a great and powerful despotic state, with a strong military force, subjugating nearly all the people of central Mexico, and eventually ruling 400–500 small tribute-paying states (probably 5–6 million people), which provided them with raw materials and produce. People captured in wars were offered as human sacrifice to the Aztec gods. The Aztecs were famous for their agriculture, cultivating all available land, introducing irrigation, draining swamps, and creating artificial islands in the lakes. Their best-known ruler was **Montezuma II**. They developed a form of hieroglyphic writing, a complex calendar system, and built famous pyramids and temples. The Aztec empire was finally destroyed by the Spanish under **Cortés** in 1521.

B

Bacon's Rebellion (1675–6)
A rising against the royal governor in the American colony of Virginia, rooted in a conflict between small frontier farmers and the indigenous Native Americans. The rebellion reflected the rift between the western farmers and the eastern aristocracy represented by the colonial government. When Governor Berkeley, perhaps protecting trading interests with the Native Americans, failed to respond to an attack by some of them against western settlers, Nathaniel Bacon led a misguided reprisal against innocent Native Americans. In 1676 Berkeley sought to bring the farmers to trial, but the opposition escalated, resulting in the burning of **Jamestown**. After Bacon's death, the rebellion collapsed.

Bagley, Sarah (fl.1835–47)
US labour leader. She was active in the mills of Lowell, Massachusetts, where she led 'turn-outs' (strikes) and organized the Female Labor Reform Association. Bagley played a major role in the successful campaign for a 10-hour working day in Massachusetts.

Bagot, Sir Charles (1781–1843)
British diplomat and Governor-General of Canada. On taking office in 1842, he was advised by the British Colonial Secretary to depend on the **Family Compact**. However he discovered that 'you cannot rule Canada without the French', and that the **Durham–Sydenham** programme of anglicization was causing great resentment amongst the French Canadians. He therefore appointed as advisers Louis H **Lafontaine** and Robert **Baldwin**, and invariably listened to their advice. Since these two men held a majority in the Assembly, this almost amounted to ministerial government or collective responsibility, but Bagot still retained the ultimate decision-making power. In 1843 a fatal illness forced him to resign.

Baker, James Addison (1930–)
US public official. He was educated at Princeton and the University of Texas. Baker served President Ford as Under-Secretary of Commerce, and President **Reagan** as White House Chief of Staff (1981–5) and Secretary of the Treasury (1985–8) before resigning to manage George **Bush**'s campaign for the presidency. After winning the election, Bush made him Secretary of State.

Baker v Carr (1962)
The US Supreme Court decision that state electoral districts must contain approximately the same voting population, bringing to an end the long-standing rural domination of state legislatures.

Bakke v Regents of the University of California (1978)
The US Supreme Court decision that universities could not set explicit quotas for racial minorities and thus exclude white applicants who might be better qualified. The controversial decision did however allow that race could be considered a factor in deciding admissions.

Baldwin, Robert (1804–58)
Canadian lawyer and politician. He was the leader of the **Canada West** reforming clique who formed a coalition with Louis H **Lafontaine** to establish a reform party, which became a precursor of the **Liberal Party**. With his father, William Baldwin, he devised the theory of **Responsible Government**. This was rejected initially by the British government and governors such as Sir Francis Bond **Head** and Sir Charles **Metcalfe**, although Sir Charles **Bagot** accepted a level of participation by the Executive Council in government. Metcalfe's autocratic government led both Baldwin and Lafontaine to resign. In 1848 Baldwin came into power again as a partner with Lafontaine in the 'Great Ministry', during the period of transition from colonial rule to self-government.

Baltimore and Ohio Railroad
The first US passenger-carrying railroad. Its foundation stone was laid on 4 July 1828 by the last surviving signatory of the **Declaration of Independence**. In 1830 its first section was opened, running horse-powered vehicles over the 13 miles from Baltimore to Ellicott's Mills. Later that year the railroad turned to steam after Peter Cooper's Tom Thumb covered the distance in one

hour. By the Civil War the system had become a major element in the transportation links between the mid-west and the east coast.

Baltimore Incident (1891)

A brief but serious dispute between the USA and Chile, stemming from the death of two US sailors from the cruiser *Baltimore* in a brawl in Valparaiso. A war between the two countries was averted by a Chilean apology.

Bancroft, George (1800–91)

US historian and politician. Educated at Harvard, and an ardent Democrat, he is best known for his monumental and intensely patriotic *History of the United States* (1834). He served as US minister in London and Berlin. ▷ **Democratic Party**

Bank War (1832)

An anti-national bank policy adopted by US President Andrew **Jackson**, when he vetoed the re-charter of the Second Bank of the United States which had been passed through Congress under the patronage of the **National Republican Party**. Like many Americans, especially in the West, Jackson believed that the bank had been responsible for the depression of the 1820s. He accused the bank of being a monopoly and representing big business, of allowing foreigners too much influence, of showing favour to congressmen, and of having too much power over state banks. Jackson refused, against the advice of two Secretaries of the Treasury, to allow any more federal revenues to be deposited with the bank, placing them instead with favoured state banks. Flush with new deposits and without the restraints which the national Bank had placed on their activities, the state banks encouraged another speculative boom which collapsed in the Panic of 1837, after Jackson had been succeeded by Martin **Van Buren**.

Barnburners

A faction within the US **Democratic Party** in New York State (1843–50), which arose through opposition to extending **slavery** into western territory conquered during the **Mexican War**. Many Barnburners, led by former President **Van Buren**, joined the **Free-Soil Party** in 1848. Their name derived from the story of a Dutch farmer who burned down his barn (the Democratic Party) in order to drive out rats (slavery).

Barton, Clara (Clarissa Harlowe) (1821–1912)
US humanitarian and founder of the American Red Cross. A schoolteacher (1836–54) and clerk in the Patent Office in Washington DC (1854–7), during the **American Civil War** she organized the distribution of hospital supplies and nursed the wounded, becoming known as the 'Angel of the battlefield'. She worked for the International Red Cross in Europe during the Franco-Prussian War (1870–1). After returning to the USA she established the US branch of the Red Cross in 1881 and became its first President (1881–1904). As a result of her campaigning, in 1882 the USA signed the Geneva Convention for the humane treatment of the wounded and prisoners of war.

Baruch, Bernard Mannes (1870–1965)
US financier. In 1918 he was appointed by President Woodrow **Wilson** to head the War Industries Board, with sweeping powers to establish priorities and increase production. His appointment symbolized a new alliance between a Democratic administration which had previously acted against the excesses of big business, and industry which now wished to combine patriotism with its own interests. A conservative Democrat and supporter of Al **Smith**, Baruch was one of the few speculators who anticipated the **Wall Street Crash** and so preserved his fortune. Often critical of the more radical aspects of the **New Deal**, he nevertheless frequently advised President Franklin D **Roosevelt**. In 1946 he presented the US plan for atomic energy control to the UN.

Batista (y Zaldívar), Fulgencio (1901–73)
Cuban dictator. In 1933 he organized a military coup (the 'Sergeants' Revolt'), consolidated his power, and became President (1940–4). In 1952 he overthrew President Prio Socorras, and ruled as dictator until his overthrow by Fidel **Castro** (Jan 1959), when he found refuge in the Dominican Republic.

Bay of Pigs (Apr 1961)
The failed invasion of Cuba by anti-**Castro** Cuban exiles sponsored by the USA. The invasion force of 1 500 men landed at Bahía de Cochinos ('Bay of Pigs') on the southern coast, but failed

to win local support and was rapidly overwhelmed and defeated by Cuban troops. The episode was an embarrassment to John F **Kennedy**'s administration.

Beauregard, Pierre Gustave Toutant (1818–93)

US Confederate general. He graduated from the US Military Academy at West Point (1838), served with distinction in the **Mexican War**, and was appointed by the Confederate government to the command at Charleston, where he commenced the war by the bombardment of **Fort Sumter** (12 Apr 1861). He fought at **Bull Run** (1861), then took command at **Shiloh** (1862), and later defended Charleston and Richmond. ▷ **American Civil War**

Beecher, Catharine (Esther) (1800–78)

US author and educator. Born into a famous New England family of religious leaders, she was the sister of Harriet Beecher Stowe. She campaigned throughout her life against feminism and in favour of domesticity, but in her own life was strongly independent.

Begin, Menachem (1913–   )

Israeli Zionist politician. In 1973 three parties combined to form the nationalist Likud Front with Begin as its leader, and in the 1977 elections he became Prime Minister at the head of a coalition government. In the late 1970s he attended peace conferences in Jerusalem (Dec 1977) and at Camp David (Sep 1978) at the invitation of President **Carter**. In 1978 he and President Anwar **Sadat** of Egypt were jointly awarded the Nobel Peace Prize. He resigned the premiership in 1983. ▷ **Camp David Accords**

Beijing, Treaty of (1860)

The treaty which gave Tsarist Russia all the territory it wanted between the Ussuri River and the Pacific coast in order to establish a strong presence in the Far East. Russia had been expanding towards the Pacific at China's expense since the 17c. Alexander II took advantage of China's weakness in face of British and French military attacks and US diplomatic pressure to secure peaceably the territory on which he then built the port and naval base of Vladivostok (literally, 'Ruler of the East').

Bemis Heights, Battle of (7 Oct 1777)
A preliminary conflict during the Saratoga campaign, in the US
War of Independence. ▷ **Saratoga, Battle of**

Benedict, Ruth (1887–1948)
US anthropologist. A student of Franz Boas, she introduced to
millions through her *Patterns of Culture* (1934) the different values
of cultures from Melanesians to Native Americans. Her study
Race: Science and Politics (1940) was one of the most influential
challenges to the doctrine of white supremacy.

Bennett, Richard Bedford, 1st Viscount (1870–1947)
Canadian politician. Educated in Nova Scotia, he trained as a
lawyer, and entered politics in 1897. He was Conservative leader
from 1927, and while Prime Minister (1930–5) convened the
Imperial Economic Conference in Ottawa (1932), from which
emerged a system of empire trade preference. He retired to England in 1938 and was made a peer in 1941. ▷ **New Deal (Canada);
Price Spreads Commission**

Benton, Thomas Hart (1782–1858)
US politician. He was a Missouri Senator for 30 years, and a
leader of the **Democratic Party**, becoming known as 'Old Bullion'
from his opposition to paper currency. In his later years, he
adopted an anti-slavery position which finally lost him his seat in
the Senate.

Berlin Airlift (1948–9)
A massive airlift of essential supplies flown in to **Cold War** Berlin
by British and US aircraft in round-the-clock missions. It was
carried out in response to the action of the Soviet military authorities in Berlin, who had attempted to isolate the city from the
West by severing all overland communication routes (June 1948).
Stalin lifted the blockade in May 1949.

Bethune, Mary McLeod (1875–1955)
US educator and administrator. She was founder and President of
the National Council of Negro Women and of Bethune-Cookman
College. Serving as adviser to President Franklin D **Roosevelt**'s
New Deal administration, she worked to expand awareness of
minority issues within government agencies. She was director of

23

the division of Negro Affairs within the National Youth Administration at a time when 40 per cent of black youths were suffering unemployment. As such she was quietly insistent that the number of blacks enrolled in the programme be increased despite the reluctance of state administrators. Black college students also benefited from the Special Negro Fund which she administered. In 1945 she was accredited by the State Department to attend the San Francisco Conference to establish the **UN**.

Bilingualism and Biculturalism, Royal Commission on (1963–71) Canadian governmental inquiry. Instituted by the **Pearson** administration, it was a response to the increasing separatist pressure in Quebec. Its aims were to research the origins of the crisis and to propose measures which would lead to a more equitable relationship between francophones and anglophones. Joint presidents of the commission were André Laurendeau, editor of the newspaper *Le Devoir*, and A Davidson Dunton, President of Ottawa's Carleton University. The final report revealed the extent to which French-Canadians were disadvantaged, both economically and culturally, by their origins. It recommended the adoption of both French and English as official languages throughout the federal bureaucracy and in business. Whilst the report refused to advocate separate nationhood for Quebec, it did propose the concept of a two-nation federation, and the establishment of a ministry for multiculturalism, which was enacted in 1972.

bill of rights
A list of citizens' rights set out in constitutional documents. Usually accompanying the document is an elaboration of the institutional means and powers by which such rights may be enforced. The best-known example is the one adopted in 1791 as the first 10 amendments to the **US Constitution**. The American Bill of Rights protects the liberties of private citizens in relation to the federal and state governments in such matters as freedom of speech, religion, the press and assembly, and legal procedure. It was adopted because of popular pressure during the campaign to ratify the constitution (1787–8), and its meaning has been expounded in many cases decided by the Supreme Court.

Billy the Kid ▷ **Bonney, William H**

Black Codes

Laws enacted in 1865–6 by Southern state legislatures following the **American Civil War** which severely restricted many rights of the newly freed slaves. Varying significantly from state to state, these laws were interpreted by the North as Southern unwillingness to change its racial attitudes. The Freedman's Bureau prevented their implementation and they were later repealed.

Black Friday

The name given to 24 Sep 1869, the day of a US financial crisis, when the price of gold dropped severely as a result of an attempt by such financiers as Jay **Gould** (1836–92) and James Fisk (1834–72) to corner the gold market. Many speculators lost their fortunes in the ensuing panic.

Black Hawk War (1832)

A military conflict between the USA and Sauk and Fox peoples, which led to the completion of the policy of removing Native Americans from 'the Old North-West' to beyond the Mississippi River. ▷ **Indian Wars**

Black, Hugo Lafayette (1886–1971)

US jurist. He practised law in his home state of Alabama and became a police court judge. In 1927 he entered the US Senate and as a liberal leader promoted the Tennessee Valley Authority as well as legislation that would set minimum wages and impose limits on working hours. In 1937 he was appointed to the US Supreme Court, where he served until his death. Black, a libertarian, opposed undue economic regulation by the states or the federal government. Central to his philosophy was the conviction that the Fourteenth Amendment made the **Bill of Rights** generally applicable to the states and that the First Amendment's guarantees of freedoms were absolute. Late in his career he supported civil rights legislation.

Black Muslims

A black religious movement in the USA, also known as the Nation of Islam, founded in 1930 by Wali Farad (Wallace D Fard), who proclaimed that black Americans are descended from an ancient Muslim tribe. Followers adopted Muslim names and believed Farad to be an incarnation of God. Following Farad's mysterious disappearance in 1934, Elijah **Muhammad** became leader of the movement until his death in 1975. Muhammad urged his followers to avoid contact with whites and demanded a separate state for blacks as well as reparation for past injustices. **Malcolm X** was one of the movement's most inspiring preachers, while the boxer Muhammad Ali was one of its most famous members. After Elijah Muhammad's son, Warith Dean (Wallace D), assumed leadership, the organization adopted orthodox Muslim beliefs. There were some, however, who continued to hold to the original tenets of the movement, including its separatist stance. Louis Farrakhan emerged as that faction's spokesman and has continued in that role.

Black Panthers
US militant black political party, founded by Huey P Newton and Bobby Seale in 1966, promoting the use of physical force and armed confrontation for black liberation. The party was active in the 1960s, but was split by rival groups in the 1970s and diminished in importance.

Black Power
The slogan used by black activists in the USA from the mid-1960s to reflect the aspiration of increased black political power. Its adherents formed part of the more radical wing of the **civil rights** movement, were against integrationist policies, and rejected non-violence. Some political results were achieved in terms of registering black voters, together with much wider attitudinal change.
▷ **Black Panthers; Congress of Racial Equality (CORE); SNCC; Carmichael, Stokely**

Black Thursday (24 Oct 1929)
The date of the crash of the New York stock market that marked the onset of the **Great Depression**.

Black Zionism
The term applied to quasi-nationalist, messianic movements founded among black Americans and West Indians who look to Africa as the land from which their descendants came as slaves. Characteristically, Africa is held in reverence, black history is regarded with pride, and there is a desire to return to the land of their forefathers.

Blackwell, Elizabeth (1821–1910)

US physician and feminist. Born in Bristol, UK, she received a degree in medicine from Geneva College in New York State. Blackwell, who faced hostility throughout her education and career, was responsible for opening the field of medicine to women. She also established an infirmary for the poor of New York City. In later life she returned to England, where she died at Hastings, Sussex.

Blaine, James G (1830–93)

US politician. Speaker of the House of Representatives and Senator from Maine who generated a huge personal following. He might have received the Republican nomination in the 1876 election but for the publication of the 'Mulligan Papers' which showed him ready to receive bribes from railroads. Leader of the 'Half-Breed' faction of the **Republican Party** under President Rutherford B **Hayes**, he was nominated Republican candidate for the presidential election of 1884 over the incumbent President Chester A **Arthur**, but lost to Grover **Cleveland**.

Blake, Edward (1833–1912)

Canadian lawyer and politician. A Liberal, he became Premier of Ontario in 1871 and minister without portfolio in the **Mackenzie** federal administration in 1873. Uncomfortable with Mackenzie's policies, he resigned in 1874 and with a fervent speech assumed the leadership of the **Canada First** movement. He returned to government as the Minister of Justice in 1875 and succeeded in gaining the British government's acceptance of the Supreme Court Act and a reduction in the powers of the Governor-General. Leader of the Liberals (1880–87), he resigned from the party in 1891 because he could not accept its **reciprocity** proposals. Long interested in the Irish question, he left Canada in 1892 and became an Irish nationalist MP in the British parliament, but eventually returned to Canada in 1906. ▷ **Liberal Party** (Canada)

Bleus

French-Canadian moderate reform followers of Louis Hippolyte **Lafontaine** (the term dating from 1850 in contradistinction to the radical **Rouges**). From 1854 they became the French-Canadian wing of the new Conservative Party. In 1862, with the introduction of the **Militia Bill**, the bloc split into two wings, the *Ultra-bleus*, led by Sir Hector **Langevin**, who were on the extreme right, and the moderate *Bleus*, led by Joseph Adolphe **Chapleau**. The party had problems when **Canada West** and **Canada East** were united in 1864 because the French Canadians suffered a numerical disadvantage in the legislature. However, under the leadership of George Étienne **Cartier**, the Bleus sought to protect the cultural rights of the French Canadians. The support of the party was essential to the Conservative domination of federal politics during the late 19c, but with D'Alton **McCarthy**'s Equal Rights Association and the **Manitoba Schools Act** controversy, Quebec swung its vote behind the Liberals who then won the 1896 federal election.

Bloc Populaire
Quebecois nationalist political party. It was formed in 1942 by liberals who opposed Canadian participation in **World War II** and the introduction of conscription, and by Catholic radicals like André Laurendeau who wished to base industrial relations on papal encyclicals and to forbid the entry of foreign capital. After winning four seats in the provincial elections of 1944, the party fragmented, with the **Union Nationale** having benefited considerably from its extremism.

Bloomer, Amelia (1818–94)
US suffragist. She gave her name to Turkish-style trousers tied at the ankles under a loose-fitting short skirt, which attracted a great deal of ridicule. Bloomer founded a temperance newspaper, *The Lily*, in which she also championed women's rights and suffrage.

Bonney, William H ('Billy the Kid') (1859–81)
US outlaw. He achieved legendary notoriety for his robberies and murders in the south-west, supposedly from the age of 12. He was captured by Sheriff Patrick F Garrett in 1880, and sentenced to hang. He escaped, but was finally tracked down by Garrett and shot.

Bonus Army (June 1932)
A US protest march of some 20 000 unemployed ex-servicemen on Washington DC, demanding Congressional passage of a bill authorizing the immediate payment of a bonus due to **World War I** veterans. When the bill was defeated in the Senate, some veterans

refused to return home. At the end of July, on the orders of President Herbert **Hoover**, General **MacArthur** evicted the marchers but incurred great odium by doing so with violence and cruelty.

Boone, Daniel (1735–1820)
US frontiersman. He made a trail, the 'wilderness road', through the Cumberland Gap (1767) and became one of the first to explore Kentucky (1769–73). Twice captured by Native Americans, he repeatedly repelled (1775–8) Native American attacks on his stockade fort, now Boonesboro. Boone was a successful surveyor, trapper and landowner, ushering new settlers into Kentucky. After losing his large landholdings to debt and legal mismanagement, he moved further west into Missouri, where he died.

Booth, John Wilkes (1839–65)
US assassin. An actor, he was the brother of Edwin Booth. In 1865 he entered into a conspiracy to avenge the defeat of the Confederates and shot President Abraham **Lincoln** at Ford's Theatre, Washington (14 Apr). He broke his leg while escaping, but managed to flee to Virginia. He was tracked down and was either shot by his pursuers or shot himself.

Borah, William Edgar (1865–1940)
US politician. He was elected as a Republican senator for Idaho in 1907. An advocate of disarmament and a leading isolationist, Borah was instrumental in blocking the USA's entry into the **League of Nations** in 1919.

Borden, Sir Robert Laird (1854–1937)
Canadian politician. He practised as a barrister, and became leader of the Conservative Party in 1901. As Conservative Prime Minister (1911–20), he led Canada through **World War I**, the Conscription crisis, and the introduction of income tax. At the Imperial War Conference of 1917 he called for greater recognition of the dominions' autonomy, a step towards the building of a Commonwealth. ▷ **Compulsory Service Act; Lapointe, Ernest; War Measures Act**

Boston Massacre (5 Mar 1770)

The first bloodshed of the **American Revolution**. In an atmosphere of intense resentment against British troops and regulations, on 5 Mar 1770 British guards opened fire on an unruly crowd, killing five. Of the nine British soldiers tried for murder, seven, including the commander, were acquitted and two were found guilty of manslaughter.

Boston Tea Party (1773)

During the **American Revolution**, the climactic event of resistance to British attempts at direct taxation, resulting in the destruction of 342 chests of dutied tea by working men disguised as Native Americans. Other ports had refused to let the tea ships enter. ▷ **Intolerable Acts**

Bourassa, Henri (Joseph-Napoléon-Henri) (1868–1952)

Canadian politician and journalist (as a founder and editor of *Le Devoir*). A grandson of Louis Joseph **Papineau**, he was a French-Canadian nationalist who consistently opposed French Canada's forced participation in British wars. He resigned his independent Liberal seat in the federal House of Commons when **Laurier** sent Canadian troops to the Boer War, but, since most French-Canadians felt the same way, he was returned by acclamation. Bourassa was also the focal point for French-Canadian outrage at the Naval Act of 1910, using *Le Devoir* to advocate his views and making an important contribution to the **Liberal Party** defeat in the election of 1911. He was also a vigorous opponent of Canadian involvement in **World War I**. An advocate of European liberal Catholic thinking, he was opposed to industrial capitalism and emerged as a social reformer in the 1920s and 1930s.

Bourassa, Robert (1933–)

Canadian politician. He was leader of the Quebec Liberal Party when it won an emphatic election victory in 1970, despite the nationalist unrest of the period. By refusing to give prominence to the constitutional and language controversies and promising to help the unemployment crisis by generating 100 000 jobs, his party won 41.8 per cent of the vote and 72 seats. During the **October Crisis** Bourassa was accused of being too ready to hand over power to Ottawa by those who suspected that he hoped to undermine his nationaliste and left-wing opponents. Bourassa responded by reinforcing his demands for a special status for Quebec within the Confederation. He resigned as party leader when the Liberals lost the 1976 provincial elections to the **Péquistes**, but he was re-elected in 1983 and led the party to victory in 1986, this time with a huge hydro-electric project as the electoral promise.

Bowell, Sir Mackenzie (1823–1917)

Canadian politician. In 1878, as Grand Master of the **Orange Order** (a position he filled with a certain tact towards the sensibilities of Catholics), he was included in the cabinet of Sir John **Macdonald** in order to balance the leadership of the **Bleus**. In 1895 Bowell became Prime Minister, faced not only with the Depression but also with the crisis caused by the **Manitoba Schools Act**. When the province refused to restore the rights of the Catholic minority, he introduced a Remedial Bill and seven ministers resigned. They were concerned not so much with the actual issue but to remove Bowell, whose stand had alienated the Orange Order from the party, and they returned to office when he had yielded to Sir Charles **Tupper**. Nevertheless, the Conservatives were defeated in the election of 1896, after which Bowell led their opposition in the Senate.

Bowie, Colonel James ('Jim') (1790–1836)

US adventurer. He is mainly remembered for his role in defending the **Alamo** (1836) during the Texas revolution. He was the inventor of the curved sheath knife named after him.

bracero

The term used to describe seasonal labour from Central and Southern Mexico, working on large-scale agroindustrial enterprises in California and Texas. Often 'wetbacks', who had illegally entered the USA by crossing the Rio Grande, they did not benefit from minimum wage and employee-protection legislation in either California, Texas or New Mexico. They had often been used as 'scab' or strike-breaking labour in both states, so were not easily accepted into US trade unions. Drives to unionize them began in the mid-1960s, thanks to the activities of leaders such as Cesar **Chavez**; against heavy opposition from both the **AFL–CIO** and local employers, they were supported by the Republican Governor, Ronald **Reagan**. The influx of *braceros* increased during the

1980s, in the wake of the Mexican debt crisis and the endemic civil wars of Central America.

Bradford, William (1590–1656)

English colonist and religious leader. One of the Pilgrim Fathers, he was born near Doncaster, England. A nonconformist from boyhood, he joined a separatist group in 1606 and went with them to Holland in 1609, seeking freedom of worship. In Leiden he became a tradesman and read widely. One of the moving spirits in the Pilgrim Fathers' expedition to the New World in 1620, he sailed on the *Mayflower* and signed the Mayflower Compact. In 1621 he was elected as the second governor of Plymouth colony, taking over from John **Carver**. Re-elected governor 30 times between 1622 and 1656 (elections were held yearly), he guided the fledgling colony with exemplary fairness and firmness.

Bradley, Omar Nelson (1893–1981)

US soldier. He entered the army in 1915 and served in World War I. A brigadier general from 1941, he commanded II Corps in Tunisia and Sicily in 1943. He commanded the US First Army at the Normandy invasion in 1944, and later the US 12th Army Group in Europe until the end of World War II. He became the first permanent chairman of the US Joint Chiefs of Staff (1949–53), and in 1950 was promoted to a five-star general of the army. He retired in 1953.

Brady bill

Legislation passed by Congress in Nov 1993, imposing a mandatory five-day waiting period for anyone buying a handgun to allow for police checks on the purchaser. The restriction was limited to five years, during which time additional funds would be made available to update police computer records to permit instant background checks. The bill, the most significant gun-control statute in recent years, was named after James Brady, the press secretary of Ronald **Reagan**, who was permanently disabled by gunfire during the assassination attempt on the president in 1981.

Brandeis, Louis Dembitz (1856–1941)

US judge. He was educated in the USA and in Europe and, after graduating from Harvard Law School, he practised law in Boston.

He conducted many labour arbitrations, and was frequently involved in cases challenging the power of monopolies and cartels, as well as others that dealt with the constitutionality of maximum hours and minimum wages legislation. He formulated the economic doctrine of the New Freedom adopted by Woodrow **Wilson** for his 1912 presidential campaign. Appointed to the US Supreme Court in 1916, he favoured governmental intervention to control the economy where public interest required it, but was also a strong defender of the principle of private property. Brandeis, who supported most of **Roosevelt**'s New Deal legislation, is remembered as one of the most perceptive and thoughtful Supreme Court judges.

Brandywine, Battle of the (11 Sep 1777)
A battle fought during the **American Revolution**, taking its name from the Brandywine Creek near Philadelphia, Pennsylvania. British forces under William **Howe** defeated George **Washington**'s troops, who were attempting to defend Pennsylvania.

Brant, Joseph (1742–1807)
Mohawk chief. He fought for the British in the French and Indian Wars and the American Revolution. In later years an earnest Christian, he translated St Mark's Gospel and the Book of Common Prayer into Mohawk, and in 1786 visited England, where he was received at court.

Braun, Wernher von (1912–77)
German-born US rocket scientist. He studied engineering at Berlin and Zurich and in 1930 founded a society for space travel. In 1936, with **Hitler**'s backing, he became director of a rocket research station at Peenemünde, where he perfected and launched the V-2 rockets against Britain (Sep 1944). After the war, he became a naturalized American and a director of the US Army's Ballistic Missile Agency at Huntsville, Alabama, and was chiefly responsible for the launching of the first US artificial Earth satellite (Jan 1958).

Brennan, William Joseph Jr (1906–   )
US jurist. He was educated at the University of Pennsylvania and Harvard, and after practising law he rose in the New Jersey court system to the state Supreme Court. Named to the US Supreme

Court in 1956, he took an active role in the liberal decisions handed down under Chief Justice Earl **Warren**. He retired from the Court in 1990.

Bretton Woods Conference

An international conference held at Bretton Woods, New Hampshire, USA, in 1944, which led to the establishment of the International Monetary System, including the International Monetary Fund (IMF) and the World Bank (International Bank for Reconstruction and Development). The agreement, signed by the USA, UK and 43 other nations, aimed at controlling exchange rates, which were fixed for members in terms of gold and the dollar. The system was used until 1973, when floating exchange rates were introduced.

brinkmanship

A tactic in international relations of deliberately allowing a potential crisis situation to escalate until the threat of war seems imminent. This high-risk strategy is intended to put the other side under pressure, and to force concessions out of them. The term was first coined by US strategic analyst, Thomas Crombie Schelling (1921–), drawing on a remark of John Foster **Dulles** in 1957 about going 'to the brink' of war.

British North America Act (1867)

An act passed by the British parliament which sanctioned the confederation of Nova Scotia, New Brunswick, Quebec and Ontario, thus giving rise to the Dominion of Canada. In 1982 it was renamed the Constitution Act (1867). ▷ **Canada, Dominion of**

Brooke, Edward (1918–)

US politician. A Republican Senator from Massachusetts and the first black to sit in the Senate since **Reconstruction**, he was a Boston lawyer who in 1962 was elected as Massachusetts Attorney General. Re-elected in 1964 with an overwhelming majority, Brooke was elected to the Senate in 1966 on an anti-war platform, again with a sizeable majority. In 1968 he reversed his stance on the **Vietnam War** and became alienated from Martin Luther **King**. He lost his Senate seat in 1978, and in 1979 became the Chairman of the National Low Income Housing Coalition.

Brown, George (1818–80)

Canadian politician and journalist. A supporter of **Responsible Government** in 1848, he became a member of the Canadian legislative assembly in 1851. As editor of the *Toronto Globe* he used his considerable influence to speak for the **Clear Grits**, pressing the case for representation-by-population ('rep by pop'), to give **Canada West** a majority of seats in the legislature. After the Liberal-Conservatives took over government in 1854, Brown reorganized the party, and won the 1857 elections by advocating the acquisition of the North West from the **Hudson's Bay Company**. In 1858, in alliance with A A Dorion, the leader of the Liberals of **Canada East**, he formed a government which survived only a few days. It was perhaps this experience which helped him to realize the inherent instability of provincial government under the system established by the Act of Union. He therefore played a major role with Alexander **Galt**, J A **Macdonald** and George Étienne **Cartier**, in a coalition government established to devise the constitutional reforms required for confederation. This he continued to support even after resigning in Dec 1865. Brown was also an anti-slavery activist, involved in the settlement of fugitive slaves during the 1850s. He was shot and killed by an employee sacked from the *Globe*. ▷ **Liberal Party**

Brown, John (1800–59)

US militant abolitionist. He supported himself with many different jobs while wandering through the country advocating anti-slavery. He was twice married and had 20 children. In 1859, he led a raid on the US armory at Harpers Ferry in Virginia (now West Virginia), intending to launch a slave insurrection. The raid failed, and after being convicted of treason against Virginia, he was hanged at Charles Town. The song 'John Brown's Body' commemorates the **Harpers Ferry Raid**. ▷ **abolitionism**

Brown v Board of Education of Topeka, Kansas (1954)

US Supreme Court case in which Chief Justice Earl **Warren**, speaking for a unanimous bench, declared that separate educational facilities were inherently unequal and inhumane. With this decision the court overturned **Plessy v Ferguson** (1896), which had supported 'separate but equal' facilities, and undermined the major principle upon which **Jim Crow Laws** depended. Critics contended that it encroached on **states' rights**, and that it represented judicial legislation rather than interpretation. In 'Brown

35

II' (1955) the Supreme Court acknowledged the problems faced by school boards in implementing the earlier decision; they ordered district courts therefore to integrate schools 'with all deliberate speed'. ▷ **segregation**

Bruce, Blanche Kelso (1848–98)

US politician. Born in Farmville, Virginia, he was a former slave who became a planter. He went on to become the first black American to serve a full term in the US Senate.

Bryan, William Jennings (1860–1925)

US politician. Educated at Illinois College, he entered the House of Representatives as a Democrat in 1890 and won his party's presidential nomination in 1896 on a Populist platform. He was Democratic nominee three times, and became Secretary of State under Woodrow **Wilson**. His last public act was assisting the anti-evolutionist prosecutor in the Scopes Monkey Trial in Dayton, Tennessee. ▷ **Darrow, Clarence; Democratic Party; free silver; Populist Party**

Brzezinski, Zbigniew (1928–   )

Polish-born US political scientist. Educated at McGill University (Montreal) and Harvard, he taught at Harvard and Columbia, then served as National Security Adviser under President **Carter**. He is now Professor of Political Science at Columbia University.

Buchanan, James (1791–1868)

US politician and 15th President. Educated at Dickinson College, he was admitted to the Bar in 1812. Elected to the US Senate in 1834, he became Secretary of State under President James K **Polk** (1845), an office he held during the **Mexican War**. He served as Minister to Great Britain under President Pierce (1853–6), and was elected president as a Democrat in 1856. During his administration the slavery question came to a head and he tried to maintain a balance between pro-slavery and anti-slavery forces. He supported the establishment of Kansas as a slave state, which alienated many in the North, but his moderate position also displeased radicals in the South. Defeated in the presidential election by Abraham **Lincoln**, but before Lincoln's inauguration, Buchanan was faced with the secession of the Southern states.

Determined to avert a civil war, he rejected a military response and instead pursued a policy of compromise.

Bulge, Battle of the (1944)

The last desperate German armoured counter-offensive through the Ardennes in **World War II** (beginning 16 Dec), to prevent the Allied invasion of Germany. It achieved early success, but ground to a halt, and the Germans were then pushed to retreat by the Allies by the end of Jan 1945.

Bull Moose

US political epithet applied to the **Progressive Party** after the nomination of ex-President Theodore **Roosevelt** as their presidential candidate in 1912. After he had been shot in an assassination attempt, Roosevelt refused to cancel a speaking engagement, announcing to his audience that 'it takes more than that to kill a bull moose'.

Bull Run, Battles of (21 July 1861 and 29–30 Aug 1862)

Major victories by Confederate forces in the **American Civil War**; also known as the Battles of Manassas. The first battle, which was the first major clash of the Civil War, pitted untrained Northern troops attempting to capture Richmond, Virginia (the Southern capital), against well-commanded Southerners. 'Stonewall' **Jackson**'s stand caused the Northern troops to retreat and the retreat became a rout. In the second battle, a large Northern force under John Pope was trapped by combined Confederate forces under 'Stonewall' Jackson and James Longstreet.

Bunche, Ralph (Johnson) (1904–71)

US diplomat. He studied at Harvard and the University of California, then taught political science at Howard University, Washington (1928–50). In 1944 he assisted the Swedish Nobel prize winner Gunnar Myrdal in the creation of *An American Dilemma*, a study on American blacks. He directed the **UN** Trusteeship department (1946–54), and became UN mediator in Palestine, where he arranged for a ceasefire. Awarded the Nobel Peace Prize (1950), he became a UN undersecretary for Special Political Affairs from 1957 to his death.

Bundy, McGeorge (1919–   )
US educator and administrator. Educated at Yale, he worked in public service, then taught at Harvard, where he became Dean of Arts and Sciences in 1953. As National Security Adviser to Presidents John F **Kennedy** and Lyndon B **Johnson** he was one of the architects of the **Vietnam War**. In 1989 he became professor emeritus of History at New York University.

Bunker Hill, Battle of (1775)
The first pitched battle of the **American Revolution**, technically a US defeat. The British garrison dislodged New England troops from their position overlooking occupied Boston, but very high British casualties demonstrated American fighting capacity, and forbade attempts on other American emplacements. The battle was actually fought on Breed's Hill, above Charlestown, not on nearby Bunker Hill.

Bureau of Indian Affairs (BIA)
A US government agency established in 1824 as part of the War Department and transferred in 1849 to the Department of the Interior. The BIA is in charge of the administration of Native American ('Indian') affairs, acting on behalf of the USA, which is the trustee of tribal lands and property.

Burger, Warren Earl (1907–   )
US jurist. Educated at the University of Minnesota, he taught and practised law in St Paul from 1931 before he became Assistant Attorney-General of the USA (1953) and US Court of Appeals judge for the District of Columbia in 1955. Richard **Nixon** appointed him Chief Justice of the US Supreme Court in 1969. Burger, whose philosophy inclined toward judicial restraint and caution toward change, reined in the liberal tendencies the Court had shown in previous years. He resigned from the Court in 1986.

Burgoyne, John (1722–92)
British general and dramatist. He entered the army in 1740, and gave distinguished service in the Seven Years' War (1756–63). He then sat in Parliament as a Tory MP in 1761 and 1768. He was sent to America in 1774 and fought at **Bunker Hill** in 1775. As major general he led an expedition from Canada and captured Fort Ticonderoga in 1777, but was later forced to surrender to

General Gates in **Saratoga**. He returned to England where he joined the Whigs, and was commander-in-chief in Ireland (1782–3). His plays include the comedy *The Heiress* (1786).

Burr, Aaron (1756–1836)

US politician. Educated at Princeton and called to the Bar in 1782, he became state Attorney-General (1789–91), then US Senator (1791–7), and Republican Vice-President (1801–5). His political career ended in 1804 when he killed his political rival, Alexander **Hamilton**, in a duel. Thought to be conspiring to take Louisiana and establish it as an independent republic, he was tried for treason (1807) and acquitted. In 1812 he resumed his law practice in New York City, where he died.

Bush, George (Herbert Walker) (1924–   )

US politician and 41st President. He served in the US Navy (1942–5) and after the war received a degree in economics from Yale and established an oil-drilling business in Texas. In 1966 he devoted himself to politics, and was elected to the House of Representatives. Unsuccessful in his bid for the Senate in 1970, he became US ambassador to the **UN**. During the **Watergate** scandal he was chairman of the Republican National Committee. Under President **Ford** he served as US envoy to China, and then became Director of the **CIA**. In 1980 he sought the Republican presidential nomination, but lost to Ronald **Reagan**, later becoming his Vice-President. He became President in 1988, defeating the Democratic candidate, Governor Michael Dukakis of Massachusetts. As President, he focused on US foreign policy, which was changed most dramatically by the dissolution of the USSR, and he presided over the USA-led UN coalition to defeat Iraq in the **Gulf War**. In 1992 he failed to be re-elected, perhaps because of the perception that he had ignored US domestic issues. ▷ **Republican Party**

busing

Process by which US high-school students (especially black and Asian) were taken by bus from disadvantaged urban contexts to schools elsewhere in order to achieve integration after **Swann v Charlotte-Mecklenburg Board of Education** (1971). For the first time, desegregation became a major issue throughout the North, with parents in such cities as Boston and Denver protesting, in some cases violently, that the process would bring an end to the neighbourhood school. In response, President **Nixon** asked

Congress to impose a moratorium on all busing orders by federal courts and the House of Representatives agreed. However, Nixon's anti-busing bill was blocked by a filibuster led by Senators Walter **Mondale** of Minnesota and Jacob Javits of New York. The policy was abandoned in 1972. ▷ **Milliken v Bradley**

Butler, Benjamin F(ranklin) (1818–93)

US politician, lawyer and general. He graduated from Waterville College, Maine, and was admitted to the Bar in 1840, becoming a criminal lawyer. In the **American Civil War**, he and his troops took possession of New Orleans (1862), where they crushed all opposition. Elected to Congress in 1866, he was prominent in the Republican efforts for the reconstruction of the Southern states and in the impeachment of President **Johnson**. He was Governor of Massachusetts (1882–4), and unsuccessfully ran (as the candidate for the Greenback Party) for President in 1884. ▷ **greenback; Reconstruction**

C

Cabot, John (c.1450–c.1498)
Italian navigator and explorer. Commissioned by the King of England, he made the first known landing on the North American continent since the Norsemen at a point somewhere between Maine and southern Nova Scotia in 1497, and formally claimed possession for Henry VII. It is believed that he thought he had landed in Asia, but realized his mistake when he returned the following year.

'Calamity Jane' (Martha Jane Burke) (c.1852–1903)
US frontierswoman. Of eccentric character, usually dressed in men's clothes, she was celebrated for her bravery and her skill in riding and shooting, particularly during the **gold rush** days in the Black Hills of Dakota. She is said to have threatened 'calamity' for any man who tried to court her.

Calhoun, John Caldwell (1782–1850)
US politician. He graduated from Yale (1804), studied law, then entered politics, becoming (1817) Secretary of War, Vice-President under John Quincy **Adams** and **Jackson** (1825–32), and Secretary of State under **Tyler**. He is best known for his 'nullification' theory (1828), in which he argued that states have the right to nullify laws they considered unconstitutional. He later entered the Senate, where he championed the interests of the slave-holding states.

Calles, Plutarco Elías (1877–1945)
Mexican politician. An ex-schoolmaster, he became Governor of Sonora (1917) and President of Mexico (1924–8). Anticlerical, he challenged the pretensions of the Church, implementing the 1917 constitution and provoking the **Cristero Revolt**; he dominated the presidency until 1934, enhancing the power of the state, creating the PNR but limiting agrarian reform. Defeated by his protégé,

Cárdenas, he was exiled to the USA, but was allowed to return in 1941.

Camden, Battle of (1780)

A battle of the **American Revolution**, fought in South Carolina. After the British capture of **Charleston**, Camden was the first major battle of the Southern campaign. Americans under Horatio Gates were defeated by British troops under Lord **Cornwallis**.

Caminetti, Anthony (1854–1923)

US politician. The son of Italian immigrants to California, in 1882 he was elected as a Democrat to the state legislature and from 1890 to 1895 he was a US Representative. In 1913 he returned to Washington to serve in Woodrow **Wilson**'s administration as Commissioner of Immigration, and became notorious both for the inefficiency of his department and the overzealous manner with which he screened immigrants for communist sympathies.

Camp David Accords (1978)

Documents signed by Anwar **Sadat**, President of Egypt, and Menachem **Begin**, Prime Minister of Israel, and witnessed by US President Jimmy **Carter** at Camp David, Maryland, USA, in Sep 1978. Regarded by many as a triumph of US diplomacy, they were preliminary to the signing of the formal peace treaty (1979) between the two countries, which gave Egypt back the Sinai Desert, captured in the 1967 War. ▷ **PLO**

Canada East (1841–67)

The name given to Lower Canada (Quebec) when it became a district of the united Province of Canada established by the Act of Union in 1840 as a result of the **Durham Report**. After confederation in 1867, Canada East became the Province of Quebec within the Dominion of Canada. ▷ **Canada, Dominion of; Canada, Lower; Confederation Movement; Papineau, Louis Joseph**

Canada, Dominion of

Established on 1 July 1867, by the **British North America Act** of 29 Mar, the Dominion consisted of three provinces, Canada (now divided into Quebec and Ontario), Nova Scotia and New Brunswick, all united by the **Confederation Movement**. Desire for unification had intensified because of the need for improvements in transport and because of the proximity of the USA, which instilled emulation as well as fear. The ending of **reciprocity** in 1866 and the failure of the USA to curb the **Fenians** perhaps accentuated the provinces' link with the British crown, which was a distinguishing feature of the confederation (although the term 'Dominion' was chosen rather than 'Kingdom' in deference to US republican sentiment). Manitoba joined the Dominion in 1870, British Columbia in 1871, Prince Edward Island in 1873, Alberta and Saskatchewan in 1905, and Newfoundland in 1949. ▷ **Brown, George; Cartier, George Étienne; Compact Theory of Confederation; Macdonald, John Alexander**

Canada First (1867–76)
Canadian patriotic movement. It was founded by a number of young intellectuals who were later joined by business and professional men of Toronto disenchanted by the Treaty of **Washington**. Its journal, *The Nation* (edited by Goldwin **Smith**) was noted for its political commentary and in 1874 Edward **Blake** became the chief spokesman for the movement during his temporary defection from the **Liberal Party**. The **Clear Grits** and many Liberals disliked the movement because its demand that Canada be given the authority to negotiate its own treaties seemed to imply the dissolution of the British Empire. Some of its members believed in the racial supremacy of the Anglo-Saxon inheritance, thinking French-Canada corrupt and priest-ridden and therefore likely to retard Canada's progress. Many however, like Blake, believed Canada's potential for greatness would only be realized if French Canada's cultural inheritance was recognized, so that her leaders would be free to cooperate in federal politics.

Canada, Lower (1791–1841)
The name given to Quebec by the Constitutional Act of 1791. The decision to divide Canada in two was reached with the realization that it would be impossible to establish a form of government which would satisfy both English-speaking Protestant Canadians and French-speaking Catholics. Lower Canada was dominated by French-Canadians, the Catholic Church was established and the Custom of Paris accepted as its legal system. With its borders drawn up on the old seigniorial property boundaries, Montreal,

despite being dominated by English merchants was also included. In Lower Canada the problems associated with colonial rule existed along with the friction caused by the fractious relationship between the two communities. This friction increased with the influx of English-speaking immigrants so that the French-Canadians feared for their ascendancy and the English-speaking immigrants suffered from the domination of French custom and language. In 1822 the Montreal Château Clique originated a bill which united both provinces. They aimed to bar most Frenchmen from the vote through a high property franchise and to limit the power of the Catholic Church. The bill was dropped after **Papineau** went to London to appeal. Although by 1831 control of the revenue had been given to the Assembly, the majority in the House was not given any official ministerial recognition. By 1834 the French held only a quarter of the public posts although they formed three-quarters of the population. The situation was aggravated by the depression of 1837, and rebellion broke out, but was put down fairly quickly. With the Act of Union (1840) Lower Canada became **Canada East** (in 1841), and was given equal representation within a united province, so the French were yet again at a disadvantage. ▷ **Canada, Upper; Craig, Sir James; Durham Report; Ninety-Two Resolutions**

Canada, Upper (1791–1841)
The name given to the western region of the province of Quebec when it was made, like Lower Canada, a separate province by the Constitutional Act of 1791. At that time it had a population of 14 000, but by 1812, with an influx of settlers mostly from the USA, it had grown to 90 000. The first governor was Sir John Graves **Simcoe** who initiated a system of distributing free land grants in return for a loyalty oath. However, the distribution of land according to social rank created an elite known as the **Family Compact**. Similarly the Anglican Church's semi-established status gave it advantages at the expense of the Methodist Church, although the latter's members outnumbered the Anglicans. These dissatisfactions led William Lyon **Mackenzie**, after the failure of rebellion in Lower Canada, to call settlers to action, but his inability to organize a military uprising matched the inability of the governor, Sir Francis Bond **Head**, to govern. Nevertheless it did bring the problems out into the open, and after the **Durham Report**, Upper Canada was made **Canada West** in the united Province of Canada. ▷ **Canada, Lower**

Canada West (1841–67)

The name given to Upper Canada when it became a district of the united Province of Canada established by the Act of Union in 1840 as a result of the **Durham Report**. After confederation in 1867, Canada West became the Province of Ontario within the Dominion of Canada. ▷ **Canada, Dominion of; Canada, Upper; Confederation Movement**

Canadian National Railways (CNR)

The CNR was established in 1923 through the amalgamation of the **Grand Trunk Railway**, the Canadian Trunk Pacific and the Canadian Northern with the Intercolonial railway and the National Transcontinental Railways. The federal government therefore found itself owning 22 000 miles of railway, a huge enterprise which, since all were bankrupt, presented great financial problems as well as political difficulties. The government appointed a board of 15 members and instituted a Department of Railways. The first chairman was Sir Henry Thornton, who was determined to demonstrate the viability of the project against the competition of the **Canadian Pacific Railway**. He widened the interests of the company into hotels, steamships and a telegraph system. The company still showed annual deficits, because of its inherited debts and the insistence of the government that it maintain a service to the whole community even though some sections would never become profitable.

Canadian Pacific Railway

In 1871 British Columbia was promised a railway to connect the Pacific coast with the rest of Canada as an inducement to enter the confederation. Huge land grants and cash subsidies were offered by the government in order to tempt investors. Two syndicates, one based in Montreal and one in Toronto, were organized to compete for the first offer of $30 million and 50 million acres of prime land. While the Toronto syndicate was backed by the **Grand Trunk Railway** with money raised in the London market, US money lay behind the Montreal syndicate, raising fears of US control. Within the cabinet **Cartier** was connected to the Grand Trunk, but was forced by Hugh **Allan** to switch his support to the Montreal group which then won the contract. However, the corrupt means by which it was obtained led to the downfall of the government in the 'Pacific Scandal' of 1873. The

subsequent go-slow of Alexander Mackenzie's Liberal government, which took over construction as a public work, almost
drove British Columbia into secession, but a re-chartered company completed the line in 1885.

canuck
A Canadian (slang). In US usage the term generally refers to
French Canadians, although the word is thought to be a corruption of 'Connaught' which was the name given to Irish immigrants by French Canadians.

Capone, Al(phonse) (1899–1947)
US gangster. He achieved worldwide notoriety as a racketeer
during the **Prohibition** era in Chicago. Such was his power that
no evidence sufficient to support a charge against him was forthcoming until 1931, when he was sentenced to 10 years' imprisonment for tax evasion. Released on health grounds in 1939, he
retired to his estate in Florida, where he died.

Cárdenas (del Río), Lázaro (1895–1970)
Mexican general and politician. His presidency (1934–40) shaped
modern Mexico. He promoted the return of the **ejido** in the south
and the extension of the rancho (small property) principally in
the north. His presidency also witnessed the creation of **PEMEX**
from nationalized foreign (mainly British) companies, and the
PRM (*Partido de la Revolución Mexicana*, Mexican Revolutionary Party), precursor of the **PRI**. Left-wing in his sympathies, he introduced many social reforms and reorganized the
ruling party.

Cardozo, Benjamin (1870–1938)
US jurist. He sat on the bench of the New York Court of Appeals
from 1913 to 1932, during which time the court became internationally famous. Appointed to the US Supreme Court by President Herbert Hoover, he succeeded Oliver Wendell Holmes,
serving for six years, 1932–8. Although he served for such a
relatively brief time, and although many of his opinions dissented
from the majority, he was remarkably influential because of his
eloquence and learnedness. He was generally liberal and believed
that the courts could effect social change.

Carleton, Sir Guy (Lord Dorchester) (1724–1808)

Acting Governor (1767–70) and Governor (1786–91) of Quebec and Governor-in-Chief of British North America until 1798. General James **Wolfe**'s quartermaster at the capture of **Quebec** in 1759, he realized during his first tour of duty as Governor that the 13 North American colonies were close to rebellion and that British imperial authority would require a base which he set out to establish in Quebec. His belief that the maintenance of the seigniorial system would ensure French-Canadian loyalty was embodied in the **Quebec Act** of 1774 which, despite protests from the increased English-speaking population, was pushed through the House of Commons against bitter opposition. Carleton refused to consider the English speaking settlers' demands for *habeas corpus* and other aspects of English law, but in spite of resentment against this, it was they who took up arms against the US rebels when they invaded in 1775–6. Carleton's successful defence, however, was criticized for the slowness with which he pursued the rebels and he resigned. Sent out as Governor of Quebec again in 1786, he became Governor-General after the Constitutional Act of 1791. He disliked the division of Quebec into Upper and Lower Canada, and the introduction of elected assemblies, but his advice that Montreal be retained within Lower Canada was accepted. His continued concern for the military defence of Canada was illustrated by the inflammatory speech he made to Native Americans just before **Jay's Treaty** was signed in 1794, when he was sure that war with the USA was imminent. He resigned in 1794 and left the province in 1796. ▷ **Canada, Lower; Canada, Upper**

Carmichael, Stokely (1941–   )

US civil rights activist. He came into conflict with Martin Luther **King** because his use of the emotive slogan '**Black Power**' implied violence and racial separatism. He was the most articulate speaker of **SNCC**, and under his chairmanship in 1966 it abandoned both non-violence and its policy of including white members. In 1967 he joined the **Black Panthers**, becoming the party's Prime Minister in 1968. Both he and his successor H Rap Brown became alienated from the party in 1969 because of its emphasis on class struggle.

Caroline Affair (1837)

A US/Canadian border incident on the Niagara River, growing from an attempted insurrection against the Canadian govern-

ment. The steamboat *Caroline*, carrying supplies to insur-
rectionists, was boarded, set afire, and left to drift, with the death
of one US citizen. Despite ensuing popular anglophobia, the USA
adopted official neutrality on Canadian affairs.

Carpetbaggers

A derogatory term for US Northerners who went to the defeated
South after the **American Civil War** to aid freed blacks and take
advantage of the economic opportunities offered by Reconstruction. The term derived from Southerners' characterization
of them as opportunistic transients who carried all their worldly
goods in luggage made of carpet fabric. Though many were well-
intentioned, others earned their reputation for corruption and
their rise to political power through exploitation of the black
vote.

Carranza, Venustiano (1859–1920)

Mexican politician. A senator under Porfirio **Díaz** and a supporter
of **Madero**, he emerged as the leader of Constitutionalist forces
against the dictator, Victoriano Huerta, in 1914. A fervent pro-
tagonist of Liberal aims, he was forced to accept the radical
constitution of 1917, but limited agrarian reform to military measures, destroying **Zapata** and **Villa** in the process. He was assassinated when attempting to retain the presidency.

Carson, Kit (Christopher) (1809–68)

US frontiersman. A trapper and hunter, his knowledge of Native
American habits and languages led to his becoming a guide in
1841 for John Frémont's explorations. He fought in the Mexican
War (1846), was Native American agent in New Mexico (1853),
and served the Union in the **American Civil War**.

Carter, Jimmy (James Earl) (1924–   )

US politician and 39th President. Educated at the US Naval
Academy, he served in the US Navy until 1953, when he took over
the family peanut business and other enterprises. As Governor of
Georgia (1971–5), he showed sensitivity towards the rights of
blacks and women. In the aftermath of the **Watergate** crisis he
won the Democratic presidential nomination in 1976, and went
on to win a narrow victory over Gerald **Ford**. As president (1977–
81), he arranged the peace treaty between Egypt and Israel (1979),

known as the **Camp David Accords**, and was concerned with human rights both at home and abroad. His administration ended in difficulties over the **Iran Hostage Crisis**, and the Soviet invasion of Afghanistan, and he was defeated by Ronald **Reagan** in the 1980 election.

Cartier, Sir George Étienne (1814–73)

Canadian politician. Leader of the *Bleu* bloc of **Canada East**, he served with John **Macdonald** in 1854 to form a Conservative ministry. Cartier believed that the French Canadian nation would only survive if French Canadians worked together with English-speaking Canadians. He also recognized that his people not only needed legislation to maintain their cultural identity but that their economic betterment required the development of transportation and commercial schemes. As Attorney-General for the province and solicitor for the **Grand Trunk Railway** he was able to advance his people's interests as well as his own. In 1858 the Macdonald–Cartier administration was defeated, but reformed as the Cartier–Macdonald ministry in a mutual exchange of posts (the so-called 'double-shuffle'). This lasted until 1862, and Cartier returned to government in the great coalition of 1864 which negotiated confederation. Perhaps his greatest contribution to Canadian history was to impress the need for Union upon French-Canadians, although many modern French-Canadians think of him as the first *vendu*. Because of his involvement with the **Canadian Pacific Railway** and Sir Hugh **Allan**, he was defeated in 1872, became ill and died. ▷ **Bleus; Confederation Movement**

Cartright, Sir Richard John (1835–1912)

Canadian banker and politician. Having broken with the conservatives over the railway scandal of 1873, he became Finance Minister in Alexander **Mackenzie**'s Liberal administration of 1873–8, when he was the most prominent advocate of free trade and alienated many transport and industrial interests by his opposition to tariffs. After the liberals' victory in 1896 he was made minister for trade and commerce in **Laurier**'s cabinet. ▷ **Liberal Party**

Carver, John (c.1576–1621)

Founding member and first governor of the **Plymouth Colony** in New England. He was succeeded by William **Bradford** in 1621.

Casablanca Conference (Jan 1943)

A meeting in North Africa between Franklin D **Roosevelt** and Winston Churchill during **World War II**, at which it was decided to insist on the eventual 'unconditional surrender' of Germany and Japan. Attempts to overcome friction between Roosevelt and the Free French under de **Gaulle** had only limited success. The combined Chiefs of Staff settled strategic differences over the projected invasion of Sicily and Italy.

Castors

Canadian political epithet. *Castor* (meaning 'beaver') was the signature on a pamphlet of 1882, entitled *Le Pays, le parti et le grand homme*, which attacked Joseph Adolphe **Chapleau** and J A Mousseau for becoming members of **Macdonald**'s cabinet. The name was given to right-wing conservatives in Quebec in the following year when their newspaper adopted the beaver as its emblem. *Castors* were ultramontane Catholics and racialists, the counterparts of extremist British Protestants.

Castro (Ruz), Fidel (1927–)

Cuban revolutionary. He studied law in Havana and in 1953 was imprisoned after an unsuccessful rising against **Batista**, but released under an amnesty. He fled to the USA and Mexico, then in 1956 landed in Cuba with a small band of insurgents. In 1958 he mounted a full-scale attack and Batista was forced to flee. He became Prime Minister (1959–), later proclaimed a 'Marxist-Leninist programme', and set about far-reaching reforms. His overthrow of US economic dominance and the routing of the US-connived émigré invasion at the **Bay of Pigs** (1961) were balanced by his dependence on Soviet aid. Castro became President in 1976. Although Cubans gained substantially in terms of general social provision, by the late 1980s the economic experiment had failed, and the collapse of the USSR isolated his regime.

Catt, Carrie Clinton Chapman (1859–1947)

US suffragist. In 1887 she joined the Iowa Woman Suffrage Association and quickly climbed the ranks of the national movement. Succeeding Susan B **Anthony** as president of the **National American Woman Suffrage Association** in 1900, her strategy of working on both state and national levels and through both political parties led to the ratification of the 19th Amendment in 1920 and secured the suffrage for women. She organized the Women's Peace Party during **World War I**.

caucus

A meeting, public or private, restricted to persons sharing a common characteristic, usually membership of a political party, held to formulate decisions or nominate candidates in forthcoming elections. It is most often applied to the USA, where the caucus-convention system is significant in selecting presidential and vice-presidential candidates, and where caucuses are the authoritative voice of the parties in **Congress**.

CCF (Cooperative Commonwealth Federation)

Canadian socialist political party. Founded in Calgary in 1932, with its first meeting held at Regina in 1933 by representatives of intellectual groups, organized labour, socialists and farmers, it was led by J S **Woodsworth**. The 'Regina Manifesto' included economic planning, central financial control and price stabilization, the extension of public ownership in communications and natural resources, the creation of a welfare state and an emergency relief programme. By 1934 the party had become the official opposition in Saskatchewan and in British Columbia, and hundreds of CCF clubs had sprung up throughout the country (except in the Maritimes Provinces and Quebec). The party avoided the fate of the US **Socialist Party** because of its strong adherence to parliamentary principles and the support it was given by both trade unionists and intellectuals, although it was damaged severely by **Duplessis**'s **Padlock Act**. In Ontario the CCF became the official opposition in 1943, while in the following year it was elected into government in Saskatchewan. Its challenge forced the Liberals into a far stronger emphasis on social reforms, and such federal legislation as the 1944 Families Allowances Act led to a decrease in support for CCF during the election of 1945. The continuation of this trend in **Liberal Party** policies eventually led the CCF to drop the most doctrinaire elements from its manifesto in 1956. In 1961 the party evolved into the **New Democratic Party** with 'Tommy' Douglas, the CCF Premier of Saskatchewan, as its leader.

Central Pacific Railroad

US railroad which, with the Union Pacific, connected to form the first transcontinental system. The route surveys undertaken during the 1850s all had serious sectional implications and not until after the Republican victory in 1860 was the central route chosen. This had the advantage of being straight and using the lowest mountain passes, but building was still handicapped by Native American attacks and high costs. The two railroads joined at Promontory Summit near Ogden, Utah, in 1869. Both had received huge land-grants in order to finance the project, but Leland Stanford and his associates of the CPR used their economic power as much for their own private financial gain as for national economic objectives. Their tax evasion and discriminatory freight charges contributed significantly to the establishment of the Interstate Commerce Commission (1884) and the regulatory agendas of Populist and Progressive reformers in the late 19c and early 20c.

Champlain, Samuel de (c.1570–1635)
French navigator and Governor of **New France**. In a series of voyages he travelled to North America (1603), exploring the east coast (1604–7) and founding Quebec (1608). He was appointed commandant of New France (1612), and established alliances with several Native American nations. When Quebec fell briefly to the British, he was taken prisoner (1629–32). From 1633 he was Governor of Quebec. Lake Champlain is named after him.
▷ **fur trade**

Chapleau, Sir Joseph Adolphe (1840–98)
Canadian politician. As leader of the moderate **Bleus**, John **Macdonald** invited him into the cabinet in 1882 to balance the inclusion of the extremist Sir Hector **Langevin**. The Rouge leader, Honoré **Mercier**, asked him to lead the movement of protest at the execution of **Riel** but, since he believed the sentence was just, he refused. However, he did resign in 1892 to become Lieutenant-Governor of Quebec. ▷ **Rouges**

Chapultepec, Act of (1945)
Signed in Mexico, this act established that American states should aid each other in the event of aggression from any source whatsoever. It also met the need to coordinate, by a single instrument, the various measures calling for the peaceful settlement of disputes in the Inter-American system. It was designed as a regional counterpoise to the **UN**. Its corollary was the Inter-American Treaty of Mutual Assistance (TIAR), subsequently signed in Rio

de Janeiro, and the Organization of American States (OAS), drawn up in Bogotá in 1948, as well as the Inter-American Treaty on Pacific Settlement (Pact of Bogotá) outlining procedures for the peaceful settlement of Inter-American disputes. Subsequent amendments have strengthened the economic and social functions of the OAS.

Charleston, Battles of (11 Feb–12 May 1780)
During the **American Revolution**, the victorious British siege of Charleston, South Carolina, which marked the beginning of the Southern phase of British strategy. At a small cost, the troops of Sir Henry Clinton (c.1738–95) captured a 5 400-strong American garrison and a squadron of four ships. ▷ **Pułaski, Kazimierz**

Chattanooga Campaign (Aug–Nov 1863)
A series of battles in Tennessee, during the **American Civil War**, leading to Southern victory at Chickamauga, and Northern victories at Lookout Mountain and Missionary Ridge. It was of military importance, because it placed Northern troops in a position to bisect the Confederacy on an east–west axis.

Chautauqua Movement
A late 19c and early 20c US adult education movement, organized at Lake Chautauqua, New York, under Methodist auspices by Lewis Miller (1829–99) and Bishop John H Vincent (1832–1920), with home reading programmes and lectures in the arts, sciences and humanities. At its peak it attracted up to 60 000 participants annually to regional centres in the USA and elsewhere.

Chavez, Cesar Estrada (1927–   )
US union official. A farm worker, he organized the National Farm Workers Association (NFWA) in 1962, which in 1966 merged with an agricultural group of **AFL–CIO** to form the United Farm Workers Organizing Committee (UFWOC). This later became the United Farm Workers of America (UFW), and Chavez was appointed as its president. Originally a migrant himself, he has consistently worked to improve conditions for migrant agrarian workers by means of strikes, boycotts, marches and public support. ▷ **bracero**

Cherokee
A Native American people formerly living in southeastern USA, now living in Oklahoma and North Carolina. They sided with the British in the **American Revolution**, and later, in 1827, established the Cherokee Nation with its own constitution and elected government. After gold was discovered on their land, they were removed by US troops and forced to move west to unsettled **Indian Territory** in Oklahoma. Thousands died from cold, disease and starvation during their 800-mile mid-winter march, which became known as the Trail of Tears. The survivors settled in Oklahoma with other displaced southeastern tribes. Over 250 000 Cherokee live in the USA today; most live in Oklahoma, but some who refused to leave the south-east still live in North Carolina. ▷ **Five Civilized Tribes**

Chesnut, Mary Boykin (1823–86)
US diarist. Although married into one of the great slave-owning families of South Carolina, and a fervent supporter of the South, she thought of herself as an abolitionist in view of the brutalizing effect that **slavery**'s unlimited power had on white men. She also equated the position of white women with that of slaves, denied legal freedom, **civil rights** or property, and degraded by the slave-owning husband's readiness to abuse sexually his slave women. Her powerful and perceptive civil-war diaries are a source of great value to the historian. ▷ **abolitionism**

Cheyenne
A Native American people, members of the Algonquian linguistic group, who originally lived east of the Missouri River and migrated to the Great Plains in the 17c, becoming skilled horsemen and buffalo hunters. A northern group settled along the North Platte River, while a southern contingent lived along the upper Arkansas River. Following the incursion of white prospectors and settlers on their land and attack by US troops, including a massacre at Sand Creek, Colorado, they joined the Arapaho and Sioux to fight the army, taking part in the Battle of the **Little Bighorn**. Eventually defeated, their few remaining members were assigned to reservations in Oklahoma and Montana. ▷ **Indian Wars**

Child, Lydia Mary (1802–80)
US abolitionist and novelist. In 1833 she wrote *An Appeal in Favor of That Class of Americans called Africans*. From 1841 to 1849

she edited the New York weekly *National Anti-Slavery Standard*.
▷ **abolitionism; slavery**

Chinese Exclusion (1882–1943)

A US immigration policy, growing out of strong anti-Chinese
sentiment on the West Coast, following the importation of large
numbers of Chinese as labourers. ▷ **Chinese Labour; Immigration
Legislation**

Chinese Labour (Canada)

The reputation of the Chinese for hard work meant they were in
great demand, especially by the railway interests for the building
of the British Columbian sections of the **Canadian Pacific Railway**.
Their rate of immigration into British Columbia was such that
the province attempted to restrict their entry with the introduction
of a 'head tax'. This rose from $50 in 1885 to $100 in 1900; by
1903 it had risen to $500, but still did not put off those seeking
fortune in the 'Land of the Golden Mountains'. Anti-Chinese
sentiment was pronounced among the trade unions who feared
that the labour movement would be undermined, while throughout the province there were fears that society would be destabilized. In 1902 the **Laurier** government set up a royal commission
and as a result Chinese immigration was severely restricted. In
response companies, led by the Canadian Pacific, began to bring
in East Indians and Japanese in their stead. The unions became
even more alarmed by the arrival of the Japanese, for they were
considered more competitive and were supported by a government
whom neither the Canadian nor the British government wished
to displease. With the formation of the Asiatic Exclusion League
and after the violent riots of 1907, the Laurier government introduced severe restrictions on the entry of all Oriental immigrants.
▷ **Immigration Legislation**

Chisholm, Shirley (1924–)

US politician. She was elected to the New York State Assembly
in 1964, and was the first black woman to become a member of
the House of Representatives when elected as a Democrat in 1968.
In the 1972 Democratic Convention she won a 10 per cent vote
for the presidential nomination. ▷ **Democratic Party**

Chrêtien, Joseph-Jacques-Jean (1934–   )
Canadian politician. As Chancellor in Pierre **Trudeau**'s administration he introduced two budgets in 1978 in an attempt to encourage industrial growth and fight inflation, but he failed in the latter since he also introduced tax cuts. In 1980 as Minister of Justice he fought against the concept of an independent Quebec, organizing the campaign leading up to the referendum. After Trudeau's resignation in 1984, the **Liberal Party**'s tradition of alternating francophone and anglophone leaders meant that it was John Turner who took over the leadership of the party rather than Chrêtien.

Christopher, Warren M (1925–   )
US lawyer and government official. After training as a lawyer and practising in Los Angeles, he became deputy attorney general under Andrew **Johnson** and served in the State Department during the **Carter** presidency. He was instrumental in the passing of the 1968 Civil Rights bill. As a stalwart Democrat, he was selected by Bill **Clinton** after his electoral victory to oversee his transitionary team, and subsequently as Secretary of State under the new administration.

CIA (Central Intelligence Agency)
The official US intelligence-gathering organization responsible for external security, established under the National Security Act (1947) and reporting directly to the President. The CIA was conceived as the coordinator of foreign intelligence and counter-intelligence, but it has also engaged in domestic operations. As a result of abuses of power in both the domestic (notably in the **Watergate** affair) and foreign arenas, the CIA must now coordinate domestic activities with the FBI and report on covert activities to Congress.

científicos
The pejorative term (literally, 'scientists') used to describe the intellectual supporters of Mexico's President Porfirio **Díaz** from 1876 to 1911. *Científicos* were generally Positivists, who championed the application of practical scientific (especially social sciences') methods to the solution of national problems such as

industrialization and education, arguing that 'individual absolute right is worth as much as absolute monarchy'. They were pre-eminent in the period 1876–1906, arguing that the government's duty was to assure landowners of their rights. They also believed that 'scientific-technical progress' decreed the demise of the Native American, the end to customary law which protected him, and the integration of Mexico into the international economy and European society.

Civil Rights Acts

US legislation which prohibits the states from discriminating against any citizen on the grounds of race or colour. The act of 1866 included blacks within its definition of US citizenship. President Andrew **Johnson**'s veto so angered Republican moderates in **Congress** that radicals were able to override the veto, and incorporated its provisions in the **Fourteenth Amendment**. However the act was undermined by the Supreme Court in the Slaughterhouse Cases (1873) and US v Cruikshank (1875). The act of 1875, passed as a memorial to Charles Sumner, upheld the equal rights of blacks in the use of inns, theatres and public transport (though education was specifically excluded), but was declared unconstitutional in the **Civil Rights Cases** of 1883. By the 1950s only about a quarter of those Southern blacks who were qualified to vote could actually do so because state officials were adept at preventing them from registration. The Act of 1957 therefore established the Civil Rights Commission to examine such cases. It was backed up by a new Civil Rights Division in the Justice Department which could seek injunctions to prevent denial of the right to vote. Even when bolstered in 1960 the Act did not prove very effective. By the act of 1964 the Attorney General was authorized to institute proceedings directly when voting rights were abused, and empowered to accelerate the desegregation of schools. Agencies which practised racial discrimination were liable to lose federal funding, and an Equal Opportunities Commission was set up to end job discrimination on the grounds of race, religion or sex. Discrimination was also prohibited in hotels and public transport. This legislation, together with the establishment of the Community Relations Service, indicated the federal government's awareness of the difficulties in dismantling the structures of white supremacy and was more effective than any previous **civil rights** legislation.

Civil Rights Cases (1883)

A series of seven cases in which the US Supreme Court ruled that the Civil Rights Act of 1875 was unconstitutional because **Congress** had no right to trespass on the states' internal powers of economic regulation. The judgement facilitated the development of social **segregation** by denying the federal government any direct means of protecting blacks from discrimination. ▷ **Civil Rights Acts**

civil rights movement

A movement in the USA, especially 1954-68, aimed at securing through legal means the enforcement of the guarantees of racial equality contained in the Civil War Amendments to the US **Constitution**, namely, the Thirteenth, Fourteenth, and Fifteenth Amendments, and by civil rights acts of the 1860s and 1870s. These guarantees were severely curtailed by later legislation. In particular, the Supreme Court rulings of 1883, which declared the Civil Rights Act of 1875 unconstitutional because Congress had no right to trespass on the states' internal powers of economic regulation, opened the way to racial segregation. The civil rights movement began as an attack on specific forms of segregation in the South, then broadened into a massive challenge to all forms of racial discrimination. It made considerable gains, especially at the level of legal and juridicial reform, culminating in the Supreme Court case of **Brown v Board of Education of Topeka, Kansas** (1954), in which Thurgood **Marshall** successfully argued against school segregation. The first major challenge was the Montgomery bus boycott of 1955, which was sparked by an incident in which a black woman, Rosa **Parks**, refused to give up her seat to a white man. As a result of the boycott, the buses were desegregated and Martin Luther **King**, Jr, emerged as the movement's leader. King was a major force in establishing **SCLC** (Southern Christian Leadership Conference). Forming a coalition with the **NAACP** and other organizations such as the **National Urban League**, the **Congress of Racial Equality** (**CORE**) and the Student Non-Violent Coordinating Committee (**SNCC**), he led a campaign aimed at desegregating all public facilities, including schools, restaurants, stores and transportation, by non-violent means, and at winning for blacks the unrestricted right to vote and to hold public office. Major actions included the first big clash over school desegregation (1957), which took place in Little Rock, Arkansas; the efforts of the 'freedom riders', groups of blacks and whites who challenged segregation in interstate transport (1961); the national March on Washington (1963), in which over 200 000 blacks and whites participated; and the voter registration drive in Alabama, which culminated in the march from Selma to Montgomery (1965). As white resistance grew, many participants in the marches and demonstrations were arrested, many were beaten, and some lost their lives. But by the late 1960s most of the original goals had been achieved as a result of Court decisions, major legislation and the actions of Presidents **Eisenhower**, **Kennedy** and especially Lyndon **Johnson** in enforcing the law. The Civil Rights Act of 1964 barred discrimination in public accommodations and employment; the Voting Rights Act (1965) ensured blacks' right to vote in places where it had hitherto been denied; and the Civil Rights Act of 1968 prohibited discrimination in the sale or rental of housing. One result of the 60s legislation was the increased participation of blacks in political life, even in Southern communities that were once bastions of segregation. But by the mid-60s, different problems were arising in the black ghettos of the Northern cities when blacks began rioting to protest their poverty, high unemployment and poor living conditions. Both King, who turned his attention northward in the last three years of his life, and more militant black leaders such as **Malcolm X**, recognized that the struggle for equality was moving into the economic sphere. So did **Jesse Jackson**, an associate of King's, who focused on the importance of creating jobs by investment in black businesses. But, unlike King, Malcolm X and his followers were advocating black separatism rather than integration, and the use of force to reach their goals. Significantly, widespread rioting followed King's assassination in 1968. In the decades since his death, although the economic condition of US blacks improved, the large gap between blacks and whites remained, and has led to racial tensions that have yet to be resolved.

civil rights
The rights guaranteed by certain states to its citizens. Fundamental to the concept of civil rights is the premise that a government should not arbitrarily act to infringe upon these rights, and that individuals and groups, through political action, have a legitimate role in determining and influencing what constitutes them. Historically, civil rights in the USA have been protected by the **Constitution** and **Bill of Rights**. In common usage, the term

often refers to the rights of groups, particularly ethnic and racial minorities, as well as to the rights of the individual.

Clark, Joe (Charles Joseph) (1939–)

Canadian politician. At first a journalist and then Professor of Political Science, he was elected to the Federal Parliament in 1972, becoming leader of the Progressive Conservative Party (1976) and of the Opposition (1980–83). In 1979 he became Canada's youngest-ever Prime Minister. His minority government lost the general election the following year, and he was deposed as party leader in 1983. In 1984 he became Canada's Secretary of State for External Affairs.

Clark, Mark Wayne (1896–1984)

US army officer. Chosen by Dwight D **Eisenhower** to plan the 1943 Allied invasion of North Africa, he became commander of the Allied armies in Italy in 1944. In 1945, after **World War II**, he headed the US forces occupation in Austria. During the **Korean War** he served as commander of the **UN** forces, participated in the lengthy peace talks of 1952–3, and signed the armistice.

Clay, Henry (1777–1852)

US politician. The son of a Baptist preacher, he became a lawyer (1797), entered the House of Representatives in 1811, and was chosen its speaker, a post he held for many years. He was one of the Congressional 'war hawks' active in bringing on the **War of 1812** with Britain, and was one of the commissioners who arranged the Treaty of **Ghent** which ended it. His attempts to hold the Union together in the face of the issue of slavery earned him the title of 'the great pacificator'. In 1824, 1832 and 1844 he was an unsuccessful National Republican and Whig candidate for the presidency.

Clayton–Bulwer Treaty (19 Apr 1850)

A US–British agreement on the terms for building a canal across Central America. It remained in effect until 1901, when it was superseded by the Hay–Pauncefote Treaty. Its major provision was to forbid either party to exercise exclusive control or to build fortifications. The parties involved were the US Secretary of State, John M Clayton, and the British Minister to Washington, Sir

Henry Lytton Bulwer. The Panama Canal was not completed until 1914.

CLC (Canadian Labour Congress)

Canadian labour organization. It was established in 1956 with the merger of the Trades and Labor Congress (associated with the US AFL) and the Canadian Congress of Labour (similarly associated with the US CIO). Unlike the US labour movement, the CLC was ready to take direct political action and in 1961 it united with the **CCF** (Cooperative Commonwealth Federation) to form the **New Democratic Party**. ▷ **AFL–CIO**

Clear Grits

Canadian political party. The name given to a radical reform group in Upper Canada (**Canada West**/Ontario) in the 1850s. The term derived from the group's attitude of uncompromising determination. It promoted major constitutional reform, including representation by population, direct election to executive posts, and secularization of **Clergy Reserves**. It played an important part in confederation and after 1867 it formed the core of the Canadian **Liberal Party**. ▷ **Brown, George; Canada, Upper**

Clergy Reserves

A seventh of the public land in Upper and Lower Canada (Ontario and Quebec), set aside for the future use of Protestant clergy; established under the Constitutional Act (1791). In practice, the reserves became bastions of wealth and power for the predominantly Anglican elite (the **Family Compact**) in Upper Canada, drawing fierce criticism from Methodists and disestablishmentarians. They were secularized in 1854. ▷ **Canada, Lower; Canada, Upper**

Cleveland, (Stephen) Grover (1837–1908)

US politician and 22nd and 24th President. The son of a Presbyterian minister, he became a lawyer, Mayor of Buffalo, and in 1883 Governor of New York. An honest and independent politician who abhorred machine politics, he was nominated for president by the Democrats in 1884 and won the election. In his first term he strongly advised a reduction in the high tariff. He was not re-elected in 1888, but regained the presidency in 1892. His second term began with an industrial depression that led to labour unrest and a split in the Democratic Party. In foreign affairs, he took a firm stand in the boundary dispute between Great Britain and Venezuela, asserting the US right, under the Monroe Doctrine, to determine that boundary. ▷ **political machine**

Clinton, Bill (William Jefferson) (1946–)
US politician and 42nd President. Educated at Georgetown University and Yale Law School, and a Rhodes scholar at Oxford, he taught law at the University of Arkansas (1973–6) before being elected state attorney general in 1976. A Democrat, he was elected Governor of Arkansas at the age of 32, the youngest person ever to hold that office, and served for five terms (1979–81 and 1983–92). In 1992 he was elected President, campaigning on a platform of hope and change in a climate of economic recession and voter disillusionment, ending a 12-year Republican hold on the office. His campaign and his presidency were dogged by publicity about his personal life, including the investigation into the Whitewater affair, concerning the alleged misuse of funds and tax benefits from the Whitewater development corporation and the bankrupt Madison Guaranty Savings company in Little Rock, Arkansas. Amid media speculation of a White House cover-up, Clinton set up a full inquiry into the affair. There were also calls for US intervention in difficult foreign conflicts, such as Somalia and Bosnia, and confrontation with North Korea over control of nuclear development.

Clinton, De Witt (1769–1828)
US politician. He was admitted to the bar in 1790, sat in the New York state legislature (1798–1802), US Senate (1798–1802), and was three times Mayor of New York (1803–07, 1808–10, 1811–15). He was, however, defeated by James **Madison** in the presidential election of 1812. He led the way in the fight to build the Erie Canal, known as 'Clinton's Ditch', which opened in 1825.

Clinton, Hillary Rodham (1947–)
US lawyer, known particularly for her advocacy of children's rights, and wife of President Bill **Clinton**. As an attorney in Little Rock, Arkansas, she became head of the state Rural Health Advisory Committee and later of the Children's Defense Fund (1986–92). Barred from paid office by anti-nepotism laws, she was appointed chief of a White House task force on National Health Reform, commissioned to prepare proposals on legislative

reforms to restructure the health care system of the United States. The new blueprint was unveiled to Congress in Sep 1993.

Cochise (c.1812–74)
Chief of the Chiricahua **Apache**. He lived in the American South-west and was known for his bravery and military prowess. In 1861 he was wrongfully accused of stealing and abducting a rancher's child, and was arrested by the US Army. He escaped, and after hostages were taken on both sides, and eventually killed, he began a protracted guerrilla-type war against the Army, to-gether with other tribes, that lasted for 10 years. In 1872, General Oliver Howard finally reached a peace settlement with Cochise by promising the Chiricahua a reservation on their native land.

Cody, William Frederick ('Buffalo Bill') (1846–1917)
US showman. He earned his nickname after killing nearly 5000 buffalo in 18 months for a contract to supply workers on the Kansas Pacific Railway with meat. He served as a scout in the **Sioux** wars, but from 1883 toured with his Wild West Show. The town of Cody in Wyoming stands on part of his former ranch.

Cold Harbor, Battle of (1–3 June 1864)
A battle of the **American Civil War**, fought in Virginia, with General Ulysses S **Grant**'s forces suffering heavy losses (12 000 men in one day's fighting) in an ill-advised attack on General Robert E **Lee**'s secure Confederate position. The battle, however, did serve to further Grant's strategy of keeping unrelenting pressure on the South.

Cold War
A state of tension or hostility between states that stops short of military action or a 'hot' war. The term is most frequently used to describe the relationship between the USSR and the major Western powers — especially the USA — following **World War II**. Tension was particularly high in the 1960s when the nuclear 'arms race' intensified. The process of **détente**, begun in the late 1960s, led through two decades of arms reduction and control negotiations to the 'end' of the Cold War in 1990, mainly as a result of a dramatic change in the Soviet attitude under Mikhail **Gorbachev**.

Columbus, Christopher (1451–1506)

Genoese sailor who was sent out with three ships, the *Santa Maria*, the *Pinta* and the *Nina*, by Queen Isabella of Castile (of Spain), to find a westward route to India. He explored much of the Caribbean on his four voyages, reaching the continental mainland on his last two journeys, but failing to recognize it as such. The name America was derived from that of another Italian, the merchant Amerigo Vespucci.

Comanche

Shoshonean-speaking Native American Plains people. Among the first to acquire horses from the Spanish, they migrated south into Colorado, Kansas, Oklahoma, Texas and New Mexico. They dominated the Plains and warred against both Apache and white settlers. By the 1870s the Comanche were settled on reservations in Oklahoma, where today they number about 3 500.

'Commercial Union'

A Canadian movement for economic union with the USA which became a major political issue in 1887. Confederation had failed to generate growth, probably because the number of outlets for Canadian staples had not increased, while John A **Macdonald**'s policy of protection resulted in retaliatory tariffs in the USA. Britain, an advocate of free trade, already took half of Canada's export trade, whilst there seemed little chance that trade with other European countries or South America would expand. Canadian manufacturers, anxious to maintain their protected position, argued that 'Commercial Union' was akin to Annexation, and would lead to Washington dictating fiscal policy to Ottawa. The **Liberal Party** itself was initially split, with **Laurier** for **reciprocity** rather than 'Commercial Union' and Richard **Cartright** for free trade, and in 1888 it committed itself not to 'Commercial Union' but to 'unrestricted reciprocity'.

Committees of Correspondence

In the **American Revolution**, an informal network linking towns for the purpose of sharing political information. Committees, which held town meetings, began to appear in 1772. During the crisis over independence (1775–6) they assumed active power in many places.

Commonwealth of Nations

A voluntary organization of autonomous states which had been imperial possessions of Britain. Its head is the reigning British monarch. It was formally established by the Statute of **Westminster** (1931) and meets frequently to discuss matters of mutual interest and concern. While most states, on independence, chose to become members of the Commonwealth, three have left (Irish Republic, 1949; Pakistan, 1972; Fiji, 1987).

communism

A political ideology which has as its central principle the communal ownership of all property, and thereby the abolition of private property. Although examples of early social and religious groupings based upon communal sharing of property have been cited, modern communism is specifically associated with the theories of Karl Marx. Marx saw the emergence of a communist society as being the final stage in a historical process that was rooted in human material needs, preceded by feudalism, capitalism and (a transitional stage) socialism. Communism, according to Marx, would abolish class distinctions and end the exploitation of the masses inherent in the capitalist system. The working class, or proletariat, would be the instrument of a revolution that would overthrow the capitalist system and liberate human potential. A fully developed communist system would operate according to the principle of 'from each according to his ability, to each according to his need', and as there would be no cause for the state to regulate society, it would 'wither away'. Marx's writings provided a powerful ideological basis for communist and many socialist parties and governments, which legitimized the implementation of their policies by reference to Marxism or some variant of it. ▷ **Communist Party of the USA**

Communist Party of the USA (CPUSA)

Established in 1919 by left-wing socialists and members of the **IWW**, it was bitterly harassed during the Red Scare and only in 1923–4 did a unified, coherent and legal structure emerge. This was dominated by Jay Lovestone, deposed on **Stalin**'s orders in 1929 for 'American exceptionalism'. During 1930s membership increased from about 7 000 to 90 000 during **World War II**, in spite of mass defections in response to Stalin's purges and the German–Soviet Pact; and the leadership of Earl Browder followed the 'Comintern' line, opposing other left-wing 'social fascists' until

1935, and then building a popular front with much use of the slogan 'Communism is twentieth-century Americanism'. Browder himself was expelled in 1946, after the condemnation (by Jacques Duclos, the French communist leader) of his attempt to reorient the party to the post-war world by re-forming it as the Communist Political Asociation (CPA). William Z Foster, a veteran of the 1920s, then took over during the onset of the **Cold War** and the intense domestic anti-communist campaign driven by the investigations of **HUAC** and Senator Joseph **McCarthy**. The party's leadership was jailed for five years under the Smith Act (1940), which prohibited the 'teaching and advocating' of subversive doctrines, and by the time of their release, its membership numbered no more than 17 000, and its credibility had been almost totally destroyed by the Soviet invasion of Hungary in 1956. Until this time the party had exerted an influence (both by action and reaction) out of all proportion to its tiny numbers, its often vindictive discipline, its political impotence, and even, perhaps, the contempt of Moscow. In spite of its aging leadership (almost all of the founding generation) it also showed a remarkable ability to renew its cadres. Unlike the major parties, it took with deadly seriousness two of the great questions of 20c America, industrial organization and race. It also insisted on relating politics to culture (and thus made a particular appeal to artists and intellectuals). If its answers were unacceptable to the vast majority of Americans, they still proceeded not from a conspiracy to subvert the American way, but from a vision of its regeneration.

Compact Theory of Confederation
Canadian constitutional theory. An interpretation of the **British North America Act** which argued that confederation meant the entrusting of certain powers to Ottawa while the provinces still retained their autonomy. As a compact, the agreement could not be altered without the acceptance of the signatories and could even be nullified if they so wished. The theory was supported in the 1880s by Quebeckers such as Honoré **Mercier** and by English-speaking provincial leaders like Mowat in Ontario and Norquay in Manitoba. The federal power which provincial governments most wanted to remove was that of disallowing provincial legislation, because, along with a policy of economic centralization, it would result in the severe limitation of provincial rights. At the 1927 Dominion-Provincial Conference the compact theory was proclaimed the true interpretation of confederation by both the

Liberal Premier of Quebec and the Tory Premier of Ontario and during the 1930s it was used to place the Prime Minister, Richard **Bennett**, under political pressure. The theory actually disintegrates under examination because the original signatories comprised only three provinces.

Compromise of 1850
A major but ultimately unsuccessful attempt by the Congress of the United States to resolve by legislation the conflict between the North and the South over slavery. Specifically involved was the expansion of slavery into new territories such as California and the South-West. Its major terms were the admission of California as a free (nonslave) state, and the passage of a strong fugitive slave law to placate the South. ▷ **American Civil War**

Compromise of 1877
An agreement for the restoration of home rule in the South and the inauguration as President of the Republican candidate Rutherford **B Hayes**, made after the contested US election of 1876. Even though the Democratic candidate Samuel J Tilden won a clear majority of the popular vote, the result hung on the electoral votes of three Southern states, Louisiana, South Carolina and Florida, where polling frauds (by both parties) produced two sets of returns. A Republican-controlled Electoral Commission awarded the votes to Hayes, while amid threats of disruption and violence from Northern Democrats in particular, informal understandings were reached between Republicans and Southern Democrats to recognize Democratic administrations in Louisiana and South Carolina, together with the promise of non-interference in the future, the appointment of a Southerner in Hayes's cabinet, and an empty recognition of civil and political equality for blacks. Contrary to legend, the compromise did not involve the withdrawal of the very few remaining federal troops in the South, but it did mean they were taken out of politics, and it is generally regarded as having brought the formal process of **Reconstruction** after the **American Civil War** to an end.

Compulsory Service Act (1917)
Canadian conscription legislation. It was introduced because Canada's voluntary militia had been unable to fulfil the commitment to provide four full divisions on the Western Front. **Borden**'s

Minister for Militia, Sir Sam Hughes, had deterred many French-Canadians from volunteering by his Ulster Protestant prejudices. The Act was particularly unpopular in Quebec, where many believed they were being asked to fight for the empire, while being denied equal rights at home. With **World War II** the government tried to maintain a policy of 'no conscription' to ensure national unity, despite continuous pressure from the English-speaking provinces, especially after the fall of France. In response Mackenzie **King** held a referendum which showed that although 80 per cent of the English-speaking population wished to free the government from its pledge, 72 per cent of French-Canadians were against doing so. King therefore retained the policy and sacked his Defence Minister when he was advised that there were not enough volunteers to maintain the Canadian commitment after the Normandy landings in 1944. But with the failure of the policy to enlist home defence draftees, King was forced to reintroduce conscription. Protest from French-Canadians, both among civilians and in the forces, was fierce, while one French-Canadian minister resigned from the government and 34 Quebec Liberals voted against it in a vote of confidence. Even so, King managed to survive the election of 1945, albeit with a reduced majority.

Comstock Lode

US gold and silver deposits discovered at Gold Hill, Nevada in 1859 by two prospectors who allowed H P Comstock, a drifter nicknamed 'Old Pancake', to talk his way into a share and give his name to the find. Instead of developing the claim, he sold for a tiny sum the greatest single deposit of precious metals in the USA. The field yielded more than US$300 000 000 within 20 years.
▷ **gold rush**

Confederacy ▷ Confederate States of America

Confederate States of America

The official name of the states that seceded in 1860–1, precipitating the **American Civil War**: Virginia, North Carolina, South Carolina, Georgia, Florida, Tennessee, Alabama, Mississippi, Louisiana, Texas and Arkansas. The Confederacy's constitution was modelled on the **US Constitution**. Its only President was Jefferson **Davis** of Mississippi. It never won foreign recognition, and collapsed after military defeat by the North in 1865. The other four slave states (Delaware, Maryland, Kentucky and Missouri) did not secede, and neither did the north-west counties of Virginia, which became West Virginia.

Confederation Movement

Canadian political movement for unification within the British North American provinces. Prefigured at various times from the **American Revolution** onwards, consideration of the project by Earl Grey, the British Colonial Secretary (1846–52), set in train discussions within the maritime provinces. At the same time a growing paralysis of government was becoming evident within the Province of Canada. A T **Galt**'s entry into the **Cartier–Macdonald** government in 1858 was only secured on condition that it sought confederation, which was rapidly being seen as a necessity. The English-speaking business community believed it to be essential for economic growth and expansion to the west against American competition, while the threat to reciprocity demanded closer trading links between Canada and the Maritimes. The British government's commitment to Canadian defence had been called into question since the Oregon dispute, and with the onset of the **American Civil War**, the provinces became aware that they were very vulnerable to retaliation from the Northern states because of British policies and because Confederates were ready to use Canada as a base for raids. In 1864 the 'great coalition' of Canadian reformers and conservatives under the leadership of Sir Étienne-Paschal Tache broached the idea of a general union at the Charlottetown Conference called by the Maritimes. Discussions continued at the Quebec Conference, where agreement was quickly reached. Acceptance by the provincial legislatures was much more difficult to obtain, and was achieved in Canada (where it needed all George Étienne Cartier's political acumen to persuade the French-Canadians) only after lengthy debate. In the Maritimes, Newfoundland and Prince Edward Island rejected confederation, but Samuel **Tilley** and Charles **Tupper** eventually secured its adoption in New Brunswick and Nova Scotia. The final resolutions were agreed at the London Conference of 1866 and embodied in the **British North America Act** of 1867. ▷ **Canada, Dominion of**

Congress

The national, or federal, legislature of the USA, consisting of two elected chambers: the Senate and the House of Representatives.

The Senate contains two members from each state (irrespective of size), serving six-year terms, with a third of the terms expiring every two years. Representation in the House is for a two-year term, and is calculated on the basis of population. Congress initiates legislation, and significantly amends or rejects presidential legislative proposals. The **US Constitution** endows it with the 'power of the purse', and all revenue bills must originate in the House. For a bill to become law it must be passed in identical form by both chambers and signed by the President. A presidential veto may be overturned by a two-thirds majority in each chamber. Legislation receives detailed consideration in the powerful Congressional committees. Although the chambers are organized along party lines, party discipline is weak. The majority party leader of the House occupies the influential position of Speaker.

Congress of Racial Equality (CORE)
US **civil rights** organization founded in 1942. In the 1960s CORE sponsored sit-in demonstrations, the freedom riders' challenge to segregation in interstate public buses, and registration of black voters in the South.

Connecticut Compromise
The 'Great Compromise' by which the deadlock reached in the 1787 **Constitutional Convention** was broken, and the way paved for the adoption of the **US Constitution** in its final form. It was proposed by Roger Sherman, a delegate from Connecticut, to meet the fear of the small states that they would be overwhelmed in a national government by the larger states. Nationalists such as James **Madison** had wanted representation in both houses of **Congress** to be based on population. Sherman accepted this system for the lower house, the House of Representatives, but proposed equality of representation in the upper house, the Senate, to which each state, irrespective of size or population, should send two members who would vote as individuals, not as a delegation.

conquistador
Literally 'conqueror', this is the standard term for the leaders of the Spanish expeditions of the early 16c which undertook the invasion and conquest of America. ▷ **Cortés**

Constitution Act of 1982

The statute which 'patriated' the constitution of Canada, adding a Charter of Rights and Freedoms, and a general amendment procedure. It was the result of 18 months of hectic negotiation following the 1980 Quebec referendum on independence during which the federal government had promised a national settlement of constitutional issues. Through the summer of 1980 a series of very public discussions explored the items of a prepared agenda for a First Ministers' conference in Sep. After this broke down in acrimony, the federal government announced a unilateral approach to the British parliament, a resolution whose validity was finally accepted by the Supreme Court in Sep 1981 as allowable though objectionable. 'Constitutional convention plus constitutional law equal the total constitution of the country,' it said in a judgement that was used to support the arguments of both sides. At a final conference in Nov 1981, the so-called Kitchen Meeting paved the way for compromise, which was however, rejected by Quebec. ▷ **Meech Lake Accord**

Constitutional Convention (1787)

A gathering at Philadelphia that drafted the **US Constitution**; 12 of the original 13 states were represented (Rhode Island did not send a delegate). The term, by extension, is also used for any political meeting empowered to write a state or national constitution. The plans to draw up a new system of government were jeopardized by failure to reach agreement on the issue of representation. ▷ **Connecticut Compromise**

Constitutional Union Party

A political party formed to fight the US election in 1860. It aimed to overcome the crisis between North and South by upholding 'the enforcement of the laws'. Its presidential candidate, John Bell (1797–1869) of Tennessee, came last in the popular vote and third in the electoral vote in a four-way race.

containment

The policy adopted by the USA and thereafter her Western allies aimed at containing, by political, economic, and diplomatic means, the 'expansionist tendencies' of the USSR. The policy, first advocated in 1947 by George **Kennan**, also involved the provision of technical and economic aid to non-communist countries.

Continental Congress (1774–8)

The federal legislature in North America consisting of delegates from each of the 13 colonies (the United States after 1776). The First Continental Congress met from 5 Sep to 26 Oct 1774, in response to Britain's passing the **Intolerable Acts**, and its delegates petitioned the King. When no appropriate response was received, the Second Continental Congress convened in May 1775, shortly after the Battles of **Lexington and Concord**, and created an army. Agreeing to seek independence in the summer of 1776, the Congress formally adopted the **Declaration of Independence** on July 4. The Congress remained the political voice of the young country under the **Articles of Confederation** until the US **Constitution** took effect in 1789. ▷ **American Revolution; Ordinance of 1787**

Contreras, Battle of (1847)

An engagement in the **Mexican War** (1846–8) in which the Mexican army under **Santa Anna** was badly defeated by a smaller US force under Winfield Scott (1786–1866), opening the way to Mexico City and leading to the collapse of Mexican resistance.

Coolidge, (John) Calvin (1872–1933)

US politician and 30th President. He became a lawyer, and was Governor of Massachusetts (1919–20) when he gained national attention for his firm handling of the Boston police strike. Elected Vice-President (1921–3), on Warren G Harding's death he became President (1923). A strong supporter of US business interests, he was triumphantly re-elected in 1924, but refused renomination in 1928. Coolidge's policies were successful while he was in office, but were partly responsible for the **Great Depression** that followed.

Copperhead

A term for Northern members of the US **Democratic Party** who opposed the **American Civil War**, derived from the name of a poisonous snake. In the election of 1864, Copperheads included a peace plank in their party platform, but this was repudiated by the presidential candidate, George McClellan.

Cornwallis, Charles, 1st Marquis (1738–1805)
British general and politician. He served in the Seven Years War, although he was personally opposed to taxing the American colonists, accepting a command in the war. He defeated **Gates** at **Camden** (1780), but was forced to surrender at **Yorktown** (1781). In 1786 he became Governor-General of India, and was made marquis in 1793.

Cortés, Hernán (1485–1547)
Spanish conqueror of Mexico. He studied at Salamanca, then accompanied Velázquez in his expedition to Cuba (1511). In 1519 he commanded an expedition against Mexico, fighting his first battle at Tabasco. He founded Vera Cruz, marched to Tlascala, and made allies of the natives. He then marched on the Aztec capital, capturing King **Montezuma**, but the Mexicans rose and Cortés was forced to flee. He then launched a successful siege of the capital, which fell in 1521. He was formally appointed Governor and Captain-General of New Spain in 1522, but his authority was later superseded. He spent the years 1530–40 in Mexico, then returned to Spain. ▷ **Aztecs**

Coureurs du bois
The French-Canadian term for fur-traders who 'went Indian'. Native Americans began to realize that their identity was threatened through contact with settlements and trading posts. They also grew to understand that they were in a strong position to play off the French against English fur-traders from Albany. French-Canadian fur-traders therefore made annual trips into the hinterland or *pays d'en haut* to deal directly with the Native Americans, and frequently decided not to return to the settlements.

cowboys
Cattle herders in 19c USA who flourished on the trans-Mississippi plains during the 'open range' period of the cattle industry (c.1865–85). They were particularly important in the 'long drive' from Texas to the railheads in Missouri and Kansas. Cowboys included many Confederate veterans, as well as former slaves and Mexicans. Contrary to popular imagery, the cowboy's life was one of hard work and privation. In the popular mind the cowboy remains the embodiment of the American hero who stands for rugged self-sufficiency and frontier justice.

Cowpens, Battle of (1781)

During the **American Revolution**, an engagement in South Carolina in which a small American army under Daniel Morgan (1736–1802) defeated a British force under Banastre Tarleton (1754–1833).

Craig, Sir James Henry (1748–1812)

British soldier and colonial administrator. He fought in the **American Revolution**, being wounded at the Battle of Bunker Hill (1775) and serving with distinction in the invasion of the Hudson River Valley. After playing a prominent part in the capture of the Dutch colony of the Cape of Good Hope, he was made the colony's temporary governor from 1795 to 1797. After further commands in India, England and in the Napoleonic Wars, he became Governor-General of Canada (1807–11). There, with the backing of London and the English-speaking Montreal merchants, he sought to anglicize the province. To that end he dissolved the assembly, and cashiered many French officers from the militia. In 1810 the printers and proprietor of the critical newspaper, *Le Canadien*, were arrested for treason and, when war broke out with the USA, he introduced a special Act which enabled him to suppress the newspaper altogether. This provoked both riots and the election of an increased number of radical French-Canadian deputies. The British government drew back from its policy and Craig was recalled. His name is still hated in the province, and the period of his governorship is known as the 'Reign of Terror'.

Crandall, Prudence (1803–89)

US educator. Her private school at Canterbury, Connecticut lost most of its white pupils when she admitted a black girl in 1833. She decided to keep the school open for blacks only, and for 18 months withstood insults and vandalism. The Connecticut state legislature then passed a law which made the establishment of schools for non-resident blacks illegal, unless permission had been granted from the town's selectmen. She was arrested and jailed. Eminent abolitionists took up her cause, but the main issue was evaded when her sentence was reversed by the state Supreme Court on a technicality. ▷ **abolitionism**

Crazy Horse (Ta-Sunko-Witko) (c.1849–77)

Oglala **Sioux** Chief, regarded as the foremost Sioux military leader. He defeated General **Custer** at the Battle of **Little Bighorn**

(1876), leading a combined force of Sioux and **Cheyennes**. He and his followers surrendered the following year, and he died in custody at Fort Robinson, Nebraska, stabbed in the back, according to a well-known Indian pictograph.

Créditistes

French-Canadian partner of the **Social Credit Party**. After a revival in their fortunes the party gained 26 seats in the 1962 federal elections but declined to 24 seats in 1963 when the Quebec representatives set up their own organization. The party's popularity subsequently declined with the size of the rural population and by 1980 it was eliminated.

Creek

Native Americans originally organized in a confederacy living in Georgia and Alabama. Members of the Muskhogean linguistic group, they were an agricultural people with a highly developed social system. During the colonial period they gave assistance to both the French and the British. They rose up in the Creek War of 1813–14 to stop white invasion of their territory, but were defeated and forced to cede much of their land. In the 1830s they were part of the Native American 'removal' of the **Five Civilized Tribes** to Oklahoma, where most of the remaining Creeks continue to live today.

Crerar, Thomas Alexander (1876–1975)

Canadian politician. Founder of the **Progressive Party** when he bolted from the Liberals in protest against their high tariff budget of 1920, he led the party to second place in the 1921 elections with 65 seats. Preferring to hold the balance of power, he left official opposition to the Conservatives. Within a year he resigned as leader, at least in part because he insisted on conventional principles of party organization and representation in conflict with those of his Alberta and Ontario membership. He re-entered politics, becoming Minister of Railways and Canals in Mackenzie **King**'s administration in 1929. Although he lost his seat in 1930, he won again with the Liberals in 1933, and served in the government as Minister of Mines and Resources. In 1945 he became a Senator and resigned in 1966.

Crisis

US **civil rights** journal. Produced by the **NAACP**, it was a monthly magazine aimed at the black middle and professional classes. W

E B **Du Bois** was its editor (1910–34), increasing its circulation from 1 000 to 16 000 in one year. Du Bois declared its purpose was to 'set forth those facts and arguments which show the danger of race prejudice, particularly as manifested toward colored people'. The magazine was also particularly important in providing a mouth-piece for the Harlem Renaissance.

Cristero Revolt (1927–9)

Rural guerrilla warfare against the Mexican government. Confined to the states of Guadalajara, Morelos, Colima, Jalisco and Michoacán, the rebels fought under the banner 'Viva Christo Rey!'. Unlike their predecessors, they did not merely seek to restore the traditional pre-eminence of the Church in Mexico, but also to carry through social reforms; they thus presented a fundamental challenge to the revolutionary governments led by **Calles** and Obregón. By the end of 1927, Church and State were at stalemate: the Church suspended public worship and the State persecuted the clergy. In June 1929 the Vatican and US Ambassador Dwight Morrow achieved a compromise by which Church property was returned to the clergy and religious instruction was permitted in the Churches.

Crittenden Compromise (1860)

In the months preceding the **American Civil War**, this was an attempt by Senator John J Crittenden of Kentucky to resolve the crisis between North and South by writing into the constitution a formal recognition of **slavery** in territories south of 36°30′ and other terms. None of these were new and were therefore unacceptable to Abraham **Lincoln**, whose election as President was causing secession by the slave-holding South.

Crockett, Davy (David) (1786–1836)

US frontiersman. He distinguished himself against the **Creek** in Jackson's campaign of 1814, and was elected to the US House of Representatives from Tennessee (1827–31 and 1833–5). He died fighting for Texas at the Battle of the **Alamo**. Highly embellished stories of his exploits have assumed mythological proportions.

Croker, Richard (1841–1922)

Irish-born US politician. As a prize-fighter and gang leader he came to the notice of 'Honest John' **Kelly** in the 1860s and succeeded him as the boss of **Tammany Hall** in 1885. By turning over patronage to district leaders acting under his close supervision, and by using his expertise as a tax-collector, Croker built a machine which maintained his political control in New York until 1901. ▷ **political machine**

Croly, Herbert (1869–1930)
US political philosopher. In 1909 he wrote *The Promise of American Life*, a powerful condemnation of contemporary US political life. He called for Jeffersonian ends to be achieved by Hamiltonian means: that is, for a democratic and egalitarian society to be achieved through government intervention. His ideas may have influenced Theodore **Roosevelt**'s **New Nationalism** speech at Osawatomie, Kansas in 1910. In 1914, together with Walter Weyl and Walter **Lippmann**, Croly launched *The New Republic*, which aimed to encourage 'a more thoughtful and radical form of **progressivism**'. The magazine followed Croly's new liberalism in demonstrating a concern for the individual within the conformity demanded by contemporary technological society.

Cuauhtémoc (c.1495–1525)
Last Aztec ruler. He was the successor to **Montezuma II**, who resisted the Spaniards under **Cortés** at the siege of Tenochtitlán (now Mexico City) in 1521. He was later executed while on an expedition with Cortés to Honduras. ▷ **Aztecs**

Cuban Missile Crisis (Oct 1962)
A period of acute international tension and potential military confrontation between the USA and USSR, following the USA's discovery of Soviet nuclear missile sites in Cuba. President John F **Kennedy** demanded the dismantling of the base and the return of the missiles, and threw a naval blockade around the island. The crisis ended on 28 Oct, when Soviet leader **Khrushchev** agreed to Kennedy's demands, in return for the withdrawal of US missiles from Turkey.

Cuban Revolution (1895–8)
Sometimes known as the War of Independence, the nationalist revolt against Spanish imperialism started in Apr 1895 when a force landed by Marti and Gomez in Oriente province joined that of Maceo near Santiago. A provisional government was proclaimed and, although Marti was killed soon afterwards, Gomez and Maceo triumphed everywhere until 'Butcher' Weyler, the Spanish Commander-in-Chief, resorted to a policy of terror.

Weyler's atrocities, however, provoked popular sympathy for the rebel cause in the USA and when the USS *Maine* blew up in Havana harbour (Feb 1898), the Americans blamed the Spanish authorities and instituted a military intervention, the **Spanish–American War** (1898).

Culpeper's Rebellion (1677–80)

An attempt by settlers in North Carolina to establish a government in opposition to 'proprietors' who claimed control of the province on effectively feudal terms. It was named after John Culpeper, the settlers' chief spokesman, who was subsequently acquitted on a charge of treason, and who died, as he was born, in obscurity.

Cuomo, Mario (1932–   )

US politician. Educated at St John's University, New York, he became Governor of New York State. The most charismatic Democrat of his generation, he was strongly boosted for the presidency in 1984 and 1988.

Curley, James Michael (1874–1958)

US politician, boss of the Boston Democratic machine. In 1902 he entered the state legislature and began to build a political organization based mainly on Irish support. This machine, together with a extrovert personality, enabled him to dominate Boston politics until the end of the 1940s. In 1910 he was elected to the US House of Representatives, but in 1914 returned to Boston as mayor, a position he held during 1914–18, 1922–6, 1930–4 and 1947–50. He also served as Governor of Massachusetts (1935–7) and as US congressman (1943–7). In 1947 he was convicted of mail fraud, serving nearly six months in jail before President Harry S **Truman** commuted his sentence. ▷ **political machine**

Custer, George Armstrong (1839–76)

US army officer. He graduated from the US Military Academy at West Point (1861), and after a brilliant career as a cavalry commander in the **American Civil War** served in the campaigns against the Native American peoples of the Great Plains. His actions were controversial, but his gift for self-publicity made him a symbol of the cavalry. He and over 200 of his men were killed at the Battle of **Little Bighorn**, Montana (25 June 1876), by a combined force of Sioux and Cheyenne. ▷ **Indian Wars**

D

Daley, Richard J (1902–76)
US politician. As Democratic mayor of Chicago (1955–76) and city boss, his **political machine** was so powerful that Democratic candidates at both the state and national level sought his backing. He became notorious during the 1968 Democratic Convention in Chicago, when the city's police force clubbed and gassed demonstrators protesting against the **Vietnam War**. By 1972 his influence had waned as a result of reforms which increased the representation of women, blacks and other minorities in the Democratic Party.

Danish West Indies, Sale of (1917)
The result of an agreement reached in Jan 1916 between the governments of Denmark and the USA concerning the Danish West Indian colonies, the main islands being St Croix, St Jan and St Thomas, acquired in the 18c. The agreement stipulated that the US government would pay the Danish government $25 million for the islands, which the US considered part of its sphere of influence and of strategic importance after the opening of the Panama Canal. To the agreement was annexed a declaration in which the US government recognized the sovereignty of Denmark over the whole of Greenland. On 14 Dec 1916 a referendum about the agreement was held in Denmark with 64.3 per cent of the votes in favour of the sale and 35.7 per cent, a surprisingly high proportion, against. On 1 Apr 1917 — five days before the US declared war on Germany — the islands were handed over by the Danish government to the USA and renamed the 'Virgin Islands of the US'.

Darrow, Clarence Seward (1857–1938)
US civil liberties lawyer. In 1907 he successfully defended 'Big Bill' **Haywood** and Charles Moyer of the Western Federation of Miners implicated in the murder of Frank Steunenberg, ex-governor of Idaho. In 1924, his defence of Richard Loeb and

Nathan Leopold in the most sensational murder trial of the age saved them from the death penalty; and in the Monkey Trial of 1925, at Dayton, Tennessee, he defended the high school biology teacher John Scopes who was charged under the Tennessee state law forbidding the teaching of Darwin's Theory of Evolution. Although Scopes was found guilty and fined US$100, Darrow demolished the views which lay behind the law and the arguments of the prosecution, led by William Jennings **Bryan**, the elderly champion of Protestant fundamentalism. In 1934 Darrow was appointed to investigate Senator Gerald Nye's charge that the codes introduced by the National Recovery Board were favouring monopolies. His scathing report led eventually to the demise of price control.

Daughters of the American Revolution (DAR)
A patriotic society organized in the USA in 1890; members must be directly descended from soldiers or patriots of the revolutionary period. It has three divisions: historical, educational and patriotic. ▷ **American Revolution**

Davis, Jefferson (1808–89)
US politician. After studying at the US Military Academy at West Point, he served in several frontier campaigns. He entered the US House of Representatives for Mississippi (1845), fought in the **Mexican War** (1846–7), and became Secretary of War (1853–7). In the Senate (1847–51) he led the extreme State Rights Party and supported slavery. President of the Confederate States of America at the close of the **American Civil War** (1865), he was imprisoned for two years, then released on bail. Though indicted for treason, he was never brought to trial, and he was included in the amnesty of 1872.

Dawes Plan
A report on Germany's economic problems issued in 1924 by a committee presided over by US banker Charles Dawes. The plan laid down a schedule of annual German payments of **reparations**, outlined the reorganization of the German Reichsbank, and recommended a large foreign loan for Germany. A further report was drawn up in 1929 by an international commission chaired by US financier Owen Young (1874–1962).

Dawson, William Levi (1886–1970)
US politician. Elected alderman of the 2nd Ward in Chicago in 1933, he established a strong black **political machine** which he manipulated less to change the white-dominated city government's attitudes on schools and housing than to gain political favours and a limited patronage. In 1942 he was elected as a Democrat to the House of Representatives and he became the first black to hold the chairmanship of a major congressional committee, the House Committee on Government Operations. He was continually re-elected until 1970 when he refused re-nomination because of illness.

D-Day (6 June 1944)
The day when the Allies launched the greatest amphibious operation in history (codenamed 'Overlord'), and invaded German-occupied Europe. By the end of D-Day, 130 000 troops had been landed on five beach-heads along an 80km/50ml stretch of the coast of Normandy, at a cost of 10 000 casualties. ▷ **Normandy Campaign; World War II**

Debs, Eugene Victor (1855–1926)
US politician. He worked as a locomotive fireman, and in 1893 was founder and first President of the American Railway Union, in 1894 leading the **Pullman Strike** for higher wages. He helped to establish the Socialist Party of America, was imprisoned for labour agitation, and between 1900 and 1920 stood five times as socialist candidate for President. His indictment for violation of the Espionage Act brought him imprisonment (1918–21).

Decatur, Stephen (1779–1820)
US naval commander of French descent. He served against the French, and gained great distinction in the war with Tripoli (1801–5), burning the captured Philadelphia, and escaping under the fire of 141 guns. Promoted captain in 1804 and commodore in 1810, in the **War of 1812** with England he captured the frigate *Macedonian*, but in 1814 surrendered to the British. He was killed in a duel at Bladensburg, Maryland.

Declaration of Independence (1776)
The document adopted by the US **Continental Congress** to proclaim the separation of the 13 colonies from Britain. Drawn up

by a committee of John **Adams**, Benjamin **Franklin**, Thomas **Jefferson**, Robert R **Livingston**, and Roger Sherman, it announced the right of revolution, detailing the Americans' reasons for the break, and asserted that American government should be based on a theory of natural law, and should respect the fundamental rights of individuals.

Declaratory Act (1766)

A British Act passed by the **Rockingham** government. After much opposition in the US colonies to the introduction of taxes by the preceding George **Grenville** administration, Rockingham repealed the **Stamp Act** (1765); but this legislation reasserted the British parliament's general right to legislate for the colonies 'in all cases whatsoever'.

Delany, Martin Robinson (1812–85)

US anti-slavery activist. The grandson of slaves, he became a doctor and a journalist, his major work being *The Condition, Elevation, Emigration and Destiny of the Colored Peoples of the United States* (1852). By 1854, despairing of ever achieving black **civil rights** in the North, he began to advocate emigration of blacks to Africa. This he abandoned after travelling in West Africa on the eve of the **American Civil War**, resuming the struggle for racial equality within the USA, and becoming active in the Freedmen's Bureau.

Democratic Party

US political party. It was originally composed in the late 18c of those opposed to the economic policies of Alexander Hamilton and in sympathy with France rather than Britain (during the Anglo-French Wars of the 1790s). Its first successful presidential candidate was **Thomas Jefferson**, and in the early 1800s dominated its opponent, the **Federalist Party**. During the 1830s, under Presidents Andrew **Jackson** and Martin **Van Buren**, the party gained mass appeal among the electorate through shrewd political management, and was identified as representative of the 'common man'. The party was split over slavery and secession during the **American Civil War**, and its position of national dominance was taken over by the **Republican Party**. After the war the party became conservative, based in the South and West, achieving only intermittent success. It returned to a majority position in 1932, with Franklin D **Roosevelt**'s '**New Deal**', and added large urban areas and ethnic, racial and religious support to its conservative Southern base. It also became associated with a more liberal stance on social reform and minority rights, especially in the 1960s. It retains the preference of the majority of Americans, reflected in the Democrat-dominated House and Senate, but since the early 1960s it has had great difficulty winning the presidency, with the exception of Jimmy **Carter** (1977–81) and Bill **Clinton** (1993–   ). ▷ **Barnburners; Copperhead; Whig Party**

Department of Regional Economic Expansion (DREE)
Canadian Federal Department. In 1969 it became responsible for the administration of the Agricultural Rehabilitation and Development Act (ARDA) and the Fund for Rural Economic Development (FRED). Parliament gave the department extraordinary powers under the Regional Development Incentives Act. The choice of regions or firms which qualified for capital assistance grants was made by the minister appointed by Pierre **Trudeau**, Pierre Marchand. Up to $12 million could be allotted to the projects of his choice and soon the department was involved in many different federal/provincial development schemes, so that by 1979 the department's expenditure had grown to half a billion dollars per year.

De Priest, Oscar Stanton (1871–1951)
US politician. Born in Alabama, he ran away from home to Chicago where he was the first black to be elected to the City Council (as a Republican in 1915). He became an alderman in 1927, and the first black congressman from the North in 1928. Holding office until 1934, when he was defeated by a black Democrat, he secured passage for a bill to reduce discrimination in the Civilian Conservation Corps.

De Sapio, Carmine G (1909–   )
US politician. Selected by gangster Frank Costello to be **Tammany Hall** leader in 1949, he attempted to distance himself from the mob by introducing sweeping reforms within the machine to increase the power of party members. By 1965 he had succeeded so well that he lost his own place. In 1970 he was convicted of conspiracy to bribe a city official to obtain construction contracts from the ConEd Corporation. ▷ **political machine**

détente

An attempt to lower the tension between states as a means of reducing the possibility of war and of achieving peaceful coexistence between different social and political systems. A prominent feature of relations between the USA and USSR in the 1970s, it led to several agreements over arms (SALT) and security and cooperation (Helsinki). In the early 1980s, there was a cooling towards détente on the part of the USA, on the grounds that too many concessions had been made and that the USSR did not adhere to the spirit of such agreements; but there was a considerable improvement in relations in the later part of the decade.
▷ **Cold War; Helsinki Conference**

Dewey, George (1837–1917)

US admiral. He served with the Union naval forces in the Civil War (1861–5), and as Commodore in the **Spanish-American War** (1898) defeated the Spanish fleet at Manila Bay without losing a man.

Dewson, Mary Williams (Molly) (1874–1962)

US industrial economist and political feminist. As a social worker she was Superintendent of the Massachusetts Girls Parole Department (1900–12), Secretary to the state's Commission on Minimum Wage Legislation (1911), and a Zone Chief for the Bureau of Refugees in the US relief operation after **World War I**. As an economist she served with the National Consumers League (1920–4) and the Consumer Advisory Board of the **NRA**, and was appointed to the Social Security Board in 1937. She was an early supporter of Franklin D **Roosevelt** for the presidency, playing an important role in his election and his re-election in 1936, when she was Vice-Chair of the Democratic National Committee. A close friend of Eleanor **Roosevelt**, she was a key figure in mobilizing women for political action from the mid-1920s to the late 1930s.

Díaz, (José de la Cruz) Porfirio (1830–1915)

Mexican politician. A follower of Benito **Juárez**, he fought against the conservatives and Emperor **Maximilian**'s French-imposed rule in 1864–7. He seized power in 1876 and was President until 1880, returning in 1884 to remain in office until 1911, when he was ousted by Francisco **Madero**. His long period of office saw the impact of the changes brought about by the laws of La **Reforma**, including the emergence of a wage-earning rural populace, the rise of a powerful northern economy, export-led economic growth stimulated by the railroad, and extensive foreign investment. Though a master manipulator, his regime became a gerentocracy, and his patronage of the **científicos**' attempt to 'whiten the nation' meant that he was open to the accusation of having betrayed Mexico to foreign, mainly Anglo-American, interests. Nonetheless, his regime (known as the Porfiriato) did much to stimulate material progress in Mexico. He died in Paris, in the midst of a revolution whose outcome was influenced by the changes he had fomented.

Diefenbaker, John George (1895–1979)

Canadian politician. In 1940 he entered the Canadian Federal House of Commons, becoming leader of the Progressive Conservatives (1956) and Prime Minister (1957–63) after 22 years of **Liberal Party** rule. His government introduced important agricultural reforms, and extended the federal franchise to Canada's Amerindian peoples. He remained active in national politics until his death in Ottawa.

Dixiecrats

US segregationist politicians. The term refers to 30 Southern delegates who, in 1948, walked out of the Democratic Convention at Philadelphia, in response to Hubert **Humphrey**'s assertion that 'the time has arrived for the **Democratic Party** to get out of the shadow of states' rights and walk forthrightly into the bright sunshine of human rights'. They then held a convention in Birmingham, Alabama, formed the **states' rights** Democratic Party, and selected Governor J Strom Thurmond of South Carolina as their candidate on an anti-**civil rights** platform. Although they ultimately carried only Louisiana, Mississippi, Alabama and South Carolina, the party's success in the election began the disruption of the solid Democratic South.

Dole, Elizabeth Hanford (1936–)

US government official and charity administrator, the wife of Robert J **Dole**. She became a lawyer and worked in various posts in Washington, DC, including that of Deputy Director of the Office of Consumer Affairs in the White House (1971–3). She was secretary of the US Department of Transport under **Reagan**

(1983–7), and of the US Department of Labor (1989–90) in the **Bush** administration. In 1991 she resigned to take up the presidency of the American Red Cross.

Dole, Robert J (1923–   )
US Senator. He trained as a lawyer, entered the US House of Representatives as a Repbulican (1961–9), and became member of the US Senate from Kansas in 1969. In 1976 he stood as a Republican vice-presidential candidate alongside **Ford**. Between 1984 and 1986 he was majority leader of the Senate, and later minority leader, and in 1993 became senior Republican representative in Washington. He ran unsuccessfully for presidential nomination in 1980 and 1988. He is married to Elizabeth Hanford **Dole**.

Dominion of New England
A union of Massachusetts, Connecticut and Rhode Island in 1686, to which New York and the Jerseys were added by 1688, ruled by a single governor-general without representative assemblies. The apogee of later Stuart colonial policy, it was instituted under James VII of Scotland and II of England in order to assert a more centralized British rule and to solve problems of trade, political independence and defence. Taxation without consent, restriction of town meetings, royal grants of land tenure, the administration of justice and liberty of conscience all aroused opposition to arbitrary rule parallel to that in Britain. Following the Glorious Revolution, the Governor, Sir Edmund Andros, was arrested and the colonies reverted to their charter governments.

domino theory
A strategic theory first used by President **Eisenhower** in 1954, reflecting the view that, as neighbouring states are so interdependent, the collapse of one will spread to the others. Originally referring to the belief that if one country became Communist, others would follow, the theory relates to military collapse, as well as insurgence, and has been used to justify intervention in a country not immediately threatened, but whose neighbour is. It was an important element in the US policy of intervention in South-East Asia in the 1960s and 1970s, and in Central America in the 1980s. ▷ **Vietnam War**

Douglass, Frederick (c.1817–95)
US abolitionist. Born into slavery, he escaped in 1838, and in 1841 emerged as a major anti-slavery force. He founded the abolitionist paper *North Star* in Rochester in 1847 and edited it for 17 years. During the Civil War he encouraged Negroes to join Union forces. He also supported the cause of women's rights, and became US Minister to Haiti. ▷ **abolitionism**

Douglas, Stephen Arnold (1813–61)
US political leader. Appointed to the Illinois Supreme Court in 1841, he was elected to the House of Representatives, where he served from 1843–7, and then to the US Senate, serving from 1847 to 1861. In 1858 he ran against Abraham **Lincoln** in the senatorial race, participating in a number of debates that gained national attention for Lincoln. Douglas's position on slavery in the territories was that each territory should decide for itself. In 1860 he was nominated for the presidency, but was defeated by Lincoln.

Douglas, William Orville (1898–1980)
US judge. Educated at Whitman College and Columbia University, he was a law professor at Yale, then a member (1936) and chairman (1937–9) of the Securities and Exchange Commission. A strong supporter of the New Deal legislation, he was appointed to the Supreme Court in 1939 to replace Louis **Brandeis**. As a justice he strongly supported civil rights and liberties, and guarantees of freedom of speech. He wrote *We the Judges* (1956), *A Living Bill of Rights* (1961) and autobiographical works and many books on his travels.

Dow, Neal (1804–97)
US temperance leader and originator of the 'Maine Law' (1846), the first state law prohibiting the sale or manufacture of alcoholic beverages. In 1851 he became mayor of his home town, Portland, with the aim of strengthening this law which had proved difficult to enforce. It was repealed in 1855, but his re-election as mayor enabled him to secure its repassage in 1858. In 1880 he was the presidential candidate of the **Prohibition** Party.

Draft
US conscription. It was introduced first in 1777 when the number of volunteers failed to meet the quotas demanded by the **Continental Congress**. During the **American Civil War** it was enacted

first by the South in 1862, followed by the North in 1863. Both acts caused great opposition, with a major riot taking place in New York, because the draft flouted the US tradition of voluntary service, while in the South it was believed to be an abuse of states' rights. On both sides, provisions for substitution and exemption gave rise to the slogan 'a rich man's war and a poor man's fight'. The draft was introduced for **World War I** with the passage of the Selective Service Act of 1917, and again in 1940 in anticipation of the United States' entry into **World War II**, and again in various crises such as the invasion of Korea, the **Berlin Airlift**, and the **Cuban Missile Crisis**. Much of the opposition to the **Vietnam War**, especially the student protest, centred on the draft. Eventually offenders numbered 570 000, so that under President Richard **Nixon** a fairer lottery system was introduced in 1969, with the draft itself being ended in 1973.

Drapeau, Jean (1916–)

Canadian politician. He became Mayor of Montreal in 1954, backed both by those wanting improved municipal services and those who demanded the elimination of gambling and prostitution. Drapeau sought more autonomy for the city and when he was thwarted by **Duplessis** he became a strong critic of the provincial Premier. When the **October Crisis** occurred in 1970 Drapeau, along with the Montreal chief of police and Robert **Bourassa**, asked the federal government to implement the **War Measures Act**. When Pierre Laporte's body was found, Montreal public opinion was so hardened that Drapeau was given 92 per cent of the votes in the following city elections. His administration backed Expo 67 (when General de **Gaulle** delivered his notorious 'Vive le Québec libre' speech), and Montreal's successful bid to hold the 1976 Olympic Games, and although the financial entanglements were still being unravelled in 1980, the increase in jobs certainly benefited the working population.

Dred Scott v Sandford (1857)

US Supreme Court case in which the slave Dred Scott sued for his freedom on the grounds of residence in a free state (Illinois) and territory (Wisconsin) to which a former owner had taken him. The US Supreme Court Chief Justice Roger B Taney ruled that slaves were not US citizens and therefore lacked standing in the court. Going beyond the case, the court also ruled that the **Missouri Compromise**, which excluded slavery from the northern territories, was unconstitutional. This decision and other remarks by Taney, such as his comment that blacks had no rights which a white man was bound to respect, increased sectional tension and helped to bring on the **American Civil War**.

Du Bois, William Edward Burghardt (1868–1963)
US civil rights activist, historian and sociologist. He studied at Fisk, Harvard and Berlin, and in his writings explored the history and lives of black Americans. In politics he campaigned for full equality, opposing the tactics of Booker T **Washington**. He helped found the National Association for the Advancement of Colored People (**NAACP**), and in his later years lived in Ghana, where he died.

Dulles, John Foster (1888–1959)
US politician. Educated at Princeton and the Sorbonne, he became a lawyer. During **World War II** he advocated a world governmental organization, and in 1945 advised at the Charter Conference of the **UN**, thereafter becoming US delegate to the General Assembly. In 1953 he became US Secretary of State, and was known chiefly for his aggresssive anti-communist rhetoric and his policy of **brinkmanship**.

Duplessis, Maurice le Noblet (1890–1959)
Canadian politician. He led the **Union Nationale** to power in Quebec in 1936, gaining power through a methodical exploitation of *nationalisme* and fear of anglicization; yet he encouraged further encroachments by US corporations on Quebec's economic life. His campaign against radical reformers gained him the support of the Catholic Church, which he retained almost throughout his political career. His attitude towards labour was expressed in the notorious **Padlock Act** (1937) which crippled the **CCF**, but it was his antagonistic attitude towards federal government (which he claimed was invading provincial rights through the **War Measures Act**) which contributed most to his defeat in 1939, when Ernest **Lapointe** and other French-Canadian ministers threatened to resign if he was returned to office. He did regain power in 1944, defeating both the incumbent Liberals under Adélard **Godbout** and the extremist **Bloc Populaire**, and maintained his pre-war policies. An alliance between labour, professionals, academics and even some churchmen eventually succeeded in demonstrating the scale of corruption in his government and although Duplessis

himself died suddenly in 1959, the *Union Nationale* was defeated by the Liberals in 1960.

Durham, John George Lambton, 1st Earl of (1792–1840)
British Whig politician. As Governor-General of Canada (1838) his measures were statesman-like, but the House of Lords voted disapproval of his amnesty to several of the French-Canadian rebels, and he resigned. His report on Canada (1839) advocated the union of Upper and Lower Canada, which was accepted in 1841.

Durham Report
A British government report of 1839 recommending the union of Upper and Lower Canada into a single political structure; produced by Lord Durham, the Governor-General of Canada, it called for the assimilation of French-Canadian into English-Canadian economic and linguistic culture. It also recommended responsible government. ▷ **Canada, Lower; Canada, Upper**

Dutch West India Company
The organization of Dutch merchants responsible for the settlement of New Netherland, now New York. The company was established in 1621, and was dissolved in 1674. It was later reorganized as a trading venture.

E

Earp, Wyatt (Berry Stapp) (1848–1929)
US lawman and frontiersman. He led a somewhat itinerant life-style, and worked as a police officer (1876–7) and assistant marshal (1878–9) in Dodge City, where he became renowned as a lawman and gambler. He went to Tombstone, Arizona in 1878 where, along with his brothers Virgil and Morgan, he was involved in the legendary 'Gunfight at the OK Corral'. He was later accused of murder and fled to the West, eventually ending up in California.

Eisenhower Doctrine (1957)
US declaration to protect the Middle East against communist aggression, intended to reassure the Western allies after the Suez Crisis. Addressing Congress, President **Eisenhower** stated that the USA regarded the Middle East as vital to its security and that it should give economic and military aid to any country in the region that requested it.

Eisenhower, Dwight David ('Ike') (1890–1969)
US general and 34th President. He graduated from the US Military Academy at West Point, and by 1939 had become chief military assistant to General Douglas **MacArthur** in the Philippines. In 1942 he commanded Allied forces for the amphibious descent on French North Africa. His ability to coordinate the Allied forces and staff led to his selection as Supreme Commander of the Allied Expeditionary Force which spearheaded the 1944 invasion of Europe. In 1950 he was made Supreme Commander of the NATO forces in Europe. In 1952 the popularity that he had gained as a war hero swept him to victory in the US presidential election, in which he ran as a Republican; he was re-elected in 1956. During his administration (1953–61) he negotiated a truce in the **Korean War** (1953) and continued US efforts to contain **communism**. During his second term the administration became more active in civil rights issues, sending troops to Little Rock,

Arkansas to enforce a school desegregation order. ▷ **Republican Party; World War II**

ejido

A traditional form of communal landholding in Mexico: *ejido* lands existed in the Valley of Mexico at the time of the conquest and were areas claimed as common or *cabildo* properties outside the settlement or village, which were to be protected from alienation to private holders. The idea of the ejido as a communal property was revived by the followers of Emiliano **Zapata**, who believed that title to lands should be vested in the village. Communal ejidos were created under Lázaro **Cárdenas**, who expropriated large integrated haciendas created under Porfirio **Díaz**, as a means of forming loyal peasant communities immune to pressure from the Cristeros and supporting the PRM (*Partido de la Revolución Mexicana*). Some 16.8 million hectares were distributed.

Ellis Island

An island in Upper New York Bay. Formerly a fort and arsenal, from 1892 until 1943 it was the main US centre for the control of immigration. It has been part of the Statue of Liberty National Monument since 1965. After restoration to the main buildings during the 1980s the Ellis Island Immigration Museum was opened in 1990.

Emancipation Proclamation (1 Jan 1863)

A document issued by President Abraham **Lincoln** during the **American Civil War**, that declared the freedom of all slaves in areas then in rebellion against the US government. Originally set forth in a preliminary statement on 22 Sep 1862, it was intended as a war measure to reduce the reserves of manpower in the South. It freed the slaves in the Confederacy but did not free the slaves in areas that supported the US government (the Union).

Equal Rights Amendment

Proposed amendment to the US Constitution stating that equal rights shall not be denied on account of sex. First introduced in 1923, it was not approved by Congress until 1972. Although the adoption deadline was extended from 1979 to 1982, the amendment fell just short of ratification by the required 38 states.

Erie Railroad

US railroad linking the Great Lakes with New York City. Its construction became a by-word for fraud, financial manipulation and political corruption by speculators Jim Fisk and Jay **Gould**, who also issued millions of dollars of watered stock in order to beat off a takeover bid from Cornelius **Vanderbilt** in 1868. The railroad collapsed under this burden of debt in the depression of 1893, but underwent several subsequent reorganizations and bankruptcies.

Estrada Palma, Tomás (1835–1908)

Cuban nationalist and politician. A commander in the Ten Years War, he was captured by the Spanish in 1877 and on his release moved to New York where he became Principal of the Central High School for Boys and leader of the Cuban exiles in the USA. For his work for the struggle for Cuban independence in the USA, he was elected President of the new republic (1901 and 1905) but, after having to call in US troops in 1906 to put down a rebellion against his government, was forced into retirement.

Evers, Medgar (1925–63)

US **civil rights** activist. Field Secretary of the **NAACP** with responsibility for registering black voters and organizing boycotts of establishments which practised racial discrimination, he was shot dead outside his home in Jackson, Mississippi. His murder illustrated the dangers faced by black civil rights activists working in the South. A white man, Byron de la Beckwith, boasted of and was indicted for his murder, but was freed after two trials ended in hung juries.

F

Fair Deal
The name adopted by US President Harry S **Truman** for his post-**World War II** liberal and pro-labour domestic policies. ▷ **New Deal**

Fair Employment Practices Committee (FEPC)
Established (1941) by President Franklin D **Roosevelt**, the FEPC was created to eliminate racial discrimination in the war production industries and in government employment. President Harry S **Truman**'s efforts to establish permanent status for the committee were met with rejection by the Senate in 1946. In 1964 the Fair Employment Opportunity Commission was established to prevent discrimination in employment. ▷ **Randolph, A Philip**

Family Compact
The high Tory political and social elite of Upper Canada. The phrase was coined in 1828 by Marshall Spring Bidwell, speaker of the House of Assembly, but it described a situation that had been developing from the first years of the 19c. The regulations which governed land grants were not only complicated but designed to serve the 'well-affected and respectable classes' already established. The Family Compact also controlled the seats in the two councils and most of those in the elective assembly. Its members monopolized patronage and obtained canal and bank charters as well as land. This political control also ensured that only the Anglican Church benefited from the **Clergy Reserves**, and denied financial support for the fledgling public education system. Reform agitation resulted in the expulsion of the leaders from the province, while London refused even to acknowledge petitions of protest. The resulting social tensions fuelled the radical leadership of William Lyon **Mackenzie** and were a major cause of the **Rebellions of 1837**. ▷ **Bagot, Charles; Canada, Upper; Durham Report**

Farragut, David Glasgow (1801–70)
US naval commander. He entered the navy in 1810 and saw service against the British in the War of 1812, and against pirates in 1820. In the **American Civil War** he served with the Federal forces and commanded the armament fitted out for the capture of New Orleans (1862). He took part in the siege and capture of **Vicksburg** (1863), and destroyed the enemy's gunboats in Mobile Bay, leading to the town's surrender. He was made Vice Admiral, the rank being created for him by special Act of Congress, as was also that of Admiral (1866).

FBI (Federal Bureau of Investigation)
The US organization primarily concerned with internal security or counter-intelligence operations, although it also has responsibility for investigating violations of federal law not remitted by the federal government to any other organization. The FBI is a branch of the Department of Justice. ▷ **Hoover, J Edgar**

Federal Constitutional Convention ▷ **Constitutional Convention**

Federalist Papers
A series of 85 essays defending the **US Constitution**, most of which were published in New York newspapers between Oct 1787 and Aug 1788, and subsequently collected in book form. Under the pen name of 'Publius', Alexander **Hamilton** and James **Madison** were the major contributors, with John **Jay** writing five of the articles. The papers provide important insights into the objectives sought by the framers of the US Constitution. They discuss the importance of establishing a strong centralized government while preserving state and individual freedoms. Although written in an effort to win over the citizens of New York to the constitution, the Federalist essays have become one of the most important US contributions to democratic political philosophy. ▷ **Federalist Party**

Federalist Party
US political party that favored a strong centralized government. It was formed in support of the domestic policies of Secretary of the Treasury, Alexander **Hamilton**, who represented the interests of merchants and men of property, and President **Washington**'s

foreign policy. **Washington** (in office 1789–97) and John **Adams** were Federalist Presidents, but after Thomas **Jefferson**'s victory in the 1800 election the Federalists never again held the presidency, and the party's opposition to the War of 1812 led to its demise. ▷ **Hartford Convention**

Federal Reserve System (FRS)
The US central banking system, set up in 1913. Under the system, the USA is divided into 12 districts, each with its own Federal Reserve Bank. The system is supervised by a central board of governors called the Federal Reserve Board. Its responsibilities include maintaining credit and monetary conditions as well as monitoring member banks. Less than half of the 14 000 banks in the USA are members of the 'Fed'.

Fenian Raids
A series of attacks on Canada from 1866 to 1870 led by the Fenian Brotherhood. The Fenians (mostly New York Irish immigrants) hoped to take advantage of the anti-British sentiment felt by many Northerners in the aftermath of the **American Civil War**, and to invade Britain's North American possessions. Once established in Canada, the Fenians hoped to force Britain to negotiate the independence of Ireland. Although they did capture Fort Erie before withdrawing, the Canadian militia's resistance, divisions within the Fenian organization and the US authorities' hostility left no real prospect of success. However, their threat did encourage support for the **Confederation Movement**, especially in the Maritime Provinces.

Fenians
The short title of the Irish Republican Brotherhood, a nationalist organization founded in New York in 1857. The movement quickly espoused violence as a means of achieving its objective, and is best known for attacks in Manchester and London in 1867 to rescue imprisoned supporters. The fatalities which occurred caused these to be called 'The Fenian Outrages'.

Ferraro, Geraldine Anne (1935–   )
US Democrat politician. The daughter of Italian Roman Catholic immigrants, she was educated at Marymount College, Fordham

University and New York Law School and, after marrying wealthy businessman John Zaccaro in 1960, established a successful law practice (1961–74). She served as assistant district attorney for the Queens district of New York between 1974 and 1978 and worked at the Supreme Court from 1978, heading a special bureau for victims of violent crime, before being elected to the House of Representatives in 1981. In Congress, she gained a reputation as an effective, liberal-minded politician and was selected in 1984 by Walter Mondale to be the first female vice-presidential candidate of a major party, in an effort to add sparkle to the Democrat ticket. After the Democrats' convincing defeat, she returned to private law practice and in 1992 unsuccessfully sought the New York Democratic nomination for US Senator.

Fielding, William Stevens (1848–1929)
Canadian journalist and politician. Liberal Premier of Nova Scotia, he threatened to secede in 1886 if the federal government refused to lower tariffs and redress other provincial complaints. In 1896 he became the finance minister in **Laurier**'s administration and introduced a two-tier tariff system which answered the needs of farmers for a low tariff, while still maintaining some high rates to protect manufacturers. In 1910 he negotiated a trade agreement with the USA which, like his earlier system, took into account the needs of both agriculture and industry. While the US Congress ratified it in the summer, the Conservatives under Robert Laird **Borden** filibustered the bill in the House of Commons. In response Laurier called an election, the government was defeated, and Fielding lost his seat. ▷ **Liberal Party** (Canada)

Fifth Amendment (1791)
Amendment to the **US Constitution** which protects against self-incrimination. This gained notoriety during the **Cold War** anti-communist investigations, when 'taking the Fifth' became synonymous with an admission of guilt. More important constitutionally, however, has been the amendment's clause prohibiting the deprivation of 'life, liberty, or property without due process of law'. Before the **American Civil War** it was used to defend **slavery** (**Dred Scott v Sanford**), and afterwards, when this clause was incorporated into the **Fourteenth Amendment**, it was used as an argument (known as 'substantive due process') against economic regulation.

'Fifty-Four Forty or Fight'

US political slogan used by the **Democratic Party** in the 1844 presidential election. It referred to the US claim to the Oregon country lying between the northern border of California (latitude 42°N) and the southern border of what is now Alaska (54°40'N). The UK also claimed the region for similar reasons of discovery and settlement. In spite of the expansionist arguments of Stephen Douglas and Lewis Cass in Congress, and those of President **Polk** in his inaugural speech and his first annual message to Congress, a compromise was reached with Britain in 1846 drawing the frontier along the 49th parallel.

Fillmore, Millard (1800–74)

US politician and 13th President. He educated himself, and became a lawyer. A member of the US House of Representatives from New York for eight years (1833–5 and 1837–43), he was elected Vice-President when Zachary **Taylor** won the 1848 election, becoming President (1850) on Taylor's death. A moderate on the **slavery** issue, he signed the **Compromise of 1850** and tried to enforce the Fugitive Slave Act.

Five Civilized Tribes

The Native American tribes (Chickasaws, Creeks, Choctaws, Cherokees, Seminoles) who originally inhabited the present southeast USA, so called because they adapted relatively easily to the European way of life. Nevertheless, they were forced to leave the area under the Removal Act of 1830, and were relocated west of the Mississippi River. Large numbers of **Native Americans** died as a result of exposure, disease and the hardships suffered en route and in the new **Indian Territory**. The name given to the Cherokee ordeal, the 'Trail of Tears', sums up the fate of these tribes.

force bills (1832, 1890)

US laws asserting the power of the federal government over the states. The first became law during the **Nullification** Crisis. The second was introduced to protect voting rights for black Southerners against the **Jim Crow Laws**. It passed the House of Representatives, but failed in the Senate.

Ford, Gerald Rudolph (1913–)

US politician and 38th President. Educated at the Universities of Michigan and Yale, he served in the US Navy during **World War**

II. He became a Republican member of the House of Representatives (1949–73), and on the resignation of Spiro **Agnew** in 1973 became the first appointed Vice-President. He became President (1974–6) when Richard **Nixon** resigned because of the **Watergate** scandal. The full pardon he granted to Nixon the same year, combined with an economic recession and inflation, made him unpopular, and he was defeated in the 1976 presidential election by Jimmy **Carter**. ▷ **Republican Party**

Fort Stanwix, Treaties of (1768, 1784)
North American agreements with Native American tribes. The first established a boundary between British crown lands and the **Iroquois Confederacy**. The second, forced upon the **Iroquois** after their defeat in the **American Revolution**, brought the cession of all of their lands west of the Niagara River. However, the tribes of the Ohio county rejected it. ▷ **Indian Wars**

Fort Sumter (12–13 Apr 1861)
The US federal installation in Charleston (South Carolina) harbour, bombarded in the first military engagement of the **American Civil War**. Shortly after President Abraham **Lincoln**'s inauguration, the fort's commanding officer, Captain Robert Anderson, informed the Union government that he had only enough supplies to last until early Apr. On 6 Apr 1861 Lincoln informed the Governor of the seceded state of South Carolina that he intended to provision the garrison. Confederate General Pierre **Beauregard** issued an ultimatum to surrender, which Anderson refused. On 12 Apr the fort came under fire, and Union troops departed two days later for lack of ammunition. The Confederate states thus having opened hostilities, Lincoln issued a call to the states for troops and began to blockade Southern ports.

forty-niners
Adventurers who swarmed to California in 1849, after the discovery of gold there the previous year. Their number may have been as high as 100 000. ▷ **gold rush**

Four Freedoms (1941)
Four basic human rights proclaimed in an annual message to Congress by President Franklin D **Roosevelt** as basic human

rights. They included freedom of speech and worship, and freedom from want and fear.

Fourteen Points

A peace programme outlined by US President Woodrow **Wilson** in a message to Congress in 1918, at the end of **World War I**. The programme offered the possibility of an acceptable peace to the Central Powers, and as a result Wilson came to be perceived as a moral leader. It was largely instrumental in bringing about the surrender of Germany and the beginning of peace talks. Several of the points, however, were compromised or defeated in the actual treaty.

Fourteenth Amendment (1868)

US constitutional amendment adopted during **Reconstruction** after the **American Civil War** to guarantee equality before the law to blacks and whites alike. Its first section defined federal and state citizenship for all American-born or naturalized persons specifically to include the ex-slaves, and it prohibited the states from abridging their 'privileges and immunities' and denying them the 'equal protection of the laws'. Judicial interpretation of the amendment soon turned it to purposes for which it was never intended. Since corporations were legal 'persons', the amendment became used as a shield against state regulation, particularly of railroads and working conditions. Its negative wording was also taken to allow individual discrimination, while the 'separate but equal' argument even gave the amendment's sanction to formal legislative segregation. This flagrant abuse was reversed during the 1950s and 1960s, but in the last two decades it has also been used with success against policies of affirmative action and positive discrimination. ▷ **Bakke v Regents of the University of California; Brown v Board of Education of Topeka, Kansas; Civil Rights Cases; Gaines v Canada; Lochner v New York; Munn v Illinois; Plessy v Ferguson; Sweatt v Painter**

Frankfurter, Felix (1882–1965)

Austrian-born US law teacher and judge. Educated at the College of the City of New York and at Harvard, he taught at the Harvard Law School (1914–39) and served as an associate justice of the US Supreme Court (1939–62). He was a noted supporter of civil liberties and helped found the American Civil Liberties Union, although in court he advocated judicial restraint in opposing legislative and executive policy. In constitutional cases he claimed that judges should consider whether legislators could reasonably have enacted such a law.

Franklin, Benjamin (1706–90)

US politician, author and scientist. He set up a printing house in Philadelphia, bought the Pennsylvania Gazette (1730), and built a reputation as a journalist. In 1736 he became Clerk of the Pennsylvania legislature, in 1737 Deputy Postmaster of Philadelphia, and in 1753 Deputy Postmaster-General for the colonies, and was sent on various diplomatic missions to England. In 1748 he began his research into electricity, proving that lightning and electricity are identical, and suggesting that buildings be protected by lightning-conductors. In 1776 he was actively involved in framing the **Declaration of Independence**. A skilled negotiator, he successfully won Britain's recognition of US independence (1783). He was US Minister in Paris until 1785, three times President of the State of Pennsylvania, and a member of the **Constitutional Convention**. In 1788 he retired from public life. ▷ **Albany Congress**

Fraser, Simon (1776–1862)

Canadian fur-trader and explorer. In 1792 Fraser joined the **North West Company** as a clerk, becoming a partner in 1801. In 1805 he was given responsibility for the company's operations beyond the Rockies, and established the first settlements in New Caledonia, now central British Columbia. Hoping to discover a water route which would cut the company's transport costs, in 1808 he braved the dangerous reach now known as the Fraser River Canyon. In 1815 he was arrested with other company officers at Fort William in retaliation for the Seven Oaks Incident (a North West Company attack on the **Hudson's Bay Company**'s Red River Settlement). The charges could not be sustained and Fraser had retired to Upper Canada by the time his trial took place.

Fredericksburg, Battle of (13 Dec 1862)

In the **American Civil War**, a fruitless attempt by a Northern army of well over 100 000 to capture the town of Fredericksburg, Virginia, from a Southern army that was heavily outnumbered.

free silver

A demand made within the US **Democratic Party** in 1895 for the unlimited coinage of silver at a ratio of 16:1 with gold. Intended as a reflationary solution for agrarian economic problems, in the 1896 presidential election, free silver became a major plank of the Democratic Party platform. But after Democrat William Jennings **Bryan** lost to Republican William **McKinley**, interest in the issue faded.

Free-Soil Party (1848)

A US politicial party whose slogan was 'free soil, free speech, free labor, and free men.' Opposed to the expansion of slavery into territories annexed after the **Mexican War**, it ran former President Martin **Van Buren** as its presidential candidate in 1848. Van Buren lost, but the slavery issue was later taken up by the **Republican Party**.

Frémont, John Charles (1813–90)

US explorer and politician. In 1843 he crossed the Rocky Mountains (where a peak is named after him), and found an overland route across the continent. He explored the Great Salt Lake (1843), fought in the **Mexican War** (1846), then went to California, where he made a fortune in the **gold rush**, and became a Senator. In 1856 he was the first presidential candidate of the new **Republican Party**, losing to James Buchanan, but receiving 1 million votes and making the party a major force in national politics. He later became Governor of Arizona (1878–83). ▷ **Republican Party**

French and Indian War (1756–63)

The last of the 18c wars between France and Britain for the control of North America. France accepted final defeat at the Treaty of Paris (1763).

Friends, Society of

A Christian sect founded by George Fox and others in mid-17c England, and formally organized in 1667; members are popularly known as Quakers, possibly because of Fox's injunction 'to quake at the word of the Lord'. Persecution led William Penn to establish a Quaker colony (Pennsylvania) in 1682. Belief in the 'inner light', a living contact with the divine Spirit, is the basis of its meetings for worship, where Friends gather in silence until moved by the

Spirit to speak. They emphasize simplicity in all things, and are active reformers promoting tolerance, justice and peace. Today most meetings have programmed orders of worship, though meetings based on silence (unprogrammed) still prevail in the UK and parts of the USA.

Frietschie, Barbara (1766–1862)

American patriot. She is celebrated in the poem 'Barbara Frietchie' by John G Whittier, which relates the reputedly historical incident in which she raised the Union flag in encouragement above the heads of General **Jackson**'s troops as they passed through Frederick, Maryland in Sep 1862.

Front de Libération de Québec (FLQ)

Canadian terrorist organization. On the extreme left wing and anti-capitalist, it targeted the prosperous English-speaking sector of Quebec society. The FLQ had little formal organization, although arrangements were made for its members to train with the **PLO**. It gave the impression of being a much larger conspiracy than it actually was, for its name was simply appropriated by small independent groups to indicate responsibility for terrorist attacks. The arrest of Pierre Vallière and Charles Gagnon, two of the movement's theorists, set off its most active period which culminated in the **October Crisis** of 1970.

Frontenac, Louis de Buade, Count of (1622–98)

French-Canadian politician. He served in the army, and in 1672 was appointed Governor of the French possessions in North America. He was recalled for misgovernment in 1682, but was sent out again in 1689. He extended the boundaries of **New France** down the Mississippi, launched attacks on New England villages, repulsed the British siege of Quebec (1690), and broke the power of the **Iroquois** (1696).

frontier

Movement has been one of the most fundamental characteristics of human history, and although the word frontier may mean a political boundary or the outermost line of military defence, it also has a variety of meanings associated with the expansion of a people. It may denote a physical place, a migratory process or a social situation; in these contexts the word expresses the incomers' perspective and implies the existence of some field of endeavour beyond their own organized social and political structures. It has also been taken to mean a transitory stage in social evolution before distance and isolation give way to more centrally directed integrative forces. In the ancient world of Greece and Rome, frontier encounters were conceptualized in terms of the civilized and the barbarian; while in the European medieval world they were expressed in terms of the Christian and the pagan or infidel. The overseas expansion of Europe from early modern times saw these categories overlaid by questions relating to the natural environment and the nature of indigenous peoples (eventually giving rise to the myth of the 'noble savage' and related moral controversies). By the late 19c the creation of formal empires had redefined these debates in terms of wealth and progress (both still with strong moral connotations). The first use of 'the frontier' as an organizing principle of historical analysis was in Frederick Jackson Turner's enormously influential paper of 1893 'The Significance of the Frontier in American History', where it was used to account for the evolution of democratic individualism in the USA. During the first half of the 20c the 'frontier thesis' was used by other historians to interpret the histories of Canada, Australia, New Zealand, South Africa and South America; and much of this work was synthesized by Walter Prescott Webb, whose *The Great Frontier* (1952) viewed modern history from around 1500 as a process of expansion from the European 'Metropolis' to the 'World Frontier'. All these accounts tended to emphasize the shaping influence of the frontier on the heartland, incorporating into historical explanation some of the imaginative power more usually expressed in literature. Although it has generated much professional controversy, historians today still find the frontier to be a fruitful concept and they apply it in a wide variety of temporal and geographical contexts. The stress now, however, is on the patterns of social and political organization brought to the frontier, emphasizing interaction and the themes of conquest, consolidation and mutual acculturation.

Fugitive Slave Laws (1793 and 1850)
US federal legislation requiring the return of runaway slaves who fled to states where slavery had been abolished. Enforcement was hindered by the 'personal liberty laws' of several Northern states, which allowed runaway slaves the benefit of a trial by jury, and

sometimes by popular 'rescues' of captured runaways. The laws were repealed in 1864. ▷ **Compromise of 1850**

Fulbright, James William (1905–   )
US politician. Educated at the University of Arkansas and George Washington University Law School, he was a Rhodes scholar at Oxford, and taught law in Washington and Arkansas. He was elected to the US House of Representatives as a Democrat in 1942 and to the Senate in 1944. He sponsored the Fulbright Act (1946), which established an exchange scholarship system for students and teachers between the USA and other countries. As Chairman of the Senate Foreign Relations Committee, he became a major critic of the escalation of the **Vietnam War**. He lost his Senate seat in 1974. ▷ **Democratic Party**

Fuller, (Sarah) Margaret (1810–50)
US feminist and journalist. She became part of the Transcendentalist circle that centred around Ralph Waldo Emerson, and despite a lack of higher education was known as one of its brightest stars. Her *Woman in the Nineteenth Century* (1845) is the earliest major piece of US feminist writing. She died in a shipwreck while returning to the USA after taking part in the abortive Italian revolution of 1848.

Fundamental Orders of Connecticut (1639)
US colonial charter. An agreement for self-government adopted by the Connecticut towns of Hartford, Windsor and Wethersfield, and extended to other towns. It was replaced by a royal charter in 1662.

fur trade
The history of the fur trade in North America is inextricably linked with the exploration of the continent and the struggle between France and Britain for its control. The trade was first centred along the St Lawrence River and the Atlantic coast around Newfoundland and **Acadia** during the late 16c and early 17c. The furs were brought to the fishing stations by Native Americans attracted by the exchange for relatively cheap trinkets and other manufactured goods. In 1608 Samuel **Champlain** established a base at Quebec and contacts with the **Algonquin** and **Huron**, whom he assisted against their traditional enemies the

Iroquois. With the advance of settlement and the opening up of trading routes into the interior, it became clear by the late 17c that the French were caught between the British colonies to the south and the **Hudson's Bay Company** (set up in 1670 as the result of information from two disaffected French traders) to the north and west. While the Iroquois acted as middlemen bringing the trade into British hands at Albany, the French re-established a forward position with the chain of forts and trading posts which controlled the Great Lakes region and the upper Mississippi and Ohio valleys until the cession of **New France** to Britain in 1763. In the late 18c and early 19c the north-western fur trade was bitterly contested between the independents who organized themselves as the **North West Company** (opening up new routes to the Pacific seaboard, where they found John Jacob **Astor**'s Pacific Fur Company already established) and the Hudson's Bay Company. After the amalgamation of the two Canadian companies in 1821, the HBC organized the trade on a continental basis, ceding its lands to the Dominion in 1869 but continuing as the most important economic force in the north.

G

Gadsden Purchase (1853)
A strip of land in south Arizona and New Mexico bought by the US from Mexico for US$10 000 000. The purchase was negotiated by the minister to Mexico, James Gadsden, as a feasible route for a southern railroad to the Pacific.

Gaines v Canada (1938)
US Supreme Court decision that the 'separate but equal' facilities demanded by **Plessy v Ferguson** (1896) had to be truly equal in order to be constitutional. It was an important success for the **NAACP**'s campaign to gain parity of provision for black schools in the South, particularly in regard to teachers' salaries. Their subsequent rise caused a significant increase in the cost of maintaining segregated schools. The decision marked the court's first move away from segregationist doctrine. ▷ **segregation**

Galt, Sir Alexander Tilloch (1817–93)
Canadian politician. In 1844–55 he was High Commissioner of the British American Land Company which made huge profits from lands obtained through its influence with the Château Clique and in London. As a business leader of the English-speaking community in **Canada East** his signature on the **Annexation Manifesto** in 1849 reflected fears for its future in markets no longer protected by the British **Navigation Acts**. However he recognized that **reciprocity** would only be of benefit with a more integrated Canadian economy and in 1858 he was persuaded by **Macdonald** and George Étienne **Cartier** (with whom he was involved in the **Grand Trunk Railway**) to enter politics on the understanding that they would work towards confederation. As Finance Minister in the Macdonald–Cartier administration he introduced the high tariffs of 1859, and he served in the 'great coalition' of 1864 that negotiated the terms of confederation. In 1880 he became the first Canadian High Commissioner in London. ▷ **Confederation Movement**

Garfield, James A(bram) (1831–81)
US politician and 20th President. He was a farmworker, teacher, lay preacher and lawyer before being elected to the Ohio State Senate in 1859. He fought in the **American Civil War** until 1863, when he entered the US House of Representatives, eventually becoming a leader of the **Republican Party**. After his election as President (a post he held only from Mar to Sep 1881), he alienated the 'Stalwarts', a major faction of the Republican Party, by passing them over for federal appointments. On 2 July 1881, he was shot in the Washington railroad station by a disappointed office-seeker, Charles Guiteau, and died two months later.

Garneau, Francis Xavier (1809–66)
Canadian historian. His *Histoire du Canada* (1845–8) was written to rebut Lord **Durham**'s assertions that French Canadians had neither a history nor a culture of any significance. His work provided Quebec nationalism with an intellectual basis and a body of material on which later writers drew freely.

Garnet, Henry Highland (1815–82)
US abolitionist. A former slave, who with Frederick **Douglass** helped promote racial pride and dispel popular stereotypes of blacks. A persuasive and witty speaker, he argued at the National Convention of Coloured Citizens in 1843 that a slave was justified in using violence to gain his freedom. By the 1850s, like another anti-slavery activist Martin **Delany**, he despaired of achieving racial justice and advocated the emigration of blacks to Africa.
▷ **abolitionism**

Garrison, William Lloyd (1805–79)
US abolitionist. Educated informally, he emerged in 1830 as one of the foremost anti-slavery voices in the USA. His newspaper *The Liberator* argued the case for immediate abolition, and his American Anti-Slavery Society drew thousands of people to the cause. ▷ **abolitionism**

Garvey, Marcus (1887–1940)
Advocate of black nationalism. Born and brought up in poverty in Jamaica, he promoted self-help for blacks and black pride and in 1914 founded the Universal Negro Improvement Association. Two years later, he left Jamaica for New York, his arrival in New

York coinciding with the wave of black migration into Harlem. Despite little formal education, he proved to be a gifted writer and speaker. It was in the ghettos of the northern cities that he found his greatest following, reaching blacks through his weekly *Negro World* and greatly expanding his Association, a forerunner of the black nationalist movement. However, his call for a return to Africa attracted little interest. He founded such enterprises as the Black Factories Corporation and the Black Star Line, a steamship line owned and operated by blacks, which, however, collapsed in 1921 due to mismanagement. In 1923 he was convicted of mail fraud, imprisoned, and later deported. After he left the country, his black nationalist movement went into decline. He died in obscurity in London.

Gaspée
During the **American Revolution**, a British customs schooner destroyed by Rhode Islanders after it went aground near Providence (9 Jun 1772).

Gates, Horatio (1728–1806)
British-born US general. He joined the British Army, served in America in the Seven Years War (1756–63), and then settled in Virginia. In the **American Revolution** he sided with his adoptive country and fought for its cause. In 1777 he took command of the Northern department, and forced the British Army to surrender at the Battle of **Saratoga**. In 1780 he commanded the Southern department, but his army was routed by **Cornwallis** at the Battle of **Camden**, and he was superseded. He returned to Virginia, but in 1790 emancipated his slaves and then settled near New York City.

Gaulle, Charles (André Joseph Marie) de (1898–1970)
French general and politician. As the leader of the Free French, he fought many diplomatic battles against President **Roosevelt** to ensure that France was treated as a co-belligerent, and emerged in 1944 as head of the Provisional Government. He later drew up a new constitution for the Fifth Republic which was approved by a referendum (Sep 1958) and he became its first President (1959–69). He developed a French nuclear deterrent, and removed France from its military obligations under **NATO** (1965). His supporters won by a big majority in the elections following the

'events' of 1968, but he lost a referendum on constitutional reform in 1969, and resigned.

Geneva Peace Conference (1973)
The conference, arranged by Henry Kissinger under the auspices of the **UN**, to discuss the disengagement of Israeli and Arab forces and to achieve a peace settlement after the **October War**. Despite its failure to achieve substantial results, the conference (convened 21 Dec 1973), was remarkable for its efforts towards getting Egypt, Jordan and Israel together. The USA and USSR attended in what was really an observational capacity, but the actual ceasefire arrangements were achieved by Kissinger in his so-called 'shuttle' diplomacy.

Gentlemen's Agreement (1907)
An informal pact between the USA and Japan under which Japan agreed to limit Japanese migration to the USA in return for a promise by President Theodore **Roosevelt** not to discriminate against the Japanese.

Geronimo (Goyathlay) (1829–1909)
Mexican-born Chiricahua **Apache** chief. The best-known and most fearsome of all Apaches, he led numerous raiding parties in Mexico and Arizona following the massacre of his family by Mexican soldiers. He forcibly resisted the internment of his people on a reservation, escaping from white control on several occasions, but made a final surrender in 1886. In his old age he became a Christian and a figure in public spectacles, including President Theodore **Roosevelt**'s inauguration parade. ▷ **Indian Wars**

gerrymander
A term describing the redrawing of electoral districts so as to benefit the party in power in forthcoming elections. It was first coined in the USA in 1812 by combining the last name of Elbridge Gerry, then Governor of Massachusetts, with salamander, the shape of which animal the newly created electoral district was said to resemble.

Gettysburg Address (19 Nov 1863)

A speech given by President **Lincoln** during the **American Civil War**, at the dedication of a war cemetery in Pennsylvania on the site of the Battle of **Gettysburg**. Ill-regarded at the time, it is now thought of as one of the masterpieces of US oratory, from its often-quoted opening, 'Fourscore and seven years ago our fathers brought forth on this continent a new nation', to its memorable conclusion, 'that government of the people, by the people, for the people, shall not perish from the earth'.

Gettysburg, Battle of (1–3 July 1863)

Marking the turning point in the **American Civil War**, the Gettysburg campaign began in June 1863. It consisted of a major series of engagements in Pennsylvania between the army of north Virginia (Confederate) and the army of the Potomac (Union), after Robert E **Lee**, the Southern commander, decided to take the war into the North. The Battle of Gettysburg ended with a Union victory, but with heavy losses on both sides (Union 23 000; Confederate 25 000). On 4 July, Lee's severely reduced troops retreated, with the defeat ending any prospect of foreign recognition for the Confederacy.

Ghadr Party and Movement

Originally an organization of Indian migrants, especially Punjabis, settled in British Columbia and on the West Coast of the USA, it derived its name from the title of its journal, *Ghadr* (Urdu, 'revolution'). Influenced by the activities of Irish radicals and Russian revolutionaries, a highly-organized conspiracy was hatched at the start of **World War I**, the Indian–Berlin Committee of the 'Hindustan Ghadr Party' offering money and arms to help raise a revolt against the British in India. Accordingly, large numbers of Ghadrites returned to the subcontinent. Many were arrested, but by late 1914 a substantial body of party members and suppporters was established in the Punjab. Led by men such as Rashbehari Bose and Sachin Sayal, attempts were made to foster mutiny in the Indian army; bombs were manufactured, robberies committed and arsenals raided in order to raise arms and supplies for a general uprising. However, the British pre-empted this plan, arresting large numbers of Ghadrites in Punjab, Bengal, Singapore and elsewhere. A series of trials, including the 1915 Lahore Conspiracy Case, resulted, in which Ghadrites and others accused of revolutionary activities were prosecuted under the Defence of India Act; 46 people were hanged and 194 were imprisoned. A total of 145 revolutionaries were hanged or killed by the police, and some 306 sentenced to transportation. Later, further trials of Ghadrites were held in the USA, whilst in India those revolutionary cells still active were riven by factionalism. Attempts to revive the Ghadr Movement in India after 1919 failed due to the growing popularity and success of the Gandhian Congress, although in the 1930s and 1940s returning Ghadrites, having served out their term in prison, often became activists once again in the Indian Communist movement.

Ghent, Treaty of (1814)
The treaty between the USA and Britain which ended the **War of 1812**, without any resolution of the major issues from which the conflict had grown. These had included maritime rights and military control of the Great Lakes.

Giannini, Amadeo (1870–1949)
US banker. The son of Italian immigrants, he founded the Bank of Italy in 1904. After its spectacular recovery from the 1906 San Francisco earthquake and fire, it later grew into the Bank of America, the world's largest bank. In 1919 he also founded an investment trust which became the Transamerica Corporation in 1928. Directing his operations at the small investor, the wage earner and the small businessman, he used innovative methods of advertising, branch banking, and home loans repayable in monthly instalments.

Giap, Vo Nguyen (1912–)
Vietnamese military leader. He studied law at Hanoi University, joined the Vietnamese Communist Party, and trained in China. He led the **Viet Minh** against the French after 1945, and planned and executed the decisive defeat of their garrison at **Dien Bien Phu** in 1954. As Vice-Premier and Defence Minister of North Vietnam, he masterminded the military strategy that forced US forces to leave South Vietnam (1973) and led to the reunification of Vietnam in 1975. He was a member of the politburo from 1976 to 1982. He wrote *People's War, People's Army* (1961), which became a textbook for revolutionaries. ▷ **Vietnam War**

Gilded Age
A derogatory term for a period in the latter part of the 19c in the USA. Taken from the title of a novel by Mark Twain (1835–1910) and Charles Dudley Warner (1829–1900), it referred to the widespread political corruption and scandals of the time.

Gilman, Charlotte Anna Perkins née **Perkins** (1860–1935)
US feminist and writer, born into the same family as Catharine Beecher and Harriet Beecher Stowe. She had limited schooling, an unhappy marriage and severe mental distress, then began a career as a writer, arguing in many books that women's equality required major social change. Her most notable books are *Women and Economics* (1898), *The Home* (1903) and *Man-Made World* (1911).

Godbout, Adélard (1892–1956)
Canadian politician. He became Liberal Premier of Quebec in 1939, defeating Maurice **Duplessis** and the **Union Nationale**. In 1944 his administration placed the Montreal Light, Heat and Power Company in public ownership, the first move in breaking free from the English-speaking community's hold on the economy of Quebec. ▷ **Liberal Party**

Goldman, Emma (1869–1940)
US anarchist, feminist and birth-control advocate. Her Jewish family left Russia for Germany to avoid persecution and, in 1885, she migrated to the USA, where she began her anarchist career. Imprisoned during **World War I** for opposing government policy, she was deported to the USSR and eventually settled in France.

gold rush
A burst of enthusiasm for mining, following the discovery of gold deposits in Sutter's Mill, California, in 1848. Major rushes of prospectors included California (1849), Colorado (1858–60), Idaho (1861–4), Montana (1862–4), South Dakota (1876–8) and Yukon territory (1896). ▷ **Klondike Gold Rush**

Goldwater, Barry Morris (1909–   )
US politician. Educated at the University of Arizona, he became a US Senator for that state in 1952. In 1964 he gave up his Senate seat to become Republican nominee for the presidency, but was

overwhelmingly defeated by Lyndon B **Johnson**. He returned to the Senate in 1968, serving until 1987, and was one of the architects of the conservative revival within the **Republican Party**.

Gompers, Samuel (1850–1924)

British-born US labour leader. After migrating to the USA in 1863, he followed his father's trade as a cigar maker, joining a union the following year. Self-educated, he studied and rejected Marxism and socialism, developing instead the US practice of nonpolitical trade unionism. He helped found (1886), and was long-time president of, the American Federation of Labor (AFL), and with the AFL's triumph as the main force in organized labour he became a major public figure.

Gorbachev, Mikhail Sergeevich (1931–   )

Soviet politician. In 1988 he became Chairman of the Presidium of the Supreme Soviet, ie head of state, and in 1990, the first executive President of the USSR. On becoming General-Secretary he launched a radical programme of reform and restructuring (perestroika) of the Soviet economic and political system. Greater levels of political participation, civil liberty, public debate and journalistic and cultural freedom were allowed under the policy of glasnost (openness). In defence and foreign affairs he reduced military expenditure and pursued a policy of **détente**, disarmament and arms control with the West. He met President **Reagan** in a series of Summit talks (1985–8) and signed with him the Inter-mediate Nuclear Forces (INF) treaty (1987). He ended the Soviet military occupation of Afghanistan (1989) and accepted the break-up of Comecon and the Warsaw Pact, the withdrawal of Soviet troops from Eastern Europe and the reunification of Germany. But he failed to fulfil his promise to reform the economy and improve the living standards of the Soviet people, and proved unable to cope with the rising tide of nationalism. Following the unsuccesssful coup against him in Aug 1991, he lost power to Boris Yeltsin.

Gore, Al (Albert) Jr (1948–   )

US politician. He was educated at Harvard and at Vanderbilt University, where he studied law and divinity. He worked as an investigative reporter for *The Tennessean* (1971–6) and in 1976 was elected as a Democrat from Tennessee to the US House of Representatives, a position he held for eight years. He became a

US Senator in 1984. Four years later he mounted an unsuccessful campaign for President but in 1992 made a successful bid for vice-president on the Democratic ticket with Bill **Clinton**. An ardent environmentalist, he is the author of *Earth in the Balance* (1992).

Gouin, Sir (Jean) Lomer (1861–1929)
Canadian politician. The Liberal Premier of Quebec from 1905 to 1920, many considered him to be dominated by the English-speaking business community who controlled the hydro-electric power, transport and manufacturing industries. He became federal Minister of Justice in the administration of Mackenzie **King**.
▷ **Liberal Party**

Gould, Jay (Jason)(1836–92)
US financier, one of the notorious **'Robber Barons'**. In his youth he began to speculate in small railroads, started as a broker in New York (1859), and ultimately seized the presidency of the **Erie Railroad** (1868–72) after (along with speculators Jim Fisk and Daniel Drew) manipulating shares to prevent a takeover bid by Cornelius **Vanderbilt**. He attempted to corner the gold market, causing the **'Black Friday'** stock market crash of Sep 1869. With the weight of public opinion increasingly against him, Gould was forced out of the company in 1872. He bought up huge areas of other railroad companies, however, and died worth approximately $100 000 000.

Gourlay, Robert Fleming (1778–1863)
Canadian reformer. A Scottish immigrant, disappointed by his failure to secure a large land grant, he was incensed by the bitterness of settlers at the crown and **Clergy Reserves** of Upper Canada, the lack of an emigration policy and the exclusion of Americans from settlement, complaints of which he learnt through replies to a questionnaire he had circulated to gather material for an emigrant's guide. Calling a convention of town delegates and agitating for reform, he was arrested and imprisoned when he refused to obey an order of banishment. ▷ **Canada, Upper**

Grand Army of the Republic (GAR)
US veterans organization. Established in 1866 by ex-Union soldiers, the GAR became an important force in post-**American Civil War** politics.

grandfather clause

US political manoeuvre. It was a device used by Southern US states between 1895 and 1910 to keep blacks from voting. It exempted from literacy requirements persons who were eligible to vote on 1 Jan 1867 or their descendants, thus excluding former slaves, who had not been given the right to vote by that date. It was ruled unconstitutional by the Supreme Court in 1915. ▷ **civil rights**

Grand Trunk Railway (GTR)

Canadian railway system. Incorporated in 1852, the GTR was planned to link **Canada West** and **Canada East**. It acquired the St Lawrence and Atlantic line in 1853. The Montreal to Levis section was opened in 1854 and the 'trunk' from Toronto to Montreal in 1856. At the time of confederation it was the longest railway system in the world with spectacular feats of engineering such as the Victoria Bridge over the St Lawrence at Montreal. It subsequently acquired other lines and set up the GTR Pacific to compete with the **Canadian Pacific Railway**. But this expense, coming at the same time as the upgrading of its existing system, ruined the company. Forced into bankruptcy in 1919, it was made part of the Canadian National Railways in 1923. Like the Canadian Pacific, the significance of the GTR was more than economic. Not only did they both become vast patronage machines, but they were seen by contemporaries as crucial to the achievement and maintenance of a continental union.

Granger Movement

A US organization of farmers, officially known as the Patrons of Husbandry, founded in 1867, which adopted a radical stance towards farmers' problems and big business. The name stems from the title *grange* (or farm) adopted by local units. The organization still exists. ▷ **Populist Party**

Grant, Ulysses S(impson) (1822–85)

US general and 18th President. After graduating from the US Military Academy at West Point in 1843, he fought in the **Mexican War** (1846–8), and later settled as a farmer in Missouri. On the outbreak of the **American Civil War** (1861), he rejoined the army and by 1862 was promoted to the rank of major general, leading Union forces to victory, first in the Mississippi Valley, then in the final campaigns in Virginia. He accepted Confederate general Robert E **Lee**'s surrender at **Appomattox Court House** (1865), and was made a full general in 1866. President from 1869 to 1877, he presided over the **Reconstruction** of the South, but his administration was marred by scandal.

Great Depression

The worldwide slump in output and prices, and the greatly increased levels of unemployment, which developed between 1929 and 1934. It was precipitated by the collapse of the US stock market (the Wall Street crash) in Oct 1929. This ended US loans to Europe and greatly reduced business confidence worldwide. A major Austrian bank also collapsed, producing destabilization in much of Central and Eastern Europe.

Great Migration

(1) The emigration to New England between 1630 and 1640. English Puritans undertook this hazardous journey to escape the 'personal government' of Charles I and the aggressiveness of Archbishop Laud, intending their lives to reflect their beliefs. The colonization was organized by companies to transport the emigrants. The Cambridge Agreement bound the **Massachusetts Bay Company** to get the first ships, with the governor John **Winthrop** and the company's charter on board, to Massachusetts by 1 Sep 1630. By then some 140 West Country Puritans and some 700 from the eastern counties had been despatched. Not all the 20 000 people who emigrated to Massachusetts Bay in this decade were Puritans; many were economic refugees, escaping from depression in both the wool trade and agriculture. They were also to cause friction in the Bible Commonwealths, ready to challenge the right of the Puritan 'elect' to govern the state as well as the Church. Despite these problems the foundations of the new colonies were successfully laid with the rapid establishment of what were, in contemporary terms, very stable and cohesive communities. (2) US population movement of rural Southern blacks to cities, most significantly in the North and West. Between 1910 and 1970 over 6 million left the South. New York's black population increased from 60 000 to 1 660 000, Chicago's from 30 000 to 1 103 000, Detroit's from 4 000 to 660 000 and Los Angeles' from 2 000 to 523 000. The migration was primarily an economic response to the demand for unskilled labour caused by the precipitous decline of European immigration during **World War I**,

and the very restrictive legislation in force between 1921 and 1965. Other pull factors included the production demands of the two world wars and the sustained economic boom of the 1950s and 1960s. Push factors included persistent inter-war agricultural depression, especially for tenants and the landless, and an equally persistent belief that blacks would get fairer treatment in the North than in the segregated South. The reality that the vast majority found, however, was that of the ghetto, of poverty and continuing economic and social discrimination in fact if not in law. The resulting frustration was eventually expressed in the city riots of the 1960s, in Harlem, Watts (LA), Detroit and other major cities. When Martin Luther **King** was assassinated, 70 000 troops were required to put down the riots in 125 cities whose black populations exploded in desperation and grief. During the 1970s and 1980s the decline of the northern 'rust belt' industries and the overload on welfare services reduced the North's attractiveness for Southern blacks. Together with some political and social improvements in the South this seems to have stabilized the movement.

Great Society

The name given to a legislative programme called for by US President Lyndon B **Johnson** ('LBJ') on 19 Jan 1965, which committed his administration to vigorous action on health insurance, education, housing and urban renewal. The opportunity and mandate for federal initiatives in what had previously been local responsibilities came from the extraordinary 1964 election results, which returned LBJ as President in his own right with a larger percentage of the popular vote (61 per cent) than ever before achieved, together with a two-thirds Democratic majority in both houses of Congress.

Greeley, Horace (1811–72)

US journalist and politician. The founder of the *New York Tribune*, he was the most influential Republican journalist of his day, combining support for economic development ('Go West, Young Man') with vigorous anti-slavery attitudes. It was in response to his 1862 plea for emancipation, the 'Prayer of Twenty Million', that **Lincoln** emphasized that the aim of the **American Civil War** was to preserve the union, not to destroy slavery. In 1864 he undertook an unofficial and unsuccessful effort at peacemaking. By 1872 he was advocating a general amnesty for ex-Confederates and this won him an unexpected presidential nomination in that year by the splinter **Liberal Republican Party** and the **Democratic Party**.

greenback
A popular term for paper currency in the USA, particularly in the **American Civil War** and **Reconstruction** eras, which saw strong debate about the place of currency in the monetary system. The Greenback Party was a minor party which sought a reflationary paper currency to solve the problems of farmers and working people. It ran presidential candidates in 1876 and (as the Green-back Labor Party) in 1880 and 1884. In 1892 it supported the **Populist Party**.

Green Mountain Boys
The movement of landowners and speculators who created the state of Vermont from territory disputed between New York and New Hampshire. They defied the authority of New York's government and harassed New York settlers. Of many rural insurrections in early America, that of the Green Mountain Boys was the only one to succeed. During the **American Revolution**, they redirected their energies and helped capture for the colonists the British fort at Ticonderoga, on Lake Champlain (1775). The cannon taken were important in the successful American siege of occupied Boston. ▷ **Allen, Ethan**

Greenville, Treaty of (1795)
The treaty concluded between the USA and the Confederacy of Delaware, Shawnee and Miami peoples after the victory of General Anthony Wayne at the Battle of Fallen Timbers (Ohio). The Native Americans ceded their lands east of the Wabash River (which Britain had hoped to use as a buffer zone between the USA and Canada), thus allowing safe white settlement throughout most of Ohio and south-east Indiana and encouraging immigration into the North West Territories.

Grenada Invasion (25 Oct 1983)
US 'police' action in the Caribbean. With the excuse that the lives of 1 000 US citizens were at risk in the chaos resulting from the murder of Prime Minister Maurice Bishop and the subsequent army takeover, 3 000 marines were landed on the island. It was

also claimed that the USA had been asked for help by the Organization of East Caribbean States. Bishop's readiness to accept aid from USSR and Cuba had already caused diplomatic links to be broken and the US government had become even more concerned with the building of an airport capable of offensive use. This invasion of a member of the British **Commonwealth of Nations** received widespread criticism from the USA's Western allies as well as condemnation by an 11–1 vote in the **UN** Security Council. In Dec 1984 a government that satisfied the **Reagan** administration was eventually elected.

Grenville, George (1712–70)
British politician and Prime Minister (1763–5). During his period in office, Wilkes was arrested for seditious libel under a general warrant for his attack on the King's speech (1763). The closer supervision of revenue collection (1764–5) and **Stamp Act** (1765) during his administration began the process of alienating the American colonies from British rule.

Grimké, Sarah Moore (1792–1873) and Angelina Emily (1805–79)
US abolitionists and feminists. Born into a major slaveholding family, the sisters rejected their family's way of life and joined the Quakers, who were officially anti-slavery. They moved to Philadelphia and lived quietly until, in 1836, Angelina published a letter in the anti-slavery newspaper, *The Liberator*. They became public figures, and Angelina undertook an unprecedented speaking tour. She resisted efforts to silence her, but gave up public life after her marriage to the abolitionist, Theodore Weld (1803–95). Sarah lived with the couple thereafter, and the two remained committed to social change. ▷ **abolitionism**

Groulx, Abbé Lionel (1878–1967)
French-Canadian nationalist historian and novelist. In reaction to the more moderate interpretations of the early 20c, he depicted French-Canadian history as an unremitting struggle against English domination, and in such works as *Notre maître le passé* (1944) he celebrated the clerical and agrarian elements of that past, although he never explicitly advocated separatism.

Guadalcanal, Battle of (1942)
A battle in the South Pacific in **World War II**. Following the attacks on **Pearl Harbor** and Singapore (7–8 Dec 1941), Japan

advanced into the South Pacific, reaching Guadalcanal in the Solomon Islands in May 1942. US forces reinvaded and after six months of bitter fighting, in one of the crucial actions of the war, they halted the Japanese advance.

Guadalupe Hidalgo, Treaty of (2 Feb 1848)
The agreement that settled the **Mexican War**, with Mexico yielding all of Texas, Arizona, Nevada, California and Utah, and parts of New Mexico, Colorado and Wyoming. The USA paid US$15 000 000, and assumed US$3 250 000 worth of Mexican debts.

Gulf of Tonkin Resolution (1964)
The US constitutional authorization to escalate the **Vietnam War**, passed at the request of President Lyndon **Johnson** by an overwhelming majority in Congress, after two US destroyers had reportedly been attacked by North Vietnamese torpedo boats. Its repeal in 1970, the result of mounting opposition to the war and doubts as to the wisdom of giving such discretion to the President, was unopposed by President Richard **Nixon**, who believed that he had the necessary authority to achieve US aims in the war by virtue of his powers as Commander-in-Chief.

Gulf War (16 Jan–27 Feb 1991)
A war which followed the invasion of Kuwait by Iraq in Aug 1990. A rapid air and land campaign, codenamed 'Desert Storm', was mounted by a US-led international coalition based in Saudi Arabia on the authority of George **Bush** after Iraq failed to withdraw from Kuwait by the **UN** deadline. The Bush administration gained its highest popular approval ratings during the crisis, largely due to the president's impassioned attacks on the Iraqi leader, Saddam Hussein. Iraqi forces were expelled from Kuwait and a large part of Iraq's military resources was destroyed. US casualties were set at 79 killed, 213 wounded, 45 missing and 9 captured. Casualty figures for Iraq are unavailable, although they have been estimated at 35 000 killed, 175 000 captured.

H

habitants
The peasant settlers of **New France**. Since the feudal customs transplanted from France were not suited to pioneering conditions, the *habitants* gained certain advantages such as the reduction of the *corvée* (the forced labour duty) to six days or a commutation. Another benefit they gained (though only after government pressure) was the use of the *seigneur*'s mill. Whilst the *seigneurs* still retained a certain status, their economic distinctions became increasingly less marked.

hacienda
The standard Spanish-American term for a large landed estate, usually worked by a resident population of tenant-labourers cultivating small plots of land and subject to labour obligations of various kinds. Haciendas emerged in the late 17c and early 18c due to the growth of local markets for their produce. By the mid-18c they had become clusters of buildings, including housing plus *estancias*, often held piecemeal. By the late 18c prominent families in Mexico and Peru owned strings of haciendas, organized as one substantial enterprise. These supplied an entire range of goods for domestic consumption and export. They were complemented by smaller ranchos, held by mestizo peasant farmers. A century later their position was strengthened with the growth of wage labour.

Haig, Alexander Meigs (1924–   )
US general and administrator. Educated at the US Military Academy at West Point and at Georgetown, he held a number of staff and field positions, serving in the **Vietnam War**. A full general by 1973, he then retired from the army to become White House Chief-of-Staff during the last days of Richard **Nixon**'s presidency. Returning to active duty, he became supreme NATO commander before returning again to civilian life. He served President Ronald **Reagan** as Secretary of State in 1981–2, and sought the Republican nomination for the presidency in 1988.

Hale, Nathan (1755–76)
American Revolutionary War hero. Born in Coventry, Connecticut, he joined the Continental Army in 1775 and a year later volunteered for a dangerous information-gathering mission behind British lines on Long Island. He was captured and before being hanged as a spy reportedly stated, 'I regret that I have but one life to lose for my country.'

Halsey, William F(rederick), Jr, known as **'Bull Halsey'** (1882–1959)
US naval officer. He held destroyer commands in World War I and thereafter (1919–25). He qualified as a naval pilot in 1934, and commanded the Carrier Division as rear admiral (1938) and vice-admiral (1940). During the Pacific War (1941–5) he distinguished himself in carrier battles and amphibious operations, latterly as commander of the 3rd Fleet in the battles for the Caroline and Philippine islands, and in the air strikes on the Japanese mainland. In October 1944 he led the defeat of the Japanese at the Battle of **Leyte Gulf**. He was made admiral of the fleet in 1945.

Hamilton, Alexander (1755–1804)
US politician. Educated at King's (now Columbia) College, New York, he fought in the **American Revolution**, becoming George **Washington**'s aide-de-camp (1777–81). After the war he studied law, and in 1782 was returned to Congress. He was instrumental in the movement to establish the USA in its present political form. As Secretary of the Treasury (1789–95), his policy of funding a national debt and assuming the state debts restored the country's finances to a firm footing. He was the real founder and a leader of the **Federalist Party** until his death. His successful effort to thwart the ambition of his rival, Aaron **Burr**, led to a duel in Weekauken, New Jersey, in which Hamilton was killed.

Hammer, Armand (1898–1991)
US financier and philanthropist. Using his Russian origins and business contacts, he became an intermediary between five Soviet general-secretaries and US presidents from Franklin Roosevelt to Richard **Nixon**. With **Stalin**'s accession to power, Hammer left Russia, taking with him many Russian paintings which he used to found the Hammer Galleries in New York City. Retiring to Los Angeles after building a second fortune, in 1961 he bought

123

Occidental Petroleum, a company near bankruptcy and by 1965 had made it a major force in the oil industry. Convicted of making illegal contributions to Nixon's re-election fund, he was put on a year's probation and fined US$3 000. President **Bush** pardoned him in 1989.

Hancock, John (1737–93)
American Revolutionary politician. He was a member of the Continental Congress (1775–80, 1785–6), and as its president (1775–7) he was the first to sign the **Declaration of Independence**. In 1780 he was elected first Governor of the state of Massachusetts, a post he held until 1785, and again from 1787 until his death.

Harding, Warren G(amaliel) (1865–1923)
US politician and 29th President. A successful journalist, he gained a seat in the Ohio State Senate (1899) and the lieutenant-governorship (1902), after which he returned to journalism until 1914, when he was elected to the US Senate. Emerging as a power in the **Republican Party**, he won its nomination. As President (1921–3), he campaigned against US membership of the **League of Nations**. ▷ **Prohibition; Teapot Dome Scandal**

Harpers Ferry Raid (1859)
An attack on the federal arsenal in Virginia, led by abolitionist John **Brown**, intending to launch a slave insurrection. The raiders were captured, and Brown was executed amidst great publicity. ▷ **abolitionism**

Harriman, William Averell (1891–1986)
US politician and diplomat. Educated at Yale, he became Ambassador to the USSR (1943) and to Britain (1946), Secretary of Commerce (1946–8), and special assistant to President **Truman** (1950–1), helping to organize **NATO**. He was Director of the Mutual Security Agency (1951–3), Governor of New York (1955–9), ambassador-at-large (1961 and 1965–8) and US representative at the Vietnam peace talks in Paris (1968). He negotiated the partial Nuclear Test Ban Treaty between the USA and USSR in 1963, and continued to visit the USSR on behalf of the government, making his last visit there at the age of 91. ▷ **Vietnam War**

Harrison, Benjamin (1833–1901)

US politician and 23rd President. In 1854 he became a lawyer in Indianapolis, and during the **American Civil War** fought in **Sherman**'s Atlanta campaign. He was elected US Senator from Indiana in 1881. In 1888 he defeated Grover **Cleveland** on the free-trade issue, and was President from 1889 to 1893. Failing to gain re-election, he returned to his law practice in Indianapolis, Indiana, where he died.

Harrison, William Henry (1773–1841)

US general and 9th President. He fought against the Native Americans, and when Indiana Territory was formed (1800) he was appointed Governor, serving for 12 years. He tried to avoid further **Indian Wars**, but was compelled to quell **Tecumseh**'s uprising, which ended in the Battle of Tippecanoe (1811). In the **War of 1812** he defeated the British in the Battle of the Thames (1813). In 1816 he was elected to the US House of Representatives, and in 1824 he became a Senator. With the slogan 'Tippecanoe and Tylertoo', he was elected to the presidency in 1840, but died in Washington a month after his inauguration. His grandson was Benjamin **Harrison**.

Hartford Convention (1814–15)

A gathering at Hartford, Connecticut, of delegates from the New England states to oppose the **War of 1812** and to propose changes in the **US Constitution**. The Treaty of Ghent, ending the war, and US victory at New Orleans discredited both the Convention and the **Federalist Party**, with which the Convention was associated.

Hay, John Milton (1838–1905)

US politician and writer. Educated at Brown University, he became a lawyer, and private secretary to President **Lincoln**. After Lincoln's death (1865), he served as a diplomat in Paris, Vienna and Madrid. He returned to the USA and to journalism in 1870, and went on to write poetry, fiction, and a multivolume biography of Lincoln. He became Assistant Secretary of State (1879), Ambassador to Britain (1897) and Secretary of State (1898), serving under Presidents **McKinley** and **Roosevelt**. ▷ **Open Door Policy**

125

Hay–Bunau-Varilla Treaty (1903)
An agreement between the USA and Panama creating the Panama Canal Zone under US sovereignty, and giving the USA the right to build and operate the Canal, in return for a US$10 000 000 fee and US$250 000 annual rent. The chief parties involved were US Secretary of State John **Hay** and Philippe Bunau-Varilla, representing Panama.

Hay–Herrán Treaty (1903)
An agreement between the USA and Colombia giving the USA the right to build a canal across the isthmus of Panama, then part of Colombia. Its rejection by the Colombian Senate led to the Panamanian revolt for independence, with US sponsorship. The parties involved were US Secretary of State John **Hay**, and Tomás Herrán, Colombian chargé d'affaires based in Washington. ▷ **Hay–Bunau-Varilla Treaty**

Hayes, Rutherford B(irchard) (1822–93)
US politician and 19th President. He practised law in Cincinnati (1849–61), served in the **American Civil War**, entered Congress (1865–7) as a Republican, and was elected Governor of Ohio three times (1867, 1869, 1875). The contested 1876 presidential election between Hayes and Samuel J Tilden was finally resolved in Hayes's favour, with concessions made to the Southern states in the **Compromise of 1877**. Hayes supported civil service reform but was unsuccessful in his efforts to prevent freer coinage of silver. ▷ **Republican Party**

Haymarket Square Riot (4 May 1886)
A clash between police and demonstrators at a labour union rally in Chicago at which a bomb exploded, killing seven police and injuring some 70 others. Four persons were executed by the state of Illinois for their involvement. Violent labour disputes, fueled by anarchist elements within the movement and culminating in the riot, led to a loss of public support for the union movement.

Haywood, William Dudley ('Big Bill') (1869–1928)
US labour leader. After working as a miner, homesteader and cowboy, he joined the Western Federation of Miners in 1896, and quickly achieved prominence. In 1905 he helped to found the **Industrial Workers of the World** (IWW), which was committed to

revolutionary labour politics and to the organization of all workers in one big union. An active socialist, he was convicted of sedition in 1917 for his opposition to **World War I**. He fled from the USA in 1921, and took refuge in the USSR, dying in Moscow.

Head, Sir Francis Bond (1793–1875)
British administrator. He was appointed Lieutenant-Governor of Upper Canada in 1835, but his inexperience in government and his reactionary policies (he was an advocate of the **Family Compact**) made him an unpopular leader. He faced open rebellion from reformers led by Mackenzie **King** in 1837, and although he succeeding in suppressing the uprising he left Canada the next year and retired from public life.

Helsinki Conference (1975)
A conference on security and co-operation in Europe, attended by the heads of 35 states, including the USA and USSR, with the objective of forwarding the process of **détente** through agreements on economic and technological co-operation, security, disarmament and human rights. These were set out in the Final Act within the principles of sovereignty and self-determination and existing frontiers. There have been several follow-up conferences, and there is now a permanent organization called the Conference on Security and Co-operation in Europe (CSCE).

Henry, Patrick (1736–99)
US politician. After training as a lawyer, he entered the colonial Virginia House of Burgesses, where his oratorical skills won him fame and before whom he delivered his famous lines 'Give me liberty or give me death'. He was outspoken in his opposition to British policy towards the colonies, particularly on the subject of the **Stamp Act** (1765), and he made the first speech in the **Continental Congress** (1774). In 1776 he became Governor of Virginia, and was four times re-elected. ▷ **American Revolution**

Hepburn, Mitchell Frederick (1896–1953)
Canadian politician. A farmer who came to power as the Liberal Premier of Ontario (1934–42) with the promise of a 'swing to the left' and a fight in favour of the 'dispossessed and oppressed', he soon began to fight the CIO, which was asked in to help organize the General Motors plant at Oshawa in 1937, branding them as

'foreign agitators' and communists. After Mackenzie **King** refused to send in the **Mounties**, Hepburn organized his own anti-labour force, nicknamed 'Hepburn's Hussars' or the 'Sons of Mitch's' and attacked the federal government for its 'cowardice'. Although the strikers won company recognition, Hepburn gained increased electoral support, winning 75 per cent of the seats in the subsequent election. Hepburn continued his feud with the federal administration of Mackenzie King over both provincial rights (wrecking the 1941 conference on the recommendations of the **Rowell–Sirois Commission**) and its war policies, but this fight ruined his party and destroyed his health. Resigning from office in 1942, he lost his seat in the election of 1945 in which the **Liberal Party** was decimated. ▷ **AFL–CIO**

Hidalgo (y Costilla), Miguel (1753–1811)
Mexican revolutionary. The son of a poor farmer, he became a curate in several parishes. He was known to the Inquisition as an avid reader of Rousseau, and was banished to Dolores outside Mexico City. He led a rising against the Spanish authorities (16 Sep 1810), with the cry of 'Long live our Lady of Guadelupe, death to bad government and the Spaniards'. His following, a 'horde' some 60 000 strong, sacked Guanajuato, but his 'war of revenge' terrified wealthy Creoles into support for the colonial authorities. Executed at Chihuahua, he remains a symbol of nationalism, and is often known as 'the Father of Mexican independence'.

Hincks, Sir Francis (1807–85)
Canadian politician. Editor of the *Examiner*, the **Canada West** reform party newspaper founded in 1837, he united with Louis H **Lafontaine** in the campaign for **responsible government** which Lord **Sydenham** sought to evade. He became Prime Minister in 1851, and was primarily responsible for initiating **reciprocity** negotiations with the USA. He was also a sponsor of the **Grand Trunk Railway**, but some dubious financial dealings forced him out of office in 1854.

Hiroshima, Atomic Bombing of (6 Aug 1945)
Hiroshima, the capital of Hiroshima prefecture, South Honshu Island, Japan, was chosen as the target for Little Boy, the first atomic bomb ever dropped, because of its importance as a centre of military and supply bases, shipyards and industrial plants.

Approximately 150 000 people were killed or wounded as a result, and 75 per cent of the city's buildings were destroyed or severely damaged.

Hiss, Alger (1904–)
US civil servant. He reached high office as a State Department official, then stood trial twice (1949, 1950) on a charge of perjury, having denied before a Congressional Un-American Activities Committee that in 1938 he had passed secret state documents to Whittaker Chambers, an agent for an international communist spy ring. The case roused great controversy, but he was convicted at his second trial, and sentenced to five years' imprisonment. He did not return to public life after his release. The justice of his conviction continues to be disputed. ▷ **HUAC; McCarthy, Joseph**

Hitler, Adolf (1889–1945)
German dictator and leader of the Nazi Party. He openly rearmed the country (1935), established the Rome–Berlin 'axis' with Mussolini (1936) and pursued an aggressive foreign policy which culminated in **World War II** (3 Sep 1939). His government established concentration camps for political opponents and Jews, over 6 million of whom were murdered in the course of World War II. With his early war successes, he increasingly ignored the advice of military experts and wantonly extended the war with his long-desired invasion of the USSR in 1941. After the bombing of **Pearl Harbor**, Germany and Italy declared war on the USA in 1941. The tide turned for the Allies in 1942 after victories at El Alamein and Stalingrad. When Germany was invaded, Hitler retired to his *Bunker*, an air-raid shelter under the Chancellory building in Berlin. All available evidence suggests that he and his wife committed suicide and had their bodies cremated (30 Apr 1945).

Ho Chi Minh (1892–1969)
Vietnamese politician, born Nguyen That Thanh. From 1912 he visited London and the USA, and lived in France from 1918, where he was a founder member of the Communist Party. From 1922 he was often in China and then Moscow. He led the **Viet Minh** independence movement from 1941, and directed the successful military operation against the French (1946–54). Prime Minister (1954–5) and President (1954–69) of North Vietnam, he was the leading force in the war between North and South Vietnam during the 1960s. ▷ **Vietnam War**

Holmes, Oliver Wendell (1841–1935)
US judge. Known as the 'Great Dissenter', he was the son of the writer, Oliver Wendell Holmes (1809–94). Educated at Harvard, he became a lawyer, and served in the Union army in the **American Civil War**. From 1867 he practised law in Boston, became coeditor of the *American Law Review*, and Professor of Law at Harvard (1882). He became Chief Justice (1899–1902) of the Supreme Court of Massachusetts, and Associate Justice of the US Supreme Court (1902–32). He earned his nickname because he frequently dissented from the conservative court's majority opinions, especially as the court moved to dismantle social legislation, particularly relating to regulation of the economy.

Homestead Act (1862)
A US law aimed at increasing the agricultural development of the West. It granted 160 acres of public land to settlers, who agreed to stay five years, and to cultivate their land. Homesteaders had to be US citizens or to have filed for citizenship, and either heads of families or over 21 years of age.

Homestead Steel Strike (1892)
A five-month strike, one of the bitterest industrial disputes in US labour history, which seriously weakened organized labour in the steel industry at the Carnegie Steel Company, near Pittsburgh, USA. When the union would not agree to a wage-cut, the manager, Henry Frick, refused to negotiate except with individual employees. He then recruited strike-breakers and hired 300 **Pinkerton** detectives to protect them. The union seized the works, and an armed battle broke out when the Pinkertons attempted to break in, in which several men were killed or injured. Control of the factory was regained only when the National Guard was sent in at Frick's request by the governor of Pennsylvania.

Hooks, Benjamin Lawson (1925–   )
US civil rights leader. A minister and lawyer, he was appointed by President **Nixon** to the Federal Communications Commission (FCC) in 1972 and became the first black American to serve there. After leaving the FCC in 1977, he took over the leadership of the **NAACP**.

Hoover, Herbert C(lark) (1874–1964)
US politician and 31st President. During **World War I** he was associated with food and relief efforts in Europe. In 1921 he became Secretary of Commerce. As President (1929–33), his belief in spontaneous economic recovery made him reluctant to provide massive federal assistance for the unemployed after the stock market crash of 1929. This unpopular position led to his defeat by Franklin D **Roosevelt** in 1932. Following **World War II**, he assisted **Truman** with the various US European economic-relief programs. ▷ **Great Depression; Republican Party**

Hoover, J Edgar (1895–1972)
US public official. Director of the FBI, his length of service, from 1924 until his death (because President Lyndon B **Johnson** exempted him from civil-service retirement regulations) has been interpreted both as a tribute to his national importance in the fight against crime and as a recognition that he had learnt too much about the politicians. In the early days, his force was at a disadvantage in dealing with the gangsters of **Prohibition**, but with the **Lindbergh** kidnapping case the FBI's powers were considerably strengthened. His selection and training of the 'G-Men' created an effective and efficient organization. The application of modern scientific techniques enabled him to develop counter-espionage methods of value not only during **World War II** and the **Cold War**, but also in operations against the **Mafia** and the **Ku Klux Klan**. Very sensitive to criticisms of the FBI, Hoover responded angrily to the strictures contained in the Warren Commission's report on the assassination of President **Kennedy**, but he then used the urban riots of the 1960s with great political skill to increase the Bureau's powers and funding. A fanatical anti-communist, he saw much **civil rights** protest in this light and flagrantly abused his powers in some investigations of the civil rights and anti-**Vietnam War** movements (notably that of Martin Luther **King**) .

Hopkins, Harry Lloyd (1890–1946)
US administrator. He was federal emergency relief administrator in the 1933 **Great Depression**, became Secretary of Commerce (1938–40), and supervised the Lend-Lease programme in 1941. A close friend of Franklin D **Roosevelt**, he undertook several important missions to Russia, Britain and other countries during **World War II**. ▷ **Lend-Lease Agreement; New Deal**

House of Representatives
One of the two chambers of Congress in the USA in which, under the Constitution, legislative power is vested. The 435 members of the House are elected from Congressional districts according to population, although each state has at least one representative. Many state legislatures also have a House of Representatives. Although many bills are acted on by both the Senate and the House, all revenue bills must originate in the House. ▷ **Congress; Senate**

Houston, Sam (1793–1863)
US politician. A former Governor of Tennessee, he moved to Texas in 1833 and led the force which overwhelmed the Mexican Army under **Santa Anna** at San Jacinto and won Texan independence in 1836. After Texas was admitted to the Union in 1845, he served as US Senator and later became its Governor (1859). A consistent unionist, he refused in 1861 to convene the legislature to vote on secession. Texas was therefore the last state to secede and Houston was deposed for refusing to swear allegiance to the Confederacy.

Howe, Clarence Decatur (1886–1960)
Canadian businessman and politician. In 1936 he was appointed Minister of Transport in the Liberal government of Mackenzie **King** and played a major role in establishing Trans-Canada Airlines (later Air Canada). He proved to be a superb administrator during **World War II** as director of the Wartime Prices and Trade Board and Minister for Munitions and Supply. Faced with the refusal by private companies to produce synthetic rubber, he set up the Polymer Corporation as a crown company. Its success, both financial and in research and development, enabled the government to refuse its competitors' demands to close it down. Although he always had little patience for politics and politicians, Howe became Minister of Reconstruction in **Saint Laurent**'s administration in 1951, when the Defence Production Act gave him such wide economic powers that he became known as the 'Minister of Everything'. However, his management of the Trans-Canada Pipeline project, which he rammed through parliament in 1956 over outspoken opposition and charges that he had sold out the public interest to private American companies, marked the beginning of the end of more than 20 years of Liberal federal

government and allowed the Conservatives a platform of reform on which they won the 1957 election. ▷ **Liberal Party**

Howe, Joseph (1804–73)
Canadian politician. In 1836 he entered Nova Scotia's assembly where he mobilized the reform party. His open letters to Lord John Russell, making the case for **Responsible Government**, were instrumental in winning it for Nova Scotia in 1848. As fishery commissioner Howe was out of politics during the **Confederation Movement** (which he opposed). He was Premier of Nova Scotia in 1860–3 and, after federation, entered the first Canadian government at Ottawa. In 1869 John A **Macdonald** persuaded him to join the Dominion cabinet (and increased the province's subsidy). His public opposition to administration policy caused some embarrassment and he resigned in 1873.

Howe, Julia Ward (1819–1910)
US abolitionist and reformer, author of the 'Battle Hymn of the Republic', adopted as a rally song by the Union side in the **American Civil War**. A respected writer, poet and lecturer, she was an early leader in the American women's suffrage movement. ▷ **abolitionism**

HUAC (House Committee on Un-American Activities)
A committee of the House of Representatives, it became a permanent committee in 1938 under the chairmanship of Democrat Martin Dies, with the purpose of investigating subversive activities. After the Republicans took control of the House of Representatives in 1946, the committee's focus became largely anticommunist. In the 1950s, when it became associated with Republican Senator Joseph **McCarthy**, it targeted alleged communists in the theatre, the movie industry, government and the trades. HUAC was notorious for basing its charges on loose gossip and for bullying witnesses. The committee was dissolved in 1975.

Hudson's Bay Company
A London-based corporation which was granted a Royal Charter to trade (principally in furs) in most of north and west Canada (Rupert's Land) in 1670. It annexed its main competitors, the **North West Company**, in 1821, and developed extensive sea-based

trade in otter pelts along the coast of British Columbia. Rupert's Land was purchased by the Canadian Government in 1870.

Hughes, Charles Evans (1862–1948)
US politician and jurist. Elected Governor of New York State (1907) after exposing huge frauds in the insurance industry, he served as an Associate Justice of the Supreme Court (1910–16). He resigned to run as the Republican candidate in the presidential election of 1916, when he narrowly lost to Woodrow **Wilson**. He was appointed Secretary of State in 1921 by President Warren **Harding**, and served until 1925.

Hughes, John (1797–1864)
US religious leader. The first Catholic archbishop in the USA, he led a political offensive against the Protestant monopoly over public education and sought to discourage Irish immigrants from moving away from the Eastern cities where they were close to the Church's embrace. During the **American Civil War** he visited Britain as an emissary to rally opinion behind the Union.

Hull, Cordell (1871–1955)
US politician. He became Secretary of State under **Roosevelt** in 1933, and served for the longest term in that office until he retired in 1944, having attended most of the great war conferences. He was a strong advocate of maximum aid to the Allies. He helped to organize the **UN**, for which he received the Nobel Peace Prize in 1945.

Humphrey, Hubert Horatio (1911–78)
US politician. He became Mayor of Minneapolis in 1945, and was elected Senator in 1948. He built up a strong reputation as a liberal, particularly on the **civil rights** issue, but, as Vice-President from 1965 under Lyndon B **Johnson**, alienated many of his supporters by defending the policy of continuing the **Vietnam War**. Although he won the Democratic presidential nomination in 1968, a substantial minority of Democrats opposed him, and he narrowly lost the election to Richard **Nixon**. He then returned to the Senate. ▷ **Democratic Party**

Hundred Associates

The French colonization company organized by Cardinal Riche-lieu in 1627. Its aim was to settle 4 000 colonists in **New France** within 15 years and to support them for three years after their arrival. In return the Associates were given a monopoly of the **fur trade** and a claim to the North American continent from the Arctic circle down to Florida. Their first two fleets were both captured by privateers and Quebec was lost in 1629. The profitable fur trade had to be sublet to another company and only 2 500 settlers had been sent out when the Associates' charter was revoked in 1663.

Huron

Iroquoian-speaking Native Americans, who settled in large towns and farming villages in Quebec and Ontario in the 16–17c. They supplied furs to French traders, competing with tribes of the **Iroquois Confederacy**. Defeated by the Iroquois in 1649, many were driven to the west, and eventually settled on land in Ohio and Michigan, where they were known by the British as the Wyandots. In 1867 they were moved to the **Indian Territory** in Oklahoma, where many still live.

I

ILGWU (International Ladies Garment Workers Union)

US labour organization. Founded in 1900, it saw conflict in its early years as different ethnic and political groups and skilled and unskilled workers vied for control. Massive strikes in 1909–11 in New York led to a settlement with dress manufacturers that included the 'Protocol of Peace'. Negotiated under the aegis of Louis D **Brandeis**, the protocol offered improved wages and working conditions in exchange for a ban on strikes and lock-outs and imposed impartial arbitration as a means of ending disputes. By the 1920s, the presence of a strong communist faction had caused the union's fortunes to decline, but David Dubinsky's election as President in 1932, coupled with **New Deal** legislation favourable to labour, helped it regain strength. Membership continued to grow at a rapid pace until the 1960s, but later fell with the gradual decline of the labour unions. The ILGWU's advanced social welfare programs, which included such benefits as medical and disability insurance and unemployment compensation, provided a model for other unions.

Immigration Legislation (USA)

Throughout the colonial period and the 19c, for the mixture of ideological and economic reasons symbolized by the Statue of Liberty (1886), immigration to the USA was actively encouraged rather than controlled; it was regulated by local authorities at the ports of entry rather than by the federal government, whose sole requirement before the **American Civil War** was for enumeration (1819). During the late 19c and early 20c **Congress** took control of immigration, established the reception centre on Ellis Island (1892), and began to exclude various socially undesirable categories such as prostitutes, convicts, lunatics, and sufferers from tuberculosis. Although the entry of Asians was severely restricted by the Chinese Exclusion Act (1882, passed in response to Californian fears of the 'Yellow Peril') and the 'Gentlemen's Agreement' with Japan (1907), all this legislation still left an essentially open door to Europeans. However, the massive influx from 1880 to 1910 (almost 18 million in total) aroused fears for the future character of US society, stimulated **nativism** and fuelled an increasingly effective immigration restriction movement. The Dillingham Commission (1911) compared the 'new' migrants from Southern and Eastern Europe very unfavourably with the 'old' migrants from the north and west, and recommended control by literacy tests with limits set in proportion to the size of national groups already within the country. These recommendations were followed in the xenophobia of **World War I** and its aftermath. In 1921 an annual ceiling of 385 000 p.a. was established with national quotas based on the 1910 census, thus bringing to an end an era in the social evolution of the USA. Restrictions were then tightened with the Johnson–Reed Act (1924), shifting the quota base back to the census of 1890 and so limiting the entry from South-East Europe even further; and the Oriental Exclusion Act entirely ended immigration from Asia. Further amendments in 1927 lowered the ceiling to about 150 000 p.a. and moved the quota base to 1920. Since **World War II** immigration policy has been progressively liberalized with measures allowing entry to displaced persons and refugees (1948, 1950, 1953, 1957, 1960, 1962, 1980), while the quota system itself was extended to all countries by the McCarran–Walter Act (1952), which also eliminated race as a disqualification for entry and so reversed the exclusion of Asians. A more fundamental revision took place with the Immigration Act of 1965, which replaced the national quotas with a first-come, first-served and a family preference system, together with a hemispheric distinction (totals of 120 000 for the Western Hemisphere, and 170 000 elsewhere with a limit of 20 000 for each country). These distinctions were removed in 1976 and 1978 to give a worldwide total of 290 000, a single country limit of 20 000, and a consistent family reunification system. However, since the 1920s, alongside the official immigration restriction policies has existed the problem of illegal immigration, particularly from Mexico since the ending of the **bracero** programme (which from 1942 to 1964 regulated the flow of temporary seasonal labour). By the middle of the 1980s there were probably 3–5 million illegal immigrants in the USA, and political pressure from the Hispanic and Irish communities in particular led to the passage of the 1986 Immigration Reform and Control Act which granted an amnesty to those resident since 1982 (about 2.5 million) and prohibited the employment of 'undocumented aliens', as illegal immigrants now became known. The Immigration Act of 1990 raised the overall total of admissions to 700 000 p.a., and its provisions for skill-based and diversity visas represented a significant attempt to alter the overwhelmingly Latin-American and Asian profile of the previous 25 years' immigration, by once again attracting Europeans. The USA remains, as it has been for the past 200 years, the major immigrant-receiving nation in the world.

impeachment

A legal process for removing public officials from office. Originating in medieval England, the process was revived in that country in the 17c, when the Rump Parliament voted to bring Charles I to trial, resulting in his conviction and beheading. In the USA, the Constitution provides that the House of Representatives may move to impeach for 'high crimes and misdemeanors'. The case is then tried by the Senate, where a two-thirds majority is required for conviction. It is generally agreed that impeachment is a cumbersome method because of the problem of defining unacceptable behaviour and crimes. The move to impeach President Richard **Nixon** in 1974 did, however, have the effect of forcing his resignation. Earlier, the impeachment proceedings against President Andrew **Johnson** in 1867, which were politically inspired, resulted in his acquittal by the Senate.

Imperial Conferences

The consultative arrangements devised in 1907 by which the British and Dominion governments met on a regular basis. A permanent secretariat was established and meetings at four-year intervals were organized. The Canadian Prime Minister, Sir Wilfred **Laurier**, was suspicious of both the title and its implications, but he wished to challenge the London government's right to decide the foreign policy of the empire as a whole and thereby commit Canada without proper consultation. The 1911 conference provided the first occasion for at least some briefing by the imperial government when Sir Edward Grey gave the Prime Ministers a cagey description of the European situation. By 1926 the conference at last accepted the principle that the dominions were independent nations. The Balfour Declaration recommended a new constitutional framework for the Empire in which the dominions became 'autonomous communities within the British Empire, equal in status' but still 'united by a common allegiance to the crown', and this was embodied in the Statute of **Westminster**. However, there were limits to the British government's readiness to see the dominions as equal partners. At the 1930 conference it refused to consider the Canadian Prime Minister R B **Bennett**'s plea for imperial preferential tariffs. By 1944, however, the Imperial Conference had become a genuine means by which the Prime Ministers discussed problems and suggested mutually acceptable solutions.

Imperial Federation League (1884–94)

A British pressure group, with branches in Canada, working towards federation for the British Empire. Its members saw this as answer to the challenge of industrial powers such as Germany and the USA, to Britain's isolation within Europe, and to the rivalry with other imperial powers that emerged after 1880. The British league split over the tariff in 1893 and was succeeded by the British Empire League; but this, with its Canadian counterpart, dwindled away in the early 1900s.

Indentured Servitude

A system of contract labour, developed to attract immigrants to the early American colonies, offering poor Englishmen Atlantic passage in exchange for a term of service. After serving their terms (generally four years, during which, in contrast to slaves, they retained legal rights), most indentured servants became wage-labourers on plantations or farms, although a few did succeed in becoming landowners. Through most of the 17c, some 1 500 indentured servants were brought to the Chesapeake Bay colonies every year. In the late 17c, however, the numbers declined significantly as large numbers of slaves were imported.

Independent Treasury System (1840–1)

US government financial system, independent of banks and private business. First set up under President **Van Buren**, but repealed almost immediately, it was re-established in 1846 and remained in effect until the introduction of the Federal Reserve System.

Indian Territory

The land designated by the US government as a 'permanent' homeland for Native Americans who were forced to give up their land in the southeast, which had been guaranteed by federal treaties, and relocate in the west in compliance with the Indian Removal Act of 1830. The boundaries of what was to be inviolable territory based on new treaties signed in the 1830s were redefined several times, beginning in 1834. The original area included most of Oklahoma and parts of Kansas and Nebraska. The passage of homestead and land allotment acts opened up parts of the area to white homesteaders and developers. The northern section was lost in 1854 when Kansas and Nebraska became territories, and by the end of the century most of the remaining Indian Territory had been absorbed into what is now Oklahoma. ▷ **Five Civilized Tribes**

Indian Wars (1622–1890)
The process of invasion and conquest by which white people settled the present USA. The Europeans set out to remake the New World in the image of the Old, if possible by persuasion, if necessary by force. The result was the destruction of the indigenous population, cultures and economies. Through European diseases to which the Native Americans had no natural resistance, the imposition of white culture and warfare, the native population of North America was reduced from roughly 1 million at first contact to about 250 000 by the end of the 18c. The list of specific Indian wars is very long, most of them actually being skirmishes between a local tribe and the white settlers usurping their land. They are generally accepted to have begun with the revolt of the **Powhatan Confederacy** against settlers at Jamestown, Virginia in 1622, and to have ended with the massacre at **Wounded Knee** in 1890. Specific early conflicts include the **Pequot War** (1637) and **King Philip's War** (1676) in New England and the Pueblo Revolt (1680–92) led by Popé against Spanish settlements in what is now New Mexico and Arizona. From 1689 to 1763 Indian warfare was bound up with the struggle between France and Britain for control of the continent, the **French and Indian War**. The **Algonquin** tribes sided with the French. The English, eventually victorious, enjoyed the support of the **Iroquois Confederacy** of W New York, important both for their internal strength and for their control of the Mohawk Valley and Lake Ontario plain, which formed the only natural break in the Appalachian Mountains. Further west, the Ottawa chief, Pontiac, seized almost all the British fur-trading posts from upper Michigan to New York state before the French cut off their supplies. By 1830 the US government had formalized a policy of denying Native American rights and removing tribes

from the lands east of the Mississippi to unsettled lands in the west. Despite resistance, the **Five Civilized Tribes** of the southeast and others were forced to move west and settle in **Indian Territory**. The **Seminole** people of Florida, whose number included escaped black slaves, fought for over 30 years, accepting defeat in 1842 when nearly all were lost. Some finally moved west, but a small group survived by living in the Everglades. The Indian wars generally followed the progress of white settlers as they moved their frontier westward. On the plains, the US Cavalry fought the **Sioux** and the **Cheyenne**, under such leaders as **Sitting Bull** and **Crazy Horse**. These 'Sioux Wars' lasted over 30 years until finally ended by the incident at **Wounded Knee** (1890). The massacre of warriors, women and children by the Cavalry at Sand Creek, Colorado (1864) inflamed Arapaho, **Comanche**, Kiowa and Cheyenne already fighting to avoid being placed on reservations. In the southwest, the **Navajo** conflict ended with their mass imprisonment (1864–8) at Fort Sumpter, while the **Apache** under such leaders as **Cochise** and **Geronimo** fought on until 1900. At the same time Nez Percé under Chief **Joseph** and the Modoc fought for their lands in the northwest until their eventual defeat. Throughout the wars, the Native Americans fought at material and numerical disadvantage. They were disadvantaged as well by their own concept of warfare, for they understood it in wholly different terms from their foes. Finally they were handicapped by their own lack of unity. Specific tribes approached each war in terms of their own friendships and enmities. This gave some, such as the Iroquois, more power to shape their own futures. But only on a few occasions did such confederacies surmount tribal boundaries.
▷ **Native Americans; Little Bighorn, Battle of the; Pontiac's Conspiracy**

Industrial Workers of the World (IWW)
US radical labour organization movement, whose members were known as Wobblies. An offshoot of the Western Federation of Miners, it was founded in 1905 by a group who opposed the craft unionism of the AFL and proposed instead a union of both skilled and unskilled workers. The movement was soon splintered because of the radical ideology of its leader, 'Big Bill' **Haywood**, who called for the destruction of capitalism and the formation of a new society and maintained that employers' violence must be met in kind. He was less interested in negotiation than in striking and sabotage. Lack of organization and funds meant that the

IWW had few successes in industrial conflicts although its membership reached a peak of at least 60 000. It declined rapidly after the Red Scare of 1919. ▷ **AFL–CIO**

Inouye, Daniel (1924–   )
US Senator. He was Assistant Public Prosecutor in Honolulu (1953–4) before going into private practice. He became US Senator from Hawaii in 1963, and served on the Senate Watergate Committee investigating the scandal that led to Richard **Nixon**'s resignation. He was later made chairman of the Senate committee investigating the **Iran–Contra Affair** in 1986.

intendentes
This Spanish term (literally, 'intendants') refers to well-salaried colonial officials with significant staff, responding directly to the Spanish Crown. The intendant system, instituted by the House of Bourbon in Spain, was transplanted from Spain to Cuba in 1764, the Viceroyalty of La Plata in 1782, Peru in 1784, Mexico in 1786, and in other regions in 1790. Military officers appointed for more than 10 years, in Hispanic America they were in charge of administration, finance, the military and justice: they were effectively a response to the growth and maturity of colonial society and larger changes in the international economy, principally the growth of English economic weight. Nevertheless, the system achieved centralization and rationalization, financing the growth of full-scale military forces in the Americas.

INF (Intermediate Nuclear Force) Treaty
A treaty signed (Dec 1987) in Washington by US President Ronald **Reagan** and Soviet General-Secretary Mikhail **Gorbachev**, involving the elimination of 1 286 missiles from Europe and Asia, and over 2 000 warheads. It was noted for its inclusion of the most comprehensive, stringent and intrusive verification procedures ever seen in an arms control treaty, including short-notice on-site verification, and was a major break in the arms race and a step forward in arms control generally, leading to later agreements in both the nuclear and conventional fields.

Interprovincial Conferences
A governmental consultative process in Canada. The first, in 1887, was convened by Honoré **Mercier**, and was essentially a

convention of provincial Liberals. It passed resolutions against the federal government's disallowing power and for increases in provincial subsidies. In the short term Ottawa reacted to the resolutions in a limited way, refraining from disallowing a contentious Quebec law and introducing subsidies for Nova Scotia's iron and steel industry. With the growing complexity and interdependence of the Canadian government and economy dating from the late 19c onwards, inter-governmental conferences (both federal-provincial and interprovincial) have become an increasingly important aspect of policy making and administration. Some 158 federal-provincial and 30 interprovincial bodies are now in existence, focusing mainly on economic and constitutional matters, headed by a First Ministers' Conference, with various ministerial conferences and Continuing Committees feeding up to them. Since 1960 there has also been an annual meeting of provincial premiers.

Intolerable Acts (1774)
The American name for laws passed by parliament in London to punish Massachusetts for the **Boston Tea Party** (1773). They were called the Boston Port Act, the Massachusetts Government Act, the Administration of Justice Act and a Quartering Act. The **Quebec Act**, though addressing a different problem, was also taken by colonists to add insult to the injury of the Intolerable Acts.

Inuit
The indigenous peoples of the Canadian arctic; formerly also known as the eskimos. Traditionally their eight tribes live in regional groupings of bands (about 100 strong). They have been nomadic hunters and gatherers and some maintain this way of life, though increasing numbers live in established settlements with schools, medical stations and airstrips. Their first sustained contact with Europeans came in the late 18c by way of Moravian missionaries in Labrador. Sporadic trading contacts were made during the 19c, but only after the end of commercial whaling at the time of **World War I** were permanent trading posts established. Politically they were never included under the Indian Act, but became a federal responsibility in 1939. During the 1950s exploitation of the arctic gas and oil reserves began to destabilize their communities and in 1972 the Inuit Tapirisat of Canada (ITC) was established to preserve their culture through voluntary separation

from white communities. The result of its pressure has been more government consultation and increased subsidies.

Iran–Contra Affair (1986)

A major US political scandal. It grew out of the **Reagan** administration's efforts to obtain the release of US hostages held in Lebanon by groups friendly to Iran by secretly supplying arms to Iran's strongly anti-American government. **National Security Council** officials (notably, Colonel Oliver North) had been involved in the diversion of the proceeds of the arms sales to Iran to Nicaragua, to support the anti-government Contra rebels, even though Congress had banned the supplying of arms to the Contras. Congressional hearings in 1987 centred on the legality of the arms-for-hostages deal and on whether Colonel North had acted on his own as the Administration claimed, or whether top government officials, including President Reagan himself, were involved. The issues have not been satisfactorily resolved.

Iran Hostage Crisis (1979–81)

On 4 Nov 1979 the US Embassy in Tehran, Iran, was seized by a mob and its staff of 52 were taken hostage. The action was approved by the Ayatollah Khomeini who, like many Iranians, hated Americans for the role of the **CIA** in the overthrow of the Mossadegh government (1953) and for their training of Shah Muhammad Reza Pahlavi's secret police. The price demanded for the release of the hostages was the return of the Shah and all his wealth. Neither **UN** appeals nor President Jimmy **Carter**'s move to freeze all Iranian assets induced Iran to release the hostages. In 1980 an attempted helicopter rescue operation using US marines failed, causing the Carter administration great political embarrassment. The crisis preoccupied Carter during his last months in office and may well have been the single most important factor in his defeat by Ronald **Reagan** in the 1980 election. After 444 days of captivity, the hostages were released on the day President Reagan was inaugurated, and Iranian assets were unfrozen.

Iroquois

A Native American people concentrated in the Great Lakes area. Mostly settled in villages in longhouses, the women farmed and the men hunted, fished, traded and defended the communities from attack. They fought many wars with their neighbours,

enslaving captives or absorbing them into the community. ▷
Iroquois Confederacy

Iroquois Confederacy
A confederation of Iroquois tribes during the 17–18c in northern
New York State consisting of the Mohawk, Oneida, Onondaga,
Cayuga and Seneca, later joined by the Tuscarora. Also known
as the Iroquois League or the 'Six Nations', they were united
largely for control of the **fur trade** and for war. Numbering close
to 16 000, they defeated most of their Native American rivals and
dominated the area. The league broke up during the **American
Revolution** when the tribes took sides: the four groups siding with
the British were defeated in 1779. Today most of the Iroquois
live in upstate New York, although some live on reservations
elsewhere in the USA and Canada.

isolationism
A foreign policy strategy of withdrawing from international
affairs as long as the country's interests are not affected. It is a
means of avoiding involvement in international conflicts, and
implies neutrality in most cases. It was practised most notably by
the USA, which kept out of the League of Nations and **World
War II** until attacked by the Japanese.

Iturbide, Agustín de (1783–1824)
Mexican general and politician. Born in Valladolid of a Spanish
father and Creole mother, he fought as part of Calleja's forces
against **Hidalgo (y Costilla)** and **Morelos (y Pavón)**, defeating the
latter. He seized the moment in 1821, when Mexican conservatives
were caught off balance by the radical liberal regime in Spain, to
group together the military, aristocracy and clergy in support of
Mexican independence. His manifesto, the *Plan de Iguala*,
attracted support from conservatives and rebels alike: it guaranteed the status of Catholicism, independence under a Bourbon
monarch, and equality between Creoles and Spanish-born. He
proclaimed himself Emperor as Agustín I (1822/3), after the Bour-
bons failed to provide the prince required by *Iguala*. However,
beset with political and financial problems, he was forced to
abdicate by a revolt of which one of the leaders was **Santa Anna**.
He then travelled in Europe and, on his return to Mexico, was
executed, having been sentenced *in absentia*.

IWW ▷ **Industrial Workers of the World**

J

Jackson, Andrew ('Old Hickory') (1767–1845)

US politician and 7th President. He trained as a lawyer, and became a member of the US House of Representatives for Tennessee (1796), its Senator (1797), and a judge of its Superior Court (1798–1804). In the **War of 1812** he was given command of the South, and became famous for his defence of New Orleans (1814–15). Regarded as a folk hero, he won the presidency in 1828 in a campaign that gave him a large majority in the popular vote. His emphasis on the importance of the popular vote came to be known as 'Jacksonian democracy'. His presidency (1829–37) was significant for its use of executive power, most notable in the **nullification** issue and in the **Bank War**.

Jackson, Jesse (1941–)

US **civil rights** leader and minister. As Martin Luther **King**'s lieutenant, he established a strong branch of the **SCLC** in Chicago. In 1967 he initiated Operation Breadbasket, which aimed to create jobs by attracting business investment in black enterprises in the cities. In 1971 he became the executive director of Operation PUSH (People United To Serve Humanity); these two projects helped get him national attention, and in 1983 he became a candidate for the Democratic presidential nomination. His 'Rainbow Coalition' attracted a good deal of media attention, but without an organized political base, he had little chance of success. He was the first black American to mount a serious campaign for the office. He was a candidate again in 1987, but was again unsuccessful in gaining the nomination.

Jackson, Thomas Jonathan, 'Stonewall' (1824–63)

US Confederate general. In 1851 he became a professor at the Virginia Military Institute. During the **American Civil War** he became a Confederate general. He commanded a brigade at **Bull Run**, where his firm stand gained him his nickname. He showed tactical superiority in the campaign of the Shenandoah valley

(1862), and won several victories, notably at Cedar Run, Manassas and Harpers Ferry. He was accidentally killed by his own troops at Chancellorsville.

Jamestown
A deserted 62 acre (25 hectare) town, 15 miles (24 kilometres) inland from Chesapeke Bay, Virginia, USA, the site of the first successful British settlement in America. Excavated archaeologically (1934–56), it was founded in 1607 by 105 settlers as James Fort, but after 1699 was superseded as the capital of Virginia by Williamsburg, and abandoned.

Jay, John (1745–1829)
US politician and jurist. Educated at King's (now Columbia) College, New York, he was admitted to the Bar in 1768. He was elected to the **Continental Congress** (1774–5), becoming its President in 1778. He helped negotiate (1781–3) peace with Great Britain under the Treaty of Paris, and he served as Secretary for Foreign Affairs (1784–9). Jay contributed to the **Federalist Papers** in an effort to secure ratification of the Constitution. He became the first Chief Justice of the Supreme Court (1789–95), and in that capacity negotiated **Jay's Treaty**. From 1795 to 1801 he was governor of New York. ▷ **American Revolution**

Jay's Treaty (1794)
An agreement between the USA and Britain to end the British occupation of military posts in the northwestern parts of US territory, and for altering the terms of US commerce with Britain and its colonies. Negotiated by John **Jay**, it was very unpopular with the US public, largely because of the restrictions it imposed on US trade with the West Indies.

Jefferson, Thomas (1743–1826)
US politician and 3rd President. He became a lawyer (1767) and a member of the Virginia House of Burgesses. A delegate to the Second Continental Congress (1775), he drafted the **Declaration of Independence**. Jefferson was Governor of Virginia (1779–81), Minister to France (1785) and Secretary of State (1790). He served as Vice-President under John **Adams** (1797–1801), and as President (1801–9). Important events of his administration include the

147

Louisiana Purchase (1803) and the Embargo Act of 1807. After he retired to Monticello, he founded the University of Virginia.

Jesuits' Estates Act (1888)

A Quebec statute by which Honoré **Mercier**'s administration disposed of the compensation for Jesuit property sequestrated by the crown when the order was suppressed in the late 18c. After its reestablishment in Quebec (1842), successive governments had been unable to solve the question of how to allot the compensation, which had to be spent on education. The property was valued at C$400 000 and the Act granted C$70 000 to the province's Protestant schools while the rest was to be divided within the Catholic community at the Pope's discretion. In Quebec this seemed a sensible solution, but in Ontario the **Orange Order** was enraged, and charged Mercier with inviting the Pope to intervene in Canadian affairs. John A **Macdonald**, however, refused to disallow the Act as it fell clearly within provincial powers over education.

Jim Crow Laws

A term used to characterize US state laws passed from the 1890s onwards, to segregate blacks from whites in the south in schools, public transport, housing and other areas. They were gradually abolished from the mid-20c, largely because of the **civil rights** movement, which led to Supreme Court decisions and changes in Federal policies. ▷ **Plessy v Ferguson**

Johnson, Andrew (1808–75)

US politician and 17th President. With little formal schooling, he became alderman and Mayor in Greeneville, Tennessee, and a member of the Legislature (1835), state Senate (1841) and Congress (1843). He was Governor of Tennessee (1853–7) and a US Senator (1857–62). During the **American Civil War** he was made Military Governor of Tennessee (1862), and became Vice-President when Abraham **Lincoln** was re-elected in 1864. On Lincoln's assassination (1865), he became President (1865–9). A Democrat, his **Reconstruction** policies were opposed by the Republican Congress, who wished to make reconstruction of the Southern states dependent on a measure of protection for black civil rights. After he vetoed the **Civil Rights Acts** of 1866, his popularity declined rapidly. Politically motivated impeachment proceedings were brought against him, but fell short of conviction by one vote. ▷ **Democratic Party**

Johnson, Lyndon B(aines) ('LBJ') (1908–73)

US politician and 36th President. Educated at Southwest Texas State Teachers College, he was a teacher and congressman's secretary before becoming a Democratic member of the House of Representatives in 1937. He became a Senator in 1949, and later an effective Democratic majority leader (1954). Vice-President under John F **Kennedy** in 1961, he assumed the presidency after Kennedy's assassination, and was elected to the office in 1964 with the biggest majority ever obtained in a presidential election up until that time. His administration (1963–9) passed the Civil Rights Act of 1964 and the **Voting Rights Act** of 1965, and his **Great Society** programme to reduce poverty, eliminate racial discrimination, provide medical care and improve education. However, the escalation of the **Vietnam War** led to large-scale marches and protests and to his growing unpopularity, and he decided not to seek re-election in 1968. ▷ **Civil Rights Acts; Democratic Party**

Jones, (John) Paul (1747–92)

Scottish-born American naval commander. Originally named John Paul, he was apprenticed as a cabin boy, made several voyages to America, and in 1773 inherited property in Virginia. He joined the navy at the outbreak of the **American Revolution**, and performed a number of daring exploits off the British coast, capturing and sinking several ships. Outmanned and outgunned in the famous battle against the Serapis, he refused to surrender, declaring 'I have not yet begun to fight', and through sheer grit emerged victorious.

Jones, Mary Harris ('Mother Jones') (1830–1930)

Irish-born US labour activist. She migrated to the USA via Canada, lost her family in an epidemic in 1867, and thereafter devoted herself to the cause of labour. An effective speaker, she travelled to the scenes of major strikes, especially in the coal industry, and continued to work as a labour agitator almost until her death.

Jordan, Vernon E, Jr (1935–)

US civil rights leader. After earning a law degree from Harvard University (1960), he became a field secretary for the **NAACP**, and in 1970 director of the United Negro College Fund. He was

President of the National Urban League (1972–81), and became an influential voice in politics for black concerns.

Joseph, Chief (c.1840–1904)

Leader of the Nez Percé people, born in the Wallowa Valley of Oregon. The Nez Percé had agreed to settlement on a reservation, but when whites overran their territory and the government wanted to claim even more land, they resisted. Chief Joseph opposed any conflict, but helped lead his people on a gruelling fighting retreat from US troops through approximately 1 500 miles of wilderness. They were finally overwhelmed and forced to surrender close to the Canadian border. Chief Joseph died on a reservation in Washington State.

Juárez, Benito (Pablo) (1806–72)

Mexican national hero and politician. A Zapotec, he was a clerk and lawyer and then Governor of Oaxaca (1847–52). Exiled by conservatives under **Santa Anna** (1853–5), he then returned to join the new Liberal government. Proposing fundamental change, he abolished the fueros, seized control of Church lands, and passed the anticlerical and liberal constitution of 1857. During the civil war of 1857–60 he assumed the presidency, upholding a free Church in a free state. He was elected President on the Liberal victory (1861), a post he held until his death. The French invasion under **Maximilian** forced him to the far north, from where he directed resistance until Maximilian's defeat in 1867. He then restored republican rule, creating the basis for the regime of Porfírio **Díaz**.

K

Kamehameha I ('the Great'), originally **Paiea** (1758–1819)
Hawaiian king (1795/1819). He fought his cousin Kiwalao in 1782 and took control of northern Hawaii. He then went on to conquer the rest of the islands, the last two (Kauai and Niihau) being ceded peacefully to him in 1810. An autocratic but humane leader, he organized the government of each island and brought an end to the rite of human sacrifice.

Kansas–Nebraska Act (1854)
A bill passed by the US Congress in 1854 to establish the territories of Kansas and Nebraska. Because it opened up the possibility of extending slavery into western territories, by allowing popular sovereignty, it led to bitter debates. The ensuing protests contributed to the formation of the **Republican Party**, which was hostile to the expansion of slavery.

Kefauver, (Carey) Estes (1903–63)
US Senator. He practised as a lawyer until 1939 when he became a Democratic member of Congress. He was elected to the Senate in 1949 and continued as Senator until 1963. In 1950–1 he became well known as the head of a Senate committee which investigated organized crime and exposed its findings on television. He was the Democratic candidate for Vice-President in 1956.

Kellogg–Briand Pact (27 Aug 1928)
A proposal made by French Foreign Minister Aristide Briand to US Secretary of State Frank B Kellogg that the two countries should sign a pact renouncing war as an instrument of national policy. At Kellogg's suggestion, a Paris conference in 1928 formally condemned recourse to war, and the pact was subsequently signed by 65 states (the Pact of Paris). However, no provision was made for the punishment of aggressors. ▷ **Paris, Pact of**

Kelly, 'Honest' John (1821–86)
US politician. Boss of **Tammany Hall** in the 1870s and 1880s, he revived the machine after the downfall of Boss William Tweed, by transforming it into an efficient hierarchical organization and improving its tarnished image with the recruitment of respectable business and political leaders. ▷ **political machine**

Kennan, George Frost (1904–)
US diplomat and historian. After graduating from Princeton in 1925 he joined the US foreign service. During **World War II** he served in diplomatic posts in Berlin, Lisbon and Moscow, and in 1947 was appointed director of policy planning by Secretary of State George C **Marshall**. He advocated the policy of 'containment' of the USSR by political, economic and diplomatic means, which was adopted by Secretaries of State Dean **Acheson** and John Foster **Dulles**. Kennan subsequently served as US Ambassador in Moscow (1952–3) and Yugoslavia (1961–3). From 1956 to 1974, as Professor of History at the Institute for Advanced Study at Princeton, he revised his strategic views and called for US 'disengagement' from Europe.

Kennedy, Edward Moore (1932–)
US politician. The younger brother of John F **Kennedy** and Robert F **Kennedy**, he was educated at Harvard and the University of Virginia, he was called to the Bar in 1959, and elected a Democratic Senator in 1962. In 1969 he became the youngest-ever majority whip in the US Senate, where he has established a notable record on advancing liberal issues. But his involvement the same year in a car accident at Chappaquidick, in which a companion (Mary Jo Kopechne) was drowned, dogged his subsequent political career. In 1979, he was an unsuccessful candidate for the presidency; the nomination went to Jimmy **Carter**, who became President in 1980.

Kennedy, John F(itzgerald) (1917–63)
US politician and 35th President. Educated at Harvard, he joined the US navy in 1941 and became a torpedo boat commander in the Pacific. Elected to the House of Representatives as a Democrat in 1947, he became Senator from Massachusetts in 1952 and President in 1960. He was the first Catholic, and the youngest person, to be elected President. His domestic policies called for a

'new frontier' in social legislation, involving a federal deseg-regation policy in education, and **civil rights** reform. Although criticized for his handling of the **Bay of Pigs**, he later displayed firmness and moderation in foreign policy. In 1962 he induced the USSR to withdraw its missiles from Cuba, and he achieved a partial nuclear test ban treaty with the Soviets the following year. On 22 Nov 1963, he was assassinated by rifle fire while being driven in an open car through Dallas, Texas. The alleged assassin, Lee Harvey **Oswald**, was himself shot and killed two days later, during a jail transfer. ▷ **Cuban Missile Crisis; Democratic Party; Kennedy, Robert F; Ruby, Jack**

Kennedy, Joseph Patrick (1888–1969)

US businessman and diplomat. The grandson of an Irish Catholic immigrant, he was educated at Harvard. During the 1930s, as a strong supporter of **Roosevelt** and the '**New Deal**', he was re-warded with minor administrative posts, and the ambassador-ship to Great Britain (1937–40). He had political ambitions for his sons, and placed his large fortune at their disposal for that purpose.The eldest, Joseph Patrick (1915–44), was killed in a flying accident while on naval service in **World War II**. The others achieved international political fame. ▷ **Kennedy, Edward M; Kennedy, John F; Kennedy, Robert F**

Kennedy, Robert Francis (1925–68)

US politician. Educated at Harvard and the University of Virginia, he served in the US navy during **World War II**, was admitted to the Bar (1951), and became a member of the staff of the Senate Select Committee on Improper Activities (1957–60). He managed the presidential campaign of his brother, John F **Kennedy**, and as his Attorney-General (1961–4) and closest adviser, actively sought to enforce laws that guaranteed blacks **civil rights**. In 1964 he was elected Senator for New York. On 5 June 1968, he was shot after winning the Californian primary election, and died the following day. His assassin, Sirhan Sirhan, was later convicted of murder.

Kentucky and Virginia Resolutions (1798 and 1799)

Declarations by two state legislatures that the **Alien and Sedition Acts** violated the **US Constitution**. This laid the foundation for the future development of the doctrine of 'state sovereignty' and the state's right to nullify Federal law. The resolutions were written by Thomas **Jefferson** (Kentucky) and James **Madison** (Virginia).

Khrushchev, Nikita Sergeevich (1894–1971)

Soviet politician. In 1953, on the death of Stalin, he became First Secretary of the Communist Party of the Soviet Union, though his position was not secure until 1955. In 1956, at the 20th Party Congress, he denounced Stalinism and the 'personality cult' in a well-known secret speech that fundamentally altered the course of Soviet history. He expanded the Soviet space programme, and oversaw the launch of *Sputnik*, the world's first satellite. He visited the USA in 1959 and met with President **Eisenhower** at Camp David. After the failed attempt to install missiles in Cuba (1962) he was deposed in 1964 and replaced by Leonid Brezhnev and Alexei Kosygin. ▷ **Cuban Missile Crisis**

King–Crane Commission

The commission, composed of two US members, Henry King and Charles Crane, which carried out its work in June, July and Aug 1919. Its remit — to ascertain local reactions to the proposed Middle Eastern mandatory arrangements — resulted in their reporting opposition to separation from Palestine and to the proposal for a French mandate in Syria. The commission also found that the Zionist programme for Palestine could not, at least in its extreme form, be reconciled with the Balfour Declaration in which the rights of the non-Jewish population of Palestine were enshrined. The Commission's report was published in 1922 and its findings were all but disregarded.

King, Martin Luther (1929–68)

US civil rights leader. The son of a Baptist minister, he studied at Morehouse College and Boston University and set up his first ministry in Montgomery, Alabama. In 1957 he helped found the **SCLC** (Southern Christian Leadership Council) as a base for coordinating efforts in the struggle for racial equality. Embracing M K Gandhi's message of achieving change through non-violent resistance, he mobilized the black community to challenge segregation laws in the South through non-violent marches and demonstrations, boycotts and freedom rides, and broadened support for the 1964 Civil Rights Act. His voter registration drive in Alabama, culminating in the Selma march, led to the passage of the Voting Rights Act in 1965. In 1968 he was assassinated in Memphis, Tennessee, by James Earl Ray. ▷ **civil rights movement**

King, (William Lyon) Mackenzie (1874–1950)
Canadian politician. He studied law at Toronto, and became an MP (1908), Minister of Labour (1909–11), **Liberal Party** leader (1919), and Prime Minister (1921–6, 1926–30 and 1935–48). His great ability to find common ground among differing political views made a major contribution to the Liberal domination of national politics for a whole generation, and his view that the dominions should be autonomous communities within the British Empire resulted in the Statute of **Westminster** (1931). He resigned from office in 1948. ▷ **Compulsory Service Act; Head, Sir Francis Bond; Rowell–Sirois Commission**

King Philip's War (1675–6)
US colonial war. An attempt by the Native Americans of central New England to stop further white expansion. It was led by Metacom, King Philip, or chief of the Wampanoags, who tried to build an inter-tribal coalition. The Native Americans lost, and were killed or enslaved, but not before killing hundreds of colonists. ▷ **Indian Wars**

King William's War (1689–97)
The first of the great wars between France and England for the control of North America. Known in Europe as the War of the League of Augsburg, it was settled by the Treaty of Ryswick (1697).

Kissinger, Henry Alfred (1923–)
US political scientist and politician. His family emigrated from Germany to the USA in 1938, to escape the Nazi persecution of Jews. He was educated at Harvard, served in **World War II**, and subsequently joined the Harvard faculty. He became President Richard **Nixon**'s adviser on national security affairs in 1969, was the main US figure in the negotiations to end the **Vietnam War**, and became Secretary of State in 1973, serving under Nixon and **Ford**. His 'shuttle diplomacy' during the Arab–Israeli War of 1973 helped bring about a cease-fire, and resulted in a notable improvement in Israeli–Egyptian relations. He left public office in 1977.

Kitchen Cabinet
Term used in US politics to describe an informal group of advisers surrounding a US president. It originated in the mid-19c in the administration of President Andrew **Jackson**.

Klondike Gold Rush
A flood of prospectors (largely US) when gold was discovered in Canada Yukon Territory in 1896. The rush lasted for five years, generated an estimated US$50 million in gold, established the town of Dawson, and invigorated the economies of British Columbia, Alberta, Alaska and Washington State.

Knights of Labor (1878–93)
An early US labour organization. It tried to organize all workers in support of a large-scale political and social programme, regardless of their age, race or colour. Its membership peaked at around 700 000 in 1886, but then declined. ▷ **Powderly, Terence V**

Know-Nothings (1856)
US political party. A popular name for the short-lived anti-immigrant American Party. It was so called because of the response members were instructed to give to questions from outsiders: 'I know nothing'. ▷ **nativism**

Koch, Ed(ward) (1924–)
US politician. He practised law and became a member of the City Council (1967). Elected to **Congress** as a Democrat in 1969, he became Mayor of New York in 1978, and in the 1980s was a widely known political figure in the USA. ▷ **Democratic Party**

Korean War (1950–3)
A war between communist and non-communist forces in Korea, which had been partitioned along the 38th parallel in 1945 after Japan's defeat in **World War II**. The communist North invaded the South in 1950 after a series of border clashes, and the **UN** called upon its members to help South Korea. The US and 15 other countries responded, with General Douglas **MacArthur** as supreme commander. The UN force drove the invaders back to the Chinese frontier. China then entered the war and, together with the North Koreans, occupied Seoul. The UN forces counterattacked, and by 1953, when an armistice was signed, had retaken

all territory south of the 38th parallel. The war was unpopular with the US public and **Eisenhower** was elected on a promise to end it. There were heavy casualties, with 54 000 US troops dead and 103 000 wounded, and much higher Korean and Chinese losses.

Ku Klux Klan

US white supremacist organization. The first Klan was founded after the **American Civil War** to oppose **Reconstruction** and the new rights being granted to blacks. The members, disguised in white robes and hoods, engaged in whippings, lynchings, and cross burnings to terrorize blacks and their sympathizers in the rural areas of the South. The Klan declined in influence after federal laws were passed against it, but was re-established after **World War I**. This times its influence was felt far beyond the South, and its targets were enlarged to include Catholics, foreigners, and Jews as well as blacks. It declined during the 1930s, but was revived by the fear of **communism** in the 1950s. In the 1960s its violent opposition to the **civil rights movement** led to a federal government crackdown, and the prosecution of key members. Subsequently the Klan moved toward working through traditional political channels in order to further its agenda.

L

Laffite, Jean (c.1780–c.1826)
French pirate. By 1809 he was living in New Orleans, where he established a smuggler's colony on the islands of Barataria Bay (1810–14). The British offered him money in return for his help in attacking New Orleans, but instead he betrayed their plans to American officials. In the ensuing Battle of New Orleans (Dec 1814–Jan 1815) he and his men fought on the side of the Americans. He then returned to piracy, and in 1817 established a commune on Galveston, Texas. After his men attacked US ships (1820), he was forced to leave his headquarters. He reputedly continued his marauding for several years on the coast of Spanish America (the Spanish Main).

La Follette, Robert Marion, Snr (1855–1925)
US politician. Three times Progressive Governor of Wisconsin, he began his political career by winning election as a district attorney after exposing corruption in the local Republican Party machine. From 1885 to 1891, he served in the US House of Representatives. As Governor of Wisconsin, he reformed the primary election process and the civil service, strengthened the railroad commission and introduced measures for workers' compensation and the conservation of natural resources. His widely publicized and imitated reforms became knowns as the 'Wisconsin Idea'. He would have been the **Progressive Party** presidential candidate in 1912 but for the re-entry into politics of ex-President Theodore **Roosevelt**; in 1924 he became the nominee; although he failed in his presidential bid, he received nearly 5 million votes.
▷ **political machine**

Lafontaine, Louis Hippolyte (1807–64)
Canadian lawyer and politician. He recognized that French-Canadian culture would best be served by full French-Canadian participation in politics and by achieving **Responsible Government**. Although a follower of **Papineau**, he opposed the rebellion of

158

1837, and went to London to request constitutional reform. As the leader of the French-Canadians of **Canada East**, he joined in a coalition with **Canada West**'s reform leaders, Robert **Baldwin** and **Hincks**. The British government had sought to assimilate the French-Canadians by insisting on equal representation in the provincial legislature and on the use of English as the language of debate. The French-Canadians, however, became more politically cohesive and were able to unite with the English-speaking reformers to form an alliance which became the majority party. With the arrival of the realist Sir Charles **Bagot** in 1841, Lafontaine and Baldwin were eventually accepted as the leaders of a ministry. They therefore not only introduced a semblance of a responsible government, but demonstrated the potential of bi-cultural cooperation. There was a short interruption to reform when Sir Charles **Metcalfe** replaced Bagot, but with the introduction of free elections in 1848, the Baldwin–Lafontaine coalition came into office and served until 1851.

La Guardia, Fiorello Henry (1882–1947)
US politician. He became Deputy Attorney-General (1915–17) and served seven terms in the House of Representatives as a Republican (1917–21 and 1923–33). Three times mayor of New York City (1934–46), he was a popular and effective leader who initiated broad reforms in public services, fought corruption and undertook a major rebuilding program. New York's La Guardia Airport is named after him. ▷ **Republican Party**

laissez-faire
(French 'leave alone to do') An economic doctrine advocating that commerce and trade should be permitted to operate free of controls of any kind. It was a popular view in the mid-19c. The phrase was coined by Disraeli, relating to the work of Richard Cobden and John Bright.

Langevin, Sir Hector-Louis (1826–1906)
Canadian lawyer, journalist and politician. Mayor of Quebec in 1856, and Solicitor-General in the coalition ministry that achieved confederation, he replaced George Étienne **Cartier** as the French-Canadian representative in the cabinet of John A **Macdonald**. However, he was an extremist Catholic, gaining much of his support from the intolerant ultramontane wing of the Church,

and Macdonald found it necessary to balance his power by inviting into the cabinet the Grand Master of the **Orange Order**, Mackenzie **Bowell** and later Joseph Adolphe **Chapleau**. Langevin was forced to resign in the railway scandal of 1891. ▷ **Confederation Movement**

Lansing–Ishii Agreement (2 Nov 1917)

The name given to the exchange of diplomatic notes between the Japanese ambassador to the USA, Ishii Kikujiro, and US Secretary of State, Robert Lansing, which agreed on a set of principles concerning policy towards China. The agreement helped soothe tensions between the two countries at a time when the USA was becoming increasingly critical of Japan's attempts to enhance its influence in China. Respect for China's territorial integrity and commitment to the Open Door policy (ie that all powers should have equal economic opportunities in China) were confirmed; at the same time, the USA recognized that Japan had special interests in China because of 'territorial propinquity'. The agreement was superseded by the Washington Treaties of 1921–2, which committed all the powers to respect China's independence.

Lapointe, Ernest (1876–1941)

Canadian politician. As a Liberal with **Rouge** tendencies, he was very critical of the **Borden–Meighen** stand against the **Winnipeg General Strike**. In 1921 he was appointed to a minor position in the Mackenzie **King** administration, but it was as an adviser on French-Canadian affairs and attitudes that the Prime Minister valued him. In 1924 he became Minister of Justice. Like King, he believed the unity of the country was the foremost issue and therefore put his concern for social reform to one side (accepting, for instance, the notorious anti-communist **Padlock Act** in Quebec). Although he opposed conscription, he played an important role in generating support within Quebec for Canada's participation in **World War II**, and when Maurice **Duplessis** challenged the **War Measures Act**, Lapointe's threat to resign was an effective contribution to the return of a more amenable provincial administration. ▷ **Liberal Party**

La Salle, (René) Robert Cavelier, Sieur de (1643–87)

French explorer. He settled in Canada in 1666, and descended the Ohio and Mississippi to the sea (1682), naming the area Louisiana (after Louis XIV of France). In 1684 he fitted out an expedition to establish a French settlement on the Gulf of Mexico. He spent two years in fruitless journeys, his harshness embittering his followers, and he was murdered near the Brazos River, Texas.

Laurier, Sir Wilfrid (1841–1919)
Canadian politician. He became a lawyer, a journalist and a member of the Quebec Legislative Assembly. He entered federal politics in 1874, and became Minister of Inland Revenue (1877), leader of the **Liberal Party** (1887–1919), and the first French-Canadian and Roman Catholic to be Prime Minister of Canada (1896–1911). A firm supporter of self-government for Canada, in his home policy he was an advocate of compromise and free trade with the USA. ▷ **'Commercial Union'; Imperial Conferences**

Lausanne Conference (1932)
The conference held between the Allied powers and Germany to discuss the question of German reparation payments, which had been suspended by the moratorium imposed by the unilateral decision of US President Herbert **Hoover** in 1931, after the onset of the Great Depression. A final reparation payment by Germany was agreed, but the Lausanne convention was never ratified, and no more payments were actually made.

Lease, Mary Elizabeth (1853–1933)
US reformer. She spoke out in favour of women's suffrage, **prohibition** of alcohol and other causes. Nicknamed the 'Kansas Pythoness' for the strength of her populist rhetoric, her command to 'raise less corn and more hell' became the Populist Party's slogan.

Le Duc Tho (Phan Dinh Khai) (1911–90)
Vietnamese politician. He joined the Indo-Chinese Communist Party in 1929 and was exiled to the penal island of Con Dia by the French in 1930. Released in 1937, he became head of the Nam Dinh revolutionary movement, but was then re-arrested and imprisoned (1939–44). After **World War II**, he worked for the Communist Party of Vietnam (CPV), entering its Politburo in 1955. As leader of the Vietnamese delegation to the Paris Conference on Indo-China (1968–73), he was awarded the 1973 Nobel Peace Prize, jointly with Henry **Kissinger**, but he declined to accept it. He retired from the Politburo in 1986.

Lee, Ann, known as **Mother Ann** (1736–1884)
English-born US mystic, the illiterate daughter of a Manchester blacksmith. In 1762 she married Abraham Stanley, also a blacksmith. In 1758 she had joined the 'Shaking Quakers', or 'Shakers', who saw in her the second coming of Christ. Imprisoned in 1770 for street-preaching, she emigrated with her followers to the USA in 1774, and in 1776 founded at Niskayuna, seven miles northwest of Albany, New York, the parent Shaker settlement.

Lee, Robert E(dward) (1807–70)
US general. Educated at the US Military Academy at West Point, he received a commission in the Engineer Corps. He fought in the Mexican War and later became Superintendent of West Point. He commanded the US troops that captured John **Brown** at Harpers Ferry. When the southern states seceded from the Union, he resigned from the US Army so he would be free to serve his native state of Virginia. In 1861 he accepted the position of Commander-in-Chief of the Confederate Army of Virginia. His achievements are central to the history of the **American Civil War**. He was in charge of the defences at Richmond, and halted federal forces in the **Seven Days Battles** (1862). His forces were victorious in the second battle of **Bull Run**. His first northern invasion was stopped at the Battle of **Antietam**. He repulsed the Union side in the Battle of **Fredericksburg** and was victorious at the Battle of Chancellorsville, but his second northern invasion ended in defeat at the Battle of **Gettysburg** (1863). In the Battle of **Wilderness** (1864) Lee's forces were badly battered. In Feb 1865 Lee became Commander-in-Chief of all of the southern armies, but the confederate cause was hopeless at that point and two months later he surrendered his army to General Grant at **Appomattox Court House**, Virginia. After the war, he became President of Washington College at Lexington.

Lend-Lease Agreement (1941)
The arrangement by which the USA lent or leased war supplies and arms to Britain and other Allies during **World War II**. It was a measure in which President **Roosevelt** took a close personal interest. The Lend-Lease Act was passed by Congress in Mar 1941, when British reserves were almost exhausted. By the time the agreement terminated in 1945, the allies had received about £5 000 million worth of materials.

Lesage, Jean (1912–80)
Canadian politician. He became the Liberal Premier of Quebec in 1960, carried into power on a wave of nationalist fervour, although the Liberals won only 50 out of the 95 seats. He then introduced the **Quiet Revolution** against corruption, the Catholic Church's involvement in lay issues such as education, welfare and health, and against the economic domination of the USA and of anglophone Canadians in Quebec. His demands for a more active governmental role in the province, because of its special situation within the Confederation, began to cause unease among other Canadian provinces, especially when he asked for an increased share of tax revenue. In 1966 his government was defeated by the **Union Nationale**. He remained leader of the Provincial Party until his retirement in 1970. ▷ **Liberal Party**

Lévesque, René (1922–87)
Canadian politician. He founded the **Parti Québecois** in 1968 after **Lesage**'s defeat and the refusal of the **Liberal Party** to become more nationalist. By uniting the majority of francophones who wished greater autonomy for Quebec and those who wanted complete political independence for the province, he won a stunning victory in 1976, with 41 per cent of the vote. He then introduced electoral and labour reforms, pressed hard for the completion of the huge Quebec Hydro scheme and initiated legislation to place foreign-owned and other corporations under public ownership. More controversial were Bill 101, which legislated for a unilingual province, and a referendum law on the question of Quebec's future. With the other provinces refusing to commit themselves to economic relationships with Quebec, and with Prime Minister Pierre **Trudeau**'s full involvement in the campaign, the Quebeckers voted against secession. Lévesque then began to demand enhanced provincial powers, along with Alberta's Premier Peter Lougheed. In 1981 Quebec became increasingly isolated, with Lévesque refusing to endorse Trudeau's constitutional reforms which challenged not only Bill 101 but also Lévesque's demand for compensation from Ottawa if the province opted out of federal socio-economic programmes. The party became deeply divided over the secession issue, but in 1985 Lévesque maintained his leadership with a 75 per cent vote.

Lewis and Clark expedition
A transcontinental overland expedition from St Louis to the Pacific coast and back (1804–6), made by US explorers

Meriwether Lewis (1774–1809) and William Clark (1770–1838). The first of its kind, it was made at the request of President Jefferson. It provided much information about the **Louisiana Purchase**. ▷ **Sacajawea**

Lewis, John L (1880–1969)

US labour leader. Born the son of a Welsh coalminer, he grew up to hold the presidency of the Union of United Mineworkers from 1920 to 1960. When its membership was reduced by the **Great Depression** to 150 000 in 1933, fearing a communist takeover, Lewis led a vigorous recruitment drive which increased the membership to 500 000. When, in 1935, he was unsuccessful in his attempts to change the AFL's traditional exclusion of industrial workers, he reacted by founding the Committee for Industrial Organizations, which became the CIO after its expulsion from the AFL in 1938. He took the coal miners out on several strikes during **World War II**, and his fiery personality and stubborn drive led to clashes with Presidents Franklin D **Roosevelt** and Harry S **Truman**. Although he swung the vote of organized labour behind Roosevelt in 1936, he reverted to his original Republicanism in 1940, and was a member of the isolationist **America First Committee**. ▷ **ALF–CIO**

Lexington and Concord, Battles of (19 Apr 1775)

The first battles of the **American Revolution**, fought in Massachusetts after British troops tried to seize supplies stored at the village of Concord, and were confronted by colonial militia.

Leyte Gulf, Battle of (1944)

A battle during **World War II**, when the Japanese fleet converged on the US 3rd and 7th Fleets protecting Allied landings on Leyte in the central Philippines. The Japanese suffered irreplaceable losses of 300 000 tonnes of combat ships, compared to US losses of 37 000 tonnes. The way was opened for further US gains in the Philippines and on islands nearer Japan.

Liao Zhongkai (Liao Chung-k'ai) (1878–1925)

Chinese politician. Born into an overseas Chinese family in the USA, he studied in Japan before becoming the leading financial expert of the Guomindang (Chinese Nationalist Party) after 1912. Associated with its left wing, he supported the United Front with the communists in 1923, advocating a planned economy along socialist lines. In 1924 he played an important role in setting up both the workers and peasant departments under Guomindang auspices as part of its new strategy of mass mobilization. As the leading Guomindang representative at the Whampoa Military Academy, Liao also laid the basis for the political commissar system that was to be used throughout the National Revolutionary Army. He aroused opposition from right-wing members of the Guomindang who opposed the United Front, and who may have been involved in his assassination.

Liberal Party (Canada)
This party evolved from the reform groups of **Canada East** and **Canada West** in the late 1840s and early 1850s, joined by the **Clear Grits** in 1855 and the **Rouges** after confederation. The party's early lack of cohesion and its failure to organize at a federal level meant that it was easily distracted by provincial issues, and without the Conservatives' ability to distribute patronage it could not attract new members or erode Conservative support. After the 1871 Treaty of **Washington**, however, Liberals had the necessary issues to unite their provincial groups and were ready, under the leadership of Alexander **Mackenzie**, to take advantage of the railway scandal of 1873 to win power. Their failure to negotiate a reciprocity agreement with the USA in 1874 and refusal to adopt a higher tariff policy, combined with the effects of depression and the accusation of atheism levelled by Quebec's Catholic Church, lost them the 1878 election and they remained in opposition under the leadership of Edward **Blake** in the 1880s. It was not until the end of the century that the party developed a formula for success, which essentially followed the example of the Conservatives. This was an anglo-francophone coalition, tempering reform with pragmatism, and cemented by a new emphasis on patronage. Sir Wilfrid **Laurier** led the party to success in 1896, and by recruiting provincial premiers to his cabinet he increased the government's appeal to the provinces. The party was severely damaged by the defection of Clifford **Sifton** (over reciprocity in 1911) and Henri **Bourassa** (over naval policy), and joined the union government of R L **Borden** to bring in conscription during **World War I**. After Laurier's death, W L Mackenzie **King** led the party back into office in 1921, adding to the old formula a unique ability to blur political issues which enabled distinctly antagonistic groups to remain within the Liberal fold, and which kept them in power

(with Progressive Party allies) until 1930, and from 1935 until his retirement in 1948. His successor, Louis **Saint Laurent**, was not able to maintain this unity and the party began to alienate itself from Western Canada, resulting in the defeat of 1957. Although Lester **Pearson** led the party back into minority government in 1963, it was not until Pierre **Trudeau** took the leadership that the party was successful in re-establishing itself nationally.

Liberal Republican Party (1872)

An insurgent movement in the US **Republican Party**. It was opposed to **Reconstruction** policies in the South, and to the notorious corruption in the administration of President **Grant** (in office 1869–77).

Liberty Bell

A bell which was commissioned by the Pennsylvania Provincial Assembly in 1751 for the new State House (later Independence Hall) in Philadelphia. Its circumference at its widest point measures 12 feet (3.7 metres) and it is 3 feet (0.9 metres) high. It was rung following the first public reading of the Declaration of Independence, and became a symbol of US freedom. It cracked beyond repair while being rung in 1846 on the birthday of George Washington. In 1976 it was rehoused in a new building near Independence Hall.

Lincoln, Abraham (1809–65)

US politician and 16th President. Elected to the Illinois legislature in 1834, he became a lawyer in 1836. A decade later, he was elected to a single term in Congress, where he spoke against the extension of slavery, and in 1860 was elected President as the **Republican Party**'s candidate on a platform of hostility to slavery's expansion. When the **American Civil War** began (1861), he defined the issue in terms of national integrity, not anti-slavery, a theme he restated in the **Gettysburg Address** (1863). Nonetheless, in his Emancipation Proclamation that same year he announced his intention of freeing all slaves in areas of rebellion. He was re-elected in 1864; after the final Northern victory he proposed to reunite the nation on the most generous terms, but on 14 Apr 1865 he was shot at Ford's Theater, in Washington DC, by an actor, John Wilkes **Booth**, and died next morning. He immediately became a national hero, and is regarded as one of the finest symbols of American democracy.

Lindbergh, Charles Augustus (1902–74)

US aeronaut. His 1927 flight from New York to Paris, taking $33\frac{1}{2}$ hours in his monoplane, *Spirit of St Louis*, won him a prize of US\$25 000 for the first solo transatlantic flight and instant fame. To this was added national sympathy when his son was abducted and murdered in 1932. In 1940 he became a member of the isolationist **America First Committee**, and his popularity was seriously damaged in 1941 because of his suggestion to negotiate a settlement with **Hitler**'s Germany.

Lippmann, Walter (1889–1974)

US journalist and political philosopher. His precociously brilliant *Drift and Mastery* (1914) argued for the application of 20c scientific method to political thought, and in the same year he founded *The New Republic*, with Herbert **Croly** and Walter Weyl. At the outbreak of **World War I** he became secretary of the 'Inquiry', charged with preparing America's post-war negotiating position. Although disillusioned by the Treaty of **Versailles** and the US refusal to join the **League of Nations**, he remained a consistent internationalist. For decades he was a widely influential commentator on political affairs, both domestic and international, through his editorials for the *New York Herald Tribune* and his syndicated columns.

List, (Georg) Friedrich

German political economist. A disciple of Adam Smith, he was charged with sedition in 1824, went to the USA, and became a naturalized citizen. He was US consul at Baden, Leipzig and Stuttgart successively. A strong advocate of protection for new industries, he did much by his writings to form German economic practice.

Little Bighorn, Battle of the (25–6 June 1876)

The famous battle, popularly called 'Custer's Last Stand', between US cavalry, under General **Custer**, and the **Sioux** and **Cheyenne**, under Sitting Bull and Crazy Horse. The Native Americans destroyed Custer's force. Issues behind the battle included Custer's bloody dawn attack on a Cheyenne village at the Washita in 1868, and the white invasion of the Black Hills, sacred to the Sioux. ▷ **Indian Wars**

Little Rock (Arkansas, USA)

The scene of the first major clash over school desegregation in 1957, when Governor Orval Faubus called out the National Guard to prevent nine black children from enrolling at Central High School. After the Guard was withdrawn on a court order, a white mob went on the rampage. President **Eisenhower** was eventually forced to send in an airborne division of regular troops to protect the children throughout the school year. At the beginning of the next, Faubus, backed throughout by the Citizens' Council, closed down the schools. It was not until well into 1959 that court proceedings secured their reopening.

Livingston

The name of an American family. The founder **Robert** Livingston (1654–1728) was born in Scotland. He went to America in 1673, where he settled in Albany, New York. He became a landowner, establishing a large estate, and also became involved in New York politics. Of his grandsons, **Philip** (1716–78) was a member of the Continental Congress (1774–8), and signed the Declaration of Independence; **William** (1723–90) was also a member of the Continental Congress (1774–6), and was the first Governor of New Jersey (1776–90). **Robert R** (1746–1813), a great-grandson of Robert, became a lawyer and as a member of the Continental Congress (1775–7, 1779–81) was one of the five charged with drawing up the Declaration of Independence. He served as the first US Secretary of Foreign Affairs (1781–3), was chancellor of New York state from 1777 to 1801, and US minister to France from 1801 to 1804. He also enabled Robert Fulton (1765–1815) to construct his first steamer. **Edward** (1764–1836), the brother of Robert R, also became a lawyer and sat in congress from 1795 until 1801. He then became US district attorney for New York state, and mayor of New York until 1803. He settled in New Orleans in 1804. During the second war with Britain he was aide-de-camp to General **Jackson** (1815). He represented New Orleans in Congress (1822–9) and systematized the civil code of Louisiana. In 1829 he became US Senator from Louisiana. He was appointed Secretary of State in 1831, and from 1833 until 1835 was US minister to France.

Lochner v New York (1905)

US Supreme Court ruling that New York state legislation for a 10-hour working-day was unconstitutional. According to the

majority opinion, the law violated employees' freedom to negotiate their own working conditions. Justice Oliver Wendell **Holmes**
Jnr dissented from this imposition of the judges' own **laissez-faire**
opinions on the legal process. The ruling illustrated the court's
hostility towards legislative attempts at improving working conditions, and its use of the **Fourteenth Amendment** to block them.

Lodge, Henry Cabot (1850–1924)
US politician, historian and biographer. He became a Republican
Senator from Massachusetts in 1893, and after **World War I** led
the opposition to the Treaty of **Versailles** (1919). The treaty was
not ratified, preventing the USA from joining the **League of
Nations** in 1920.

Long, Huey Pierce (1893–1935)
US politician. Flamboyant, astute and ambitious, he used the
grievances of poor whites and his record as Public Service Commissioner to win the governorship of Louisiana, and then (1928–
31) proceeded to build one of the most effective political machines
in the history of US politics. His programme of extensive public
spending on roads, educational institutions and hospitals not
only reformed and developed Louisiana's public services, but also
mitigated the impact of the Depression upon the state. Although
a ruthless manipulator of the state legislature and judiciary, Long
refused to use race as a political issue. Aiming at a national
audience, he developed the 'Share Our Wealth' plan for income
redistribution. A Democratic US Senator from 1931, by 1935 he
claimed to have a following of 7.5 million for the plan. Initially
supportive of the **New Deal** and President Franklin D **Roosevelt**,
he became a vehement critic of the president and planned to run
against him as a third-party candidate in 1936. However, he
was widely feared and reviled as a potential dictator, and was
assassinated in Sep 1935.

Louisiana Purchase (1803)
The sale by France to the USA of an area between the Mississippi
River and the Rocky Mountains for US$15 000 000. The purchase
gave the USA full control of the Mississippi Valley.

Loyalists
Colonial Americans who remained loyal to Britain during the
American Revolution. Britain defined the term carefully, since

loyalists were eligible for compensation. It was not enough to have been born or been living in the American colonies at the onset of revolution; it was necessary to have served the British cause in some substantial manner and to have left the USA before or soon after the termination of hostilities. During the revolution special corps were established for over 19 000 loyalist troops. Half of the 80 000–100 000 refugees went to Canada, especially to the Maritime Provinces, and their presence contributed to the creation of Upper Canada in 1791. Their influence was not insubstantial in the establishment of governmental, social, educational and religious institutions. In 1789 Lord Dorchester ordained that both they and their children were entitled to add the letters 'UE' after their names, indicating their belief in the Unity of Empire. They then became known as the United Empire Loyalists. ▷ **Canada, Upper; Carleton, Sir Guy**

Lundy's Lane, Battle of (1814)
The only Canadian engagement in the **War of 1812** which was not simply a skirmish. Casualties were high on both sides, with the Americans suffering more fatalities. The Americans retreated and were unable to continue their campaign in the Niagara district.

Lusitania, Sinking of the (May 1915)
A Cunard passenger liner torpedoed by a German submarine off the Irish Coast while in transit from New York to Liverpool, with 128 Americans among those lost. The German government had announced (Feb 1915) that any passenger ship caught within a designated war zone around the British Isles would be sunk without warning. President Woodrow **Wilson** declared he would hold Germany accountable for such deaths in the future. Although the German authorities argued that the *Lusitania* was carrying war munitions for the Allies, they did eventually make **reparations**. However, any US sympathy toward Germany up to this point disappeared, and many called for a declaration of war.

M

MacArthur, Douglas (1880–1964)
US general. Educated at the US Military Academy at West Point, he joined the US army, and in **World War I** served with distinction in France. In 1941 he became commanding general of the US armed forces in the Far East, and, after losing the Philippines, from Australia directed the recapture of the south-west Pacific (1942–5). He formally accepted the Japanese surrender, and commanded the occupation of Japan (1945–51). In 1950 he led the UN forces in the **Korean War**, defeating the North Korean Army, but was relieved of command when he tried to continue the war against China.

Macdonald, John Alexander (1815–91)
Scottish-born Canadian politician. His family emigrated to Canada in 1820, and he was educated in law at Kingston. Entering politics in 1843, he became leader of the Conservative Party and joint Premier in 1856. Prime Minister in 1857–8 and 1864, he played an important role in bringing about the confederation of Canada, and in 1867 formed the first government of the new dominion. The Pacific Scandal brought down his government in 1873, but he regained the premiership in 1878, retaining it until his death in office. ▷ **Jesuits' Estate Act; Tariff Policy (Canada)**

Macdonald, John Sandfield (1812–72)
Canadian politician. From an Irish background, he became Solicitor-General in Robert **Baldwin**'s ministry (1849–51), but Francis **Hincks** passed him over and he, like George **Brown**, became a bitter critic of the government. When George Étienne **Cartier** was defeated in 1862, Macdonald was asked to form a ministry. As a reformer and a Catholic, he believed in the 'double-majority' principle, requiring a government to hold majorities within each half of the province, in order to contain both Protestants and Catholics within the party. However as Reform Premier in 1862–4 he forgot his principles and voted for a Separate

171

School bill against the wishes of his Protestant supporters. He was Premier of Ontario (1867–71).

Mackenzie, Alexander (1822–92)
Canadian politician. A Clear Grit before confederation and leader of the **Liberal Party** afterwards. He came to the fore when George **Brown** retired from public life and Oliver Mowat restricted his political ambitions to Ontario. Mackenzie lacked sufficient support in parliament when he tried to form a government after the railway scandal of 1873 and he opted for a general election. A good majority established him as Prime Minister, but his tenure was cautious and inept. His go-slow public construction of the **Canadian Pacific Railway** (for which he took personal responsibility as Minister of Public Works), nearly lost British Columbia to the USA, while his inability to deal with the severe depression and his refusal to raise the tariff lost him the election of 1878. In 1880 the party threatened to rebel and he was succeeded by Edward **Blake**. ▷ **Clear Grits**

Mackenzie, William Lyon (1795–1861)
Canadian politician. He emigrated to Canada in 1820, established the *Colonial Advocate* in 1824, and entered politics in 1828. In 1837 he published in his paper the 'Declaration of the Toronto Reformers' (modelled on the US Declaration of Independence), headed a band of reform-minded insurgents, and after a skirmish with a superior force fled to the USA, where he was imprisoned. He returned to Canada in 1849, becoming a journalist and MP (1851–8). ▷ **Canada, Upper; Rebellions of 1837**

MacManes, James (1822–99)
US politician. An Irish immigrant, he became the Republican boss of the Philadelphia 'Gas Ring'. Thousands depended upon him for their jobs, voted at his direction and subscribed to his campaign funds. The city's debt rose meteorically and it was estimated that the ring had embezzled $8 million. It was swept out of office in 1876 by Democratic reformers, but their cuts in public works caused so many job losses that the ring was soon back in power. The cycle was repeated in the 1880s. ▷ **political machine**

Madero, Francisco Indalécio (1873–1913)

Mexican revolutionary and politician. The son of a wealthy land-owner, groomed in Paris and educated in the USA, he was no social revolutionary, although he greatly improved the *peons'* condition on his own estates. He unsuccessfully opposed Porfirio **Díaz**'s local candidates in 1904, and in 1908, when Díaz was quoted as saying that he would not seek another term, Madero took the dictator at his word and launched his own presidential campaign. A spiritualist, vegetarian and practitioner of homoeo-pathic medicine, he was an unlikely challenger, and at first was not taken seriously. But his popularity grew rapidly and Díaz turned to repression, imprisoning Madero and many of his sup-porters. He escaped to the USA, from where he directed a military campaign. His supporters, including **Villa**, captured Ciudad Juá-rez, where he established his capital (May 1911), and the dic-tatorship crumbled. Once elected President (Oct 1911), Madero's moderate political reform programme pleased no one and he faced a succession of revolts by Emiliano **Zapata** and others demanding land reform, as well as by supporters of the old dictatorship. On the night of 23 Feb 1913, he and his Vice-President were murdered following a military coup led by General Victoriano Huerta, plan-ned with the assistance of US ambassador Henry L Wilson.

Madison, James (1751–1836)

US politician and 4th President. He entered Virginia politics in 1776, played a major role in the **Constitutional Convention** of 1787, which framed the federal **US Constitution**, and collaborated in the writing of the **Federalist Papers**. He served as a Congressman from Virginia (1789–97) in the first federal Congress, and was a strong advocate of the Bill of Rights. He was Secretary of State under **Jefferson**, and President himself for two terms (1809–17). His period in office was dominated by the **War of 1812** with Britain. ▷ **US Constitution**

Mafia (also known as 'the Mob', 'Cosa Nostra', 'the Syndicate' or, in Chicago, 'the Outfit')

US development of the Sicilian Mafia. Evolving in the early 20c with the migration to the USA of Neapolitans, Calabrians and Sicilians, who took with them their state-suspicious structures of authority and clientage, a series of gangland wars ended with a 1931 'peace treaty' which established its modern structure. The

Mafia has flourished because it satisfied demands for alcohol during **Prohibition**, and for narcotics and gambling since. The infiltration of some labour unions has also enabled the organization to benefit from extortion. While the code of *omerta* ('silence') has protected it during repeated investigations, these have shown that some officials, at all levels of government, have been controlled by the Mafia, which now consists of at least 24 families, each led by a *capo* ('head').

Maisonneuve, Paul de Chomedey, Sieur de (1612–76)

French soldier who founded Montreal in 1642 leading an expedition of missionary priests, nuns and settlers. In their zeal they were ready to accept the challenges not only of the primitive conditions but also of the threat of attack from the neighbouring **Iroquois**.

Malcolm X (1925–65)

US militant black activist, who became the most effective spokesman for **Black Power**. Born Malcolm Little, he took the name 'X' to symbolize the stolen identities of the generations of black slaves. After an adolescence of violence, narcotics and petty crime, he came under the influence of Elijah **Muhammad** while in prison for burglary and after his release in 1952 became Muhammad's chief disciple within the **Black Muslims**, greatly expanding the organization's following. In 1963 Malcolm was suspended from the Nation of Islam after disagreements with Muhammad and gained the deep hatred of the leader's loyal followers. Malcolm founded the Organization for Afro-American Unity, dedicated to the alliance of American blacks and other non-white peoples. In the last year of his life, following a pilgrimage to Mecca, Malcolm announced his conversion to orthodox Islam and put forward the belief in the possible brotherhood between blacks and whites. Malcolm's extreme stance and the inflammatory nature of his oratory had scared many whites, appealed to many northern blacks in the urban ghettos, and had been met with criticism by moderate civil rights leaders who deplored his violent message. In 1965 Malcolm was the victim of Black Muslim assassins who retaliated against the man they viewed as a traitor.

Manhattan Project

The codename for the most secret scientific operation of **World War II**, the development of the atomic bomb, undertaken successfully in the USA from 1942 onwards. The project culminated in the detonation of the first atomic weapon near Alamogordo, New Mexico (16 July 1945).

Manifest Destiny

A term for US expansion throughout North America in the mid-19c, used particularly to rationalize the conquest of Native American and Mexican lands and southern and western settlements. The phrase was coined by the editor of the *United States Magazine and Democratic Review*, John O'Sullivan, who, in 1845, stated that it was the country's 'manifest destiny to overspread the continent allotted by Providence for the free development of our yearly multiplying millions'.

Manitoba Schools Act (1890)

Canadian educational legislation. Passed by the Manitoba provincial assembly under pressure from the campaign of D'Alton **McCarthy**, it established a non-sectarian educational system and reversed the act under which Manitoba had been admitted to the Confederation with denominational schools specified. Popular outrage among Catholics, especially in Quebec, challenged the act in the courts, but the privy council found in favour of the law. After the Supreme Court had declared remedial legislation to be within federal jurisdiction, the Conservative administration reluctantly introduced it, but not in time to be carried before the election of 1896. When the Liberals won the election, **Laurier** ensured that the matter was settled by negotiation rather than coercion. While separate schools were not re-established, denominational religious instruction was accepted, as was bilingual teaching where there were more than 10 pupils with a native language other than English. This solution satisfied all except the Catholic Church, which eventually relented after Vatican approval had been sought by the Liberals.

Mann, Horace (1796–1859)

US educator. Secretary of the Massachusetts State Board of Education from 1837, he introduced such reforms as a minimum school year, teacher-training institutes and a state association of teachers. He used his annual reports to discuss such matters as teaching methods and school management. His last report, written in 1848 against the background of European revolution, argued that public school education was the best means of ensuring social stability through the provision of equal opportunity. In 1848 he was elected to **Congress** as an anti-**slavery** Whig.

maquiladoras

A Spanish term used in Mexico (literally, 'assembly') signifying foreign-owned industrial assembly plants built on the US border, in order to take advantage of lower wage rates and less onerous labour legislation in Mexico. The growth of *maquiladora* industries was most rapid in the 1960s as both the US and Mexican authorities sought to limit the flight of the *braceros* to California and Texas, while major multinational manufacturing firms sought to take advantage of tax-breaks conceded under Mexican legislation designed to stimulate industrial growth and exports. Their effective contribution to Mexican growth is hotly debated, while their existence is also unpopular with US labour unions.

Marbury v Madison (1803)

The first US Supreme Court decision declaring a federal law unconstitutional. William Marbury had received a minor judicial appointment as one of the last acts of President John **Adams**'s administration. James **Madison**, the new Secretary of State, refused to deliver the commission and Marbury took legal action. Chief Justice John **Marshall** admonished Madison but found that the clause of the Federal Judiciary Act (1789) under which Marbury brought his case was contrary to the **US Constitution**. In a classic assertion of the doctrine of judicial review he argued that 'it is emphatically the province and duty of the judicial department to say what the law is'.

March through Georgia (1864)

A campaign in the **American Civil War** by the Northern Army under General **Sherman**, resulting in devastation of the area between Atlanta and the ocean. In military terms it completed the task of splitting the Confederacy on an east–west line.

Marquette, Jacques, 'Père Marquette' (1637–75)

French Jesuit missionary. He was sent in 1666 to North America, where he brought Christianity to the Ottawa people around Lake Superior, and accompanied Louis Jolliet (1645–1700) on the expedition which discovered and explored the Mississippi (1673).

Marshall, George Catlett (1880–1959)

US general and politician. Educated at the Virginia Military Institute, he became Chief-of-Staff (1939–45), and directed the US Army throughout **World War II**. After two years in China as special representative of President **Truman**, he became Secretary of State (1947–9), originating the **Marshall Plan** for the post-war reconstruction of Europe, and Secretary of Defense (1950–1). He retired (Sep 1951) after nearly 50 years of military and civilian service, and was awarded the Nobel Peace Prize in 1953.

Marshall, John (1755–1835)

US jurist. The foremost Chief Justice in the history of the US Supreme Court, in the 1790s he became a supporter of the Federalist measures of George **Washington** and Alexander **Hamilton**, and was named Chief Justice by the outgoing President John **Adams** in 1801. From then until his death he dominated the Supreme Court, establishing the US doctrine of Supreme Court judicial review of federal and state legislation. ▷ **American Revolution; Marbury v Madison; McCulloch v Maryland**

Marshall Plan

The popular name for the European Recovery Program, a scheme for large-scale, medium-term US aid to war-ravaged Europe, announced in 1947 by US Secretary of State, George Marshall. 'Marshall Aid' was rejected by the USSR and the Eastern bloc, but during the period 1948–50 it materially assisted Western Europe's economic revival.

Marshall, Thurgood (1908–93)

US jurist. Associate justice of the US Supreme Court and civil rights advocate. Educated at Lincoln and Howard universities, he joined the legal staff of the National Association for the Advancement of Colored People, and argued many important civil rights cases. He served as a judge of the US Court of Appeals (1961–5), and as Solicitor-General of the United States (1965–7), before becoming the first black Associate Justice of the US Supreme Court, a post he held until his retirement in 1991. ▷ **civil rights**

Mason–Dixon Line

The border between Maryland and Pennsylvania, drawn 1763–7 by the British astronomer Charles Mason (1730–87) and his colleague Jeremiah Dixon (of whom little is known). It is regarded as the boundary of 'the South'.

Massachusetts Bay Company

A joint stock company established in 1629 by royal charter to promote trade and colonization along the Merrimack and Charles rivers in New England. Its Puritan stockholders won the right to acquire all of the company's stocks. The company became self-governing, and it elected John Winthrop its first governor. Puritan settlers began what would become the Great Puritan Migration. The first group arrived in Salem in 1630, and later established a settlement in Boston. The company and the Massachusetts Bay Colony were one in the same, but in 1684 the company lost its charter, and two years later the colony became part of the Dominion of New England.

Massey, Charles Vincent (1887–1967)

Canadian politician and diplomat. In 1952 he became the first native-born Governor-General. In 1925 Mackenzie **King** invited him to join his cabinet but he failed to win a seat in 1926 and he was appointed instead as Canada's first minister to the USA. He was chairman of the 1949 Royal Commission on National Development in the Arts, Letters and the Sciences which inquired into the federal cultural agencies, such as the Canadian Broadcasting Corporation, the National Film Board, the National Gallery and the National Research Council. Its report, submitted in 1951, suggested that a Canadian Council for the 'Encouragement of the Arts, Letters, Humanities and Social Sciences be established', and that Canada's cultural institutions be supported in order to limit US influence.

Mather, Cotton (1662–1728)

US colonial minister. Educated at Harvard, he became the foremost Puritan minister in New England during his time. A polymath, he reported on American botany, and was one of the earliest New England historians. But his reputation suffered lasting disfigurement because of his involvement in the **Salem Witch Trials** of 1692.

Maximilian (Ferdinand Maximilian Joseph) (1832–67)

Emperor of Mexico (1864/7). Born in Vienna, he was the younger brother of Emperor Francis Joseph I, and was an archduke of

Austria. In 1863, supported by the French, he accepted the offer of the crown of Mexico, falsely believing that he had the general support of the people of Mexico. This offer was in fact the result of conniving between those conservative Mexicans who sought the overthrow of the government of Benito **Juárez** and the French Emperor, Napoleon III, who wished to further his own interests in Mexico. When the French troops were forced, under US pressure, to withdraw from Mexico, Maximilian refused to abdicate, seeing this as the desertion of his people. He made a brave defence at Querétaro, but his forces were starved into surrender. He was captured and executed, despite petitions for clemency by many European monarchs.

Mayas
The best-known civilization of the classic period of Mesoamerica (250–900). The Maya rose to prominence c.300 in present-day southern Mexico, Guatemala, northern Belize and western Honduras. Inheriting the inventions and ideas of earlier civilizations, such as the Olmec and Teotihuacan, they developed astronomy, calendrical systems, hieroglyphic writing and ceremonial architecture, including pyramid temples. The tropical rainforest area was cleared for agriculture, and rain water was stored in numerous reservoirs. They also traded with other distant people, clearing routes through jungles and swamps. Most people farmed, while centres such as Tikal and Bonampak were largely ceremonial and political, with an elite of priests and nobles ruling over the countryside. Maya civilization started to decline, for reasons unknown, c.900, although some peripheral centres still thrived, under the influence of Mexico.

Mayflower Compact (1620)
An agreement to establish a 'civil body politic', signed aboard the ship *Mayflower* by members of the Pilgrim party about to settle in the Cape Cod region.

McCarthy, D'Alton (1836–98)
Canadian politician. From an Ulster Protestant background, he rose to be one of John A Macdonald's lieutenants, but when Macdonald refused to disallow Quebec's Jesuit Estates Act, he established the Equal Rights Association. The association's title was curiously inappropriate since it sought to limit the use of French in Ontario's schools and to annul Ottawa's acceptance of

French as an official language in the North West Territories. The McCarthyites' assertion that they were ready to use force to maintain Anglo-Saxon Protestantism destabilized the Conservative Party, in which moderates argued that confederation required tolerance of French rights. French-Canadians also began to question the old alliance between the **Bleus** and the Ontario Tories. One of the results of his campaign was the enactment of the **Manitoba Schools Act**.

McCarthy, Joseph Raymond (1909–57)

US politician. Educated at Marquette University, Milwaukee, he became a circuit judge in 1939, and after war service was elected Senator in 1946. He achieved fame for his unsubstantiated accusations in the early 1950s that communists had infiltrated the State Department, and in 1953 became chairman of the Senate permanent subcommittee on investigations. By hectoring cross-examination and damaging innuendo he arraigned many innocent citizens and officials, overreaching himself when he came into direct conflict with the army. This kind of anti-communist witch-hunt became known as 'McCarthyism'. His power diminished after he was formally condemned by the Senate in 1954. ▷ **Fifth Amendment; HUAC**

McClellan, George B(rinton) (1826–85)

US general. Educated at the US Military Academy at West Point, when the **American Civil War** began he drove Confederate forces out of West Virginia, and was called to Washington to reorganize the Federal Army of the Potomac. His Virginian campaign ended disastrously at Richmond (1862). He forced **Lee** to retreat at the Battle of **Antietam**, but failed to follow up his advantage, and was recalled. In 1864 he opposed **Lincoln** for the presidency, and in 1877 was elected Governor of New Jersey.

McCulloch v Maryland (1819)

US Supreme Court decision which prevented a state interfering with the exercise of a legitimate federal power. McCulloch was a clerk in the Baltimore branch of the Bank of the United States who appealed against an indictment for his failure to affix a state tax stamp on US banknotes. The court sustained his appeal with Chief Justice John **Marshall** declaring that although sovereignty was divided between the national government and the states, the former was supreme 'within its sphere of action'.

McDougall, William (1822–1905)
Canadian politician. He was the first Governor of the North West Territories in 1869. A Clear Grit before confederation, he became Minister of Public Works in the **McDonald** cabinet of 1867. Exploration of the North West Territories had established the agricultural potential of the 64 000 square mile belt beyond the Red River along North Sasketchewan to the mountains. McDougall was one of the negotiators for the purchase of these **Hudson's Bay Company** lands, but the **métis** of the Red River colony were not informed either of this fact or of his appointment as Governor. Thus his entry was blocked, and the rebellion began. ▷ **Clear Grits; Red River Rebellion**

McGovern, George S (1922–   )
US politician. A Senator from South Dakota, he was nominated as Democratic presidential candidate in 1972 at a convention where the 'old pros' were comprehensively outmanoevred by a younger generation determined on revenge for 1968. The **AFL–CIO** refused to endorse the ticket largely because of his radical income-entitlement and tax-reform programme. Indecision over his running-mate's history of mental illness further damaged his prospects, while he also suffered from the Republicans' 'dirty-tricks' campaign, which included the **Watergate** break-in. He lost by 520 electoral votes to 17, a result that exaggerated the popular vote of 45.9 million to 28.4 million.

McKinley, William (1843–1901)
US politician and 25th President. He served in the **American Civil War**, then became a lawyer. As a Republican, he was elected to the US House of Representatives in 1877, and in 1892 was elected Governor of Ohio, despite his name being identified with the unpopular high protective tariff carried in the McKinley Tariff Act of 1890. During the presidential election of 1896 he secured a large majority as an advocate of the gold standard. During his term as President (1897–1901), the **Spanish–American War** (1898) broke out, culminating in the acquisition of Cuba and the Philippines. He was re-elected in 1900, but his second term ended when he was shot by an anarchist in Buffalo, New York. ▷ **Republican Party**

McKissick, Floyd (1922–91)
US **civil rights** activist and attorney. Involved in setting up the **Congress of Racial Equality (CORE)**'s workshops on non-violence

in North Carolina, he became national chairman in 1963 when many of its members were beginning to question the value of non-violence in their campaigns. After a short period out of office he again became chairman in 1966, and when **Black Power** became a controversial issue during the **Meredith** march, he took the side of Stokely **Carmichael** against Martin Luther **King**. In 1968 he lost the leadership of CORE because of its shift towards a more militant nationalism; and he lost further support by his endorsement of Richard **Nixon** in 1972.

McNamara, Robert Strange (1916–)
US politician and businessman. After service in the air force (1943–6), he worked his way up in the Ford Motor Company to the office of President by 1960. A Democrat, in 1960 he joined the J F **Kennedy** administration as Secretary of Defence, being particularly involved in the **Vietnam War**. He resigned in 1967 to become President of the World Bank (a post he held until 1981). In the 1980s he emerged as a critic of the nuclear arms race. ▷ **Democratic Party**

Meagher, Thomas Francis (1822–67)
Irish nationalist and US politician. He became a prominent member of the Young Ireland Party and a founder-member (1847) of the Irish Federation, and in 1848 was transported for life to Van Diemen's Land (Tasmania) after an abortive rising. He made his escape in 1852, and made his way to the USA, where he studied law and became a journalist. At the outbreak of the **American Civil War** (1861) he organized the 'Irish brigade' for the federals, and distinguished himself at Richmond and elsewhere. While secretary of Montana territory, and keeping the Native Americans in check, he was drowned in the Missouri.

Meech Lake Accord (1987)
Canadian constitutional amendment, which recognized French-speaking Quebec as a 'distinct society', in response to the province's demands for special status within the Confederation. The agreement was concluded in 1987 but did not receive enough support from the English-speaking provinces to be ratified. The failure of the Accord intensified Quebec separatism and also fuelled resentment among the Inuit and Native Americans at their own lack of representation. The Charlottetown Agreement, balancing concessions for greater autonomy for Quebec and the

Inuit and Native American populations with other consitutional reforms aimed at the Western provinces, was put to a referendum on 26 Oct 1992. This was defeated by 54.4 per cent to 44.6 per cent.

Meighen, Arthur (1874–1960)

Canadian lawyer and politician. A Conservative, in 1913 he became Solicitor-General in Robert **Borden**'s Union government and was the architect of much of its strategy during **World War I**: railway nationalization, conscription and the deeply-resented Wartime Elections Act. It was Meighen who also orchestrated the government's draconian response to the **Winnipeg General Strike** (1919), insisting that organized labour was revolutionary. Both the Immigration Act and the criminal code were amended so that strike leaders would face either deportation or long prison sentences. In 1920 Meighen succeeded Borden as Prime Minister and his high tariff policy was a major factor in the defeat of the Conservative Party in 1921. He became Prime Minister again in 1925 but when the Progressives deserted him, the Governor-General allowed him to dissolve parliament, a mechanism which had not been afforded to Mackenzie **King** in a similar situation. King won the election by promising to prevent such imperial intervention. Meighen then resigned as Conservative leader a few months later, and was replaced by R B **Bennett**. In 1940 the Conservatives invited him to lead the party again but he failed to win a seat and retired from politics.

melting pot

A metaphor used by the US immigrant author, and later Zionist, Israel Zangwill (1864–1926), in a play of that name (1909), to describe the process of cultural assimilation. He also suggested that this might result in the evolution of a superior race, but this connotation has been lost in popular usage.

Mennonites

The Dutch and Swiss Anabaptists who later called themselves Mennonites after one of their Dutch leaders, Menno Simons (1496–1559). They adhere to the Confession of Dordrecht (1632), baptize on confession of faith, are pacifists, refuse to hold civic office, and follow the teachings of the New Testament. Most of their one million adherents live in the USA. ▷ **Anabaptists**

Mercier, Honoré (1840–94)

Canadian politician. Leader of the Quebec liberals, he revived the **Parti National** in response to the execution of **Riel** in 1885, bringing both **Rouges** and conservatives into a 'united front' to preserve French Canadian rights. In 1887 he became Premier of Quebec, and sought the support of the Catholic Church with the passage of the **Jesuit Estates Act**. Realizing that a majority of the English-speaking provinces also sought a greater measure of autonomy, he called an **Interprovincial Conference** in 1887 which supported **Compact Theory of Confederation**. His popular premiership was curtailed by charges of corruption in 1891, when the lieutenant-governor removed him from office. The charges were unproven but the party was badly beaten in the following year and he only just retained his seat.

Meredith, James H (1933–   )

US **civil rights** activist. The first black student to enrol at the University of Mississippi in 1962, it required court injunctions and a confrontation between the State Governor, Ross Barnett, and President **Kennedy** before he was able even to attempt enrolment. Hundreds of US marshals and federalized national guardsmen were necessary to put down the riots (in which two people were killed and 375 injured) resulting from his arrival on campus. In 1966 he was shot and injured while on a one-man 'March Against Fear' through the state of Mississippi. Martin Luther **King**, Stokely **Carmichael** and Floyd **McKissick** were among those who completed the march for him.

Merritt, William H (1793–1862)

Canadian entrepreneur. He built the Welland Canal, bypassing the Niagara cataract, to provide a major route for exports and imports into the American–Canadian interior. The canal was completed by 1829 but essential improvements were not completed until 1848, when the US railways provided a satisfactory alternative which Canadians were ready to use. Merritt was also one of the foremost proponents of **reciprocity**.

Metcalfe, Charles Theophilus Metcalfe, Baron (1785–1846)

British colonial official. He went in 1808 as an envoy of Lord Minto to the Sikh ruler Ranjit Singh of Lahore, in order to cement the cracks in the East India Company's north-western front. After heading the Delhi Residency (1811–18), he was Resident in Hyderabad (1820–5), where he exposed irregularities in the Nizam's financial relations with the House of Palmer and Co, in whose Hyderabad branch Lord Hastings, the then Governor-General, was personally interested. Serving continuously in India from 1800, he was Lord Bentinck's right-hand man during most of his government and, following his retirement (1835), acted as Governor-General until the arrival of his permanent successor. He resigned from the service in 1837 and became Governor-General of Jamaica (1839) and Governor-General of Canada (1843). Having succeeded Sir Charles **Bagot** in 1843, he attempted to reverse the trend towards responsible government and reassert his independence of ministers. On his pressing the crown's right to make all appointments, the ministry, including Robert **Baldwin** and **La Fontaine**, resigned, and the assembly showed their support for them in a vote of no confidence. Metcalfe then dismissed the government and, in the following bitterly-fought election campaign, appealed to the country for support; he won, but with a dangerously narrow margin. His ministers were weak and unpopular, although they managed to remain in power for two years. With the end of the mercantile system and repeal of the Corn Laws, the need to maintain the colonies in political dependence was diminished and in 1845 Metcalfe resigned, to allow for the introduction of responsible government.

métis

Canadians of Native American and white stock (both French and Scottish, but especially the former). They thought of themselves as a separate people, with a culture which blended their French heritage with Aboriginal skills. Living a semi-nomadic life and dependent on buffalo-hunting, the semi-military structure of their society enabled them to resist the pressures of new settlements. However, the failures of the rebellions in Red River (1869–70) and Saskatchewan (1885) meant that the *métis* either sank further into poverty or were absorbed into the city, for they did not benefit even from the slender privileges which treaties bestowed on the Native Americans. ▷ **Red River Rebellion**

Mexican War (1846–8)

A war between Mexico and the USA, declared by US Congress after it received a message from President **Polk** calling for war. The culmination of a decade of friction resulting from the secession of

Texas from the republic in 1835, the war began with General
Zachary Taylor's advance into the area between the River Neuces
and the Rio Grande. US troops assaulted Mexico City in Sep
1847 and Mexico was subsequently forced to cede most of the
present-day south-west USA. This 'national catastrophe' provided the basis for the subsequent struggle between conservatives
under **Santa Anna** and liberals under **Juárez**. ▷ **Guadalupe
Hidalgo, Treaty of; Wilmot Proviso**

Mexican War (1862–7)

The Mexican government having suspended interest payments on
its foreign debt to France, Spain and Britain, Napoleon III tried
to use this default as a pretext for intervention designed to turn
Mexico into a client state of France. A joint expedition of the
three European powers in 1862 was followed by a larger French
force in 1863, and the proclamation of the Austrian Archduke
Maximilian as Emperor of Mexico. The end of the **American Civil
War** forced the French to withdraw their troops; Maximilian was
captured and executed. The war had always been unpopular in
France, and the outcome was seen as a humiliation.

Midway, Battle of (1942)

US naval victory. Admiral Chester **Nimitz**, forewarned of
Japanese intentions by the breaking of their naval codes,
reinforced Midway Island and forced the Japanese to withdraw
with the loss of four aircraft carriers. This was the first battle in
which the use of aircraft enabled engagement beyond visual range,
and together with the Battle of the **Coral Sea**, saved Australia and
Hawaii and stemmed the Japanese push into the Central Pacific.

Military Service Act (1917)

Canadian conscription legislation. It was introduced because Canada's voluntary militia had been unable to fulfil the commitment
to provide four full divisions on the Western Front. Robert Laird
Borden's Minister for Militia, Sir Sam Hughes, had deterred many
French-Canadians from volunteering by his Ulster Protestant
prejudices. The Act was particularly unpopular in Quebec, where
many believed they were being asked to fight for the empire,
while being denied equal rights at home. With **World War II** the
government tried to maintain a policy of 'no conscription' to
ensure national unity, despite continuous pressure from the English-speaking provinces, especially after the fall of France. In

response **King** held a referendum which showed that although 80 per cent of the English-speaking population wished to free the government from its pledge, 72 per cent of French-Canadians were against doing so. King therefore retained the policy and sacked his Defence Minister when he was advised that there were not enough volunteers to maintain the Canadian commitment after the Normandy landings in 1944. But with the failure of the policy to enlist home defence draftees, King was forced to reintroduce conscription. Protestation from French-Canadians, both among civilians and in the forces, was fierce, while one French-Canadian minister resigned from the government and 34 Quebec Liberals voted against it in a vote of confidence. Even so, King managed to survive the election of 1945, albeit with a reduced majority.

Militia Bill (1862)

Canadian legislation to provide better protection against incursions from the USA during their **American Civil War**, and from **Fenian Raids**. The first bill proposed a force of 50 000 at a cost of C$1 million per year. Its rejection in favour of a cheaper alternative was seen by the British government as Canadian reluctance to assume their defensive responsibilities, but it was countered by the insistence that Canadians had the right to determine their own defence and how much they would allocate to it. This argument indicated the colony's progress towards autonomy.

Milliken v Bradley (1974)

US Supreme Court decision that the **busing** of students from the inner city of Detroit to the suburbs, as required by the city's desegregation scheme, was unconstitutional. Although the court had required desegregation since **Brown v Board of Education of Topeka, Kansas**, under Chief Justice Warren **Burger** it sought also to recognize individual rights and group interests, and based this ruling on the belief that Detroit's scheme prevented local people from exerting any control over their schools. As the court's later rulings on busing in both Boston and Louisville indicate, the decision did not mean the end of the court's support for the policy.

Minnewit, Peter ▷ **Minuit, Peter**

Minuit (Minnewit), Peter (c.1580–1638)
Dutch colonial governor. He was Director-General of the Dutch colony of New Netherland (1626–31). He is best remembered for his purchase of Manhattan Island from the Native American chiefs for only 60 guilders. There he built a fort and founded New Amsterdam. He was recalled to Holland in 1631. In 1638 in the service of the Swedish West India Company he established the colony of New Sweden on the Delaware River. He again bought land from the Native Americans, and built Fort Christina (later Wilmington). He was lost at sea while on a voyage to the West Indies.

Minutemen
Militiamen, particularly in New England, who were prepared to take up arms at very short notice. They were important in the first months of the US War of Independence, before the creation of a regular continental army under George **Washington**. ▷ **Bunker Hill, Battle of; Lexington and Concord, Battles of**

Missouri Compromise (1820)
An agreement to admit Missouri, with slavery, and Maine (formerly part of Massachusetts), without it, to statehood simultaneously, in order to preserve a sectional balance in the US Senate. The compromise also forbade slavery in the rest of the **Louisiana Purchase** lands, north of 36°30′. It was in effect until 1854, when it was repealed by the **Kansas–Nebraska Act**.

Mitchell, William (Billy) (1879–1936)
US airman and advocate of air power. After serving in **World War I**, he became assistant chief of the US Air Service (1921). He tried to create an independent air force, but clashed noisily with his bureaucratic superiors, and was court-martialled for insubordination in 1926; he resigned from the army.

Molly Maguires
A secret organization of (primarily) Irish miners, involved in industrial disputes in Pennsylvania, USA, during the 1870s. The prosecution of their leaders led to hangings and imprisonments, which crushed their group.

Mondale, Walter F(rederick) (1928–)
US Democratic politician. He practised law privately and became Minnesota Attorney-General (1960) and US Senator (1964). He served as Vice-President (1977–81) under President **Carter**. In 1984 he was the Democratic presidential nominee, but was defeated in the election by Ronald **Reagan**.

Monkey Trial ▷ **Darrow, Clarence**

Monmouth, Battle of (1778)
An engagement in New Jersey between British and American troops during the US War of Independence. It was notable for Washington's suspension of General Charles Lee (1731–82) from command, and for the discipline of American troops under fire.
▷ **American Revolution; Washington, George**

Monroe Doctrine
A major statement of US foreign policy, proclaimed in 1823, attributed to President James **Monroe**, but written by Secretary of State John Quincy **Adams**. The doctrine was issued after renewed interest in the Americas by European powers, especially Britain and Russia, following the Spanish-American revolutions for independence. It announced (1) the existence of a separate political system in the Western Hemisphere, (2) US hostility to further European colonization or attempts to extend European influence, and (3) non-interference with existing European colonies and dependencies or in European affairs.

Monroe, James (1758–1831)
US politician and 5th President. After serving in the War of Independence, he entered politics, becoming a member of the Senate (1790–4), Minister to France (1794–6), Governor of Virginia (1799–1802), Minister to England and Spain (1803–7), and Secretary of State (1811–17). During his 'era of good feeling' he signed the **Missouri Compromise**, acquired Florida and set forth the principles of the **Monroe Doctrine**. He won an easy re-election in 1820. ▷ **American Revolution**

Montcalm (de Saint Véran), Louis Joseph de Montcalm-Grozon, Marquis of (1712–59)
French general. During the Seven Years War, he took command of the French troops in Canada (1756), and captured the British

post of Oswego and Fort William Henry. In 1758 he defended Ticonderoga, and proceeded to the defence of **Quebec**, where he died in the battle against General James **Wolfe** on the Plains of Abraham.

Montezuma I (c.1390–1464)
Aztec Emperor of Mexico (c.1437/64). His reign is notable for the annexation of Chalco and the crushing of the Tlascalans. ▷ **Aztecs**

Montezuma II (1466–1520)
The last Aztec Emperor of Mexico (1502/20). A distinguished warrior and legislator, he died at Tenochtitlán during the Spanish conquest. One of his descendants was Viceroy of Mexico from 1697 to 1701. ▷ **Cortés, Hernan**

Montgomery Bus Boycott (1955)
A US **civil rights** campaign concerning an Alabama state ordinance, which required blacks to vacate their bus seats on demand of the driver (most of whom were white). The local secretary of the **NAACP**, Rosa Parks, was arrested and fined for failing to give up her seat to a white man. In response, the local leader of the NAACP, Rev E D Nixon, proposed a boycott of local buses by the city's black community. The Montgomery Improvement Association was formed, with Martin Luther **King** (recently arrived in the city) as its President, to run the campaign and to resist pressure from the city's whites. A Supreme Court decision against several Alabama state laws eventually brought the campaign to a successful conclusion.

Montgomery (of Alamein), Bernard Law, 1st Viscount (1887–1976)
British field marshal. He commanded the 8th Army in North Africa, and defeated Rommel at the Battle of El Alamein (1942). He played a key role in the invasion of Sicily and Italy (1943), and was appointed Commander-in-Chief, Ground Forces, for the Allied **Normandy Campaign** (1944). In 1945, German forces in north-western Germany, Holland and Denmark surrendered to him on Lüneberg Heath. Appointed field marshal (1944) and viscount (1946), he served successively as Chief of the Imperial General Staff (1946–8) and Deputy Supreme Commander of **NATO** forces in Europe (1951–8).

Moral Majority

A US pressure group founded in 1979 which campaigns for the election of morally conservative politicians and for changes in public policy in such areas as abortion, homosexuality and school prayers. It is associated with Christian fundamentalists who in the 1980s played a prominent role in US politics.

Morelos (y Pavón), José María (1765–1815)

Mexican revolutionary. Born a mestizo in Michoacán, New Spain, his early life was spent as a muleteer before he entered the priesthood. He then joined **Hidalgo (y Costilla)** in the struggle for Mexican independence as the leader in the south and reorganized the insurgents in the period 1810–13. A brilliant guerrilla leader, he regrouped opposition to Spanish rule in 1811 under a supreme junta. In opposition to the Spanish Constitution of Cádiz, he convened a 'sovereign congress' at Chilpancingo which, though beleaguered, declared independence at Apatzingán (22 Oct 1814). This first Mexican constitution was republican, and abolished the fuero and slavery. Isolated and trapped by the royalist forces under Viceroy Felix Calleja, he was captured, defrocked and executed in Mexico City. He was one of the founders, with Vicente Guerrero, Guadelupe Victoria and Juan Álvarez, of the radical liberal tradition of Mexican politics.

Morgan, J(ohn) P(ierpont) (1837–1913)

US financier. In 1895 he founded the international banking firm of J P Morgan and Co, providing US government finance, and developing interests in steel, railroads, and shipping. He was a prominent philanthropist and art collector. His only son, John (1867–1943), helped to finance the Allies during **World War I**.

Mormons

A religious movement based on the visionary experiences of Joseph Smith, who organized it as the 'Church of Jesus Christ of Latter-Day Saints' in 1830 at Fayette, New York. Smith claimed to have been led to the Book of Mormon, inscribed on golden plates and buried 1 000 years before in a hill near Palmyra, New York. An account of an ancient American people to whom Christ appeared after his ascension, it teaches Christ's future establishment of the New Jerusalem in America. It is regarded as equal with the Bible. Subjected to persecution, the Mormons moved west, and Brigham Young finally led most of them to the valley of the Great Salt Lake (1847). Mormons actively engage in missionary work and give two years' voluntary service to the Church. There are over 5 million worldwide.

Morrill Land Grant Act (1862)
US educational legislation. The act (sponsored by Representative Justin Morrill of Vermont) provided for the sale of public lands to establish 'land-grant' colleges in every state. The majority of these were agricultural and technical colleges, many of which have grown into the state universities. The act was a major precedent for the provision of federal aid for education in the 20c.

Mosaic Theory of Ethnicity
Canadian social theory. The concept emerged in the 1920s to describe the pluralism of Canadian society. The analogy facilitated the description of each racial group, its status and influence within the whole society as well as its cultural and institutional contributions to the nation. In 1965 John Porter suggested the refinement of a vertical mosaic, with status and prestige indicated by layers, so that some ethnic groups were heavily represented in the upper strata whilst others, without power, remained in the lower strata. He believed the idea of the mosaic (as opposd to that of the **melting pot**) impeded social mobility, and thus encouraged the persistence of conservative traits within Canadian society.

Mott, Lucretia (1793–1880)
US abolitionist and feminist. A Quaker, she became deeply involved in anti-slavery agitation in the 1830s, helping to organize the Philadelphia Female Anti-Slavery Society (1833). She was one of the driving forces at the world's first women's rights convention, held at Seneca Falls, New York, in 1848. ▷ **abolitionism**

Mounties (The Royal Canadian Mounted Police)
The force was founded as the Royal North-West Mounted Police in 1873 by Lt Col George Arthur French who was the first commissioner, recruited mainly from the British Army and retaining its red jackets and pillbox hats. Organized on strictly military lines, the Mounties established tight control over the new territories as compared with law enforcement in the American West. Policing

was only one of their many roles in the North West until 1953, when the Department of Northern Affairs took over most of their civic duties. In the other provinces the Mounties were amalgamated with the federal Dominion Police in 1920 and became the Royal Canadian Mounted Police. In 1928 Saskatchewan became the first province to contract the RCMP to provide a police force, followed by Alberta and other provinces in the later decades. Ontario and Quebec have not followed their example.

Moynihan, Daniel Patrick (1927–   )
US politician. Educated at the City College of New York and Tufts University, he taught at Syracuse, Harvard, and the Massachusetts Institute of Technology. He served in the administrations of Presidents **Johnson** and **Nixon**, acquiring notoriety as the author of *The Negro Family: The Case for National Action* (1965). He became Ambassador to India (1973–4), and won a seat in the US Senate as a Democrat from New York in 1976. ▷ **Democratic Party**

muckrakers
A derogatory term coined in 1906 by President Theodore **Roosevelt** for crusading journalists, authors and critics whose accounts of social evils were attracting widespread attention. Among the most important were Ida M Tarbell (1857–1944), Lincoln Steffens (1866–1936), Ray Stannard Baker (1870–1946) and Upton Sinclair (1878–1968). ▷ **progressivism**

mugwump
US political epithet used to describe an Independent Republican in the US election of 1884 who, preferring reform to party discipline (particularly on the question of ending the **spoils system**), supported the Democrat Grover **Cleveland**, rather than the Republican James **Blaine**. The name is said to derive from an Algonquian word meaning 'chief'. ▷ **Republican Party**

Muhammad, Elijah (1897–1975)
US black leader. Born Elijah Poole, he moved to Detroit from Georgia in 1923, where eight years later he came into contact with Wali Farad, the founder of the **Black Muslims**. In 1934, Muhammad became the leader of the movement as 'Messenger of Allah'. During **World War II** he was arrested and imprisoned

for discouraging his followers from registering for the draft. After his release he initiated a period of fast expansion for the Black Muslims. ▷ **Malcolm X**

Mulroney, (Martin) Brian (1939–)
Canadian politician. The son of an Irish immigrant, he studied law and then practised as a labour lawyer in Montreal, while becoming increasingly active in the Progressive Conservative Party. In 1976 he failed to wrest the party leadership from Joe **Clark** and returned to business as President of a US-owned iron-ore company. In 1983 he replaced Clark and in 1984 became Prime Minister, with a landslide victory over the Liberals. He initiated a number of radical measures, including the **Meech Lake Accord**, settling disputes between the provinces and the centre, and negotiating a free-trade agreement with the USA. Decisively re-elected in 1988, he resigned abruptly from office in 1993. ▷ **Constitution Act of 1982**

Munn v Illinois (1877)
US Supreme Court decision sustaining state economic regulation. In 1871 the state of Illinois had passed railroad legislation fixing maximum rates, forbidding discriminatory pricing and setting up a regulatory commission. The railroads claimed that these measures trespassed on congressional power over interstate commerce and that rate-fixing violated the **Fourteenth Amendment** by depriving them of property without due process of law. Chief Justice Waite found for the state in this case, but after his retirement the court gradually moved towards the plaintiffs' argument. ▷ **Lochner v New York**

Murphy, Charles F (1858–1924)
US politician. By the age of 32 he owned four saloons which served as Tammany district headquarters. In 1902 he became leader of the 18th Assembly District in New York and also leader of **Tammany Hall**, a position he held for 22 years. Although he allowed 'honest graft' in many areas of city government, he excluded education, the police and the courts from manipulation, and occasionally proposed reform mayors.

Murray, General Sir James (1721–94)
British soldier and administrator. Military commander after the death of General James **Wolfe**, he was responsible for the

application of the 1763 Proclamation which excluded Catholics from holding public office. It was impossible for the very few Protestants to supply an Assembly, and it was also dangerous to retain the judiciary within the control of such a small number. Murray, therefore, had to make adjustments in order to establish a stable government. Already on bad terms with the English-speaking merchants (he thought them subversive, while they disliked military rule), Murray modified the proclamation to allow Catholics to sit on juries and to practise law, and introduced French legal customs into the judicial system. These concessions, as well as the lack of *habeas corpus*, angered the English-speaking merchants, who petitioned London for his replacement. In 1766 he was recalled, although the **Quebec Act** later adopted many of his administrative arrangements, and was one of the factors which prevented the colony from joining the **American Revolution**.

Muskie, Edmund S(ixtus) (1914–   )
US politician. After **World War II** service and private law practice, he entered the Maine legislature in 1947. He became Governor (1955–9) and US Senator (1959–80) for Maine, resigning to accept appointment as Secretary of State under President Jimmy **Carter**. He was Democratic candidate for the vice-presidency in 1968. ▷ **Democratic Party**

My Lai incident (Mar 1968)
The massacre of several hundred unarmed inhabitants of the South Vietnamese village of My Lai by US troops, an incident exposed by *Life* magazine photos in 1969. The officer responsible, Lieutenant Calley, was court-martialled in 1970–1. ▷ **Vietnam War**

N

NAACP (National Association for the Advancement of Colored People)

US civil rights organization established in 1910. This biracial association developed from the National Negro Committee Conference, held in 1909 in the aftermath of riots in Springfield, Illinois, in which eight people had died. Though Booker T **Washington** refused to join the association, its founding members included Jane **Addams**, William Monroe **Trotter** and W E B **Du Bois**, who became editor of its magazine, *Crisis*. The NAACP's aim was to 'make 11 000 000 Americans physically free from peonage, mentally free from ignorance, politically free from disenfranchisement and socially free from insult', through educating public opinion, lobbying for legislative reform and sponsoring court action. Its first major success came in 1915 when the Supreme Court ruled the **grandfather clause** to be unconstitutional, and a series of victories over aspects of segregation culminated in **Brown v Board of Education of Topeka, Kansas** (1954). The membership of the movement grew from 6 000 in 1914 to 500 000 in the early 1990s.

Nagasaki

The capital of Nagasaki prefecture, western Kyushu, Japan, it was the target for the second atomic bomb of **World War II** (9 Aug 1945) which killed or injured c.75 000 people and destroyed over a third of the city.

Nation, Carry Amelia (1846–1911)

US temperance advocate, born in Kentucky. After the death of her first husband from alcoholism, she moved to Kansas, where she took up the temperance cause. She gained notoriety as a prohibitionist following her numerous saloon-smashing expeditions, for which she was frequently arrested for disturbance of the peace, and during which this large and powerful woman wielded a hatchet to destroy bars and the alcohol they contained.

National American Woman Suffrage Association (NAWSA)

A US feminist organization. Founded in 1890, it united the National Woman Suffrage Association (for which the suffrage was only one cause amongst others) with the American Woman Suffrage Association (for which the suffrage was the only cause). Elizabeth Cady **Stanton** was President of the new organization for the first two years, followed by Susan B **Anthony** until 1900. By 1912, under the leadership of Carrie Chapman **Catt**, the movement had become increasingly staid in contrast with the more militant National Women's Party organized by Alice **Paul**. Nevertheless its policy of intense lobbying was instrumental in achieving passage of the 19th Amendment, giving women the vote, which was finally ratified in June 1919, and went into effect in Aug 1920.

National Labor Relations Act (Wagner Act) (1935)

US labour legislation. Instigated and steered through Congress by Senator Robert **Wagner**, the act sought to find an effective means of guaranteeing the right of collective bargaining. It established a National Labor Relations Board with legal powers to ensure compliance by employers, especially in allowing employees to elect their own bargaining agent without fear of discrimination. It also prohibited company unions and opened the way for a huge expansion in union membership. ▷ **Lewis, John L; Taft–Hartley Act; United Automobile Workers**

National Recovery Administration ▷ NRA

National Republican Party

US political party. It emerged in the winter of 1824–5 from remnants of the US Democratic-Republican Party. Opposed to Andrew **Jackson** and centred around John Quincy **Adams** (President, 1825–9) and Henry **Clay**, his Secretary of State, the National Republicans espoused active intervention in the economy. By 1836 they were absorbed into the **Whig Party**. ▷ **Republican Party**

National Road

A road built in the early 19c from Cumberland, Maryland, to Vandalia, Illinois, and eventually to St Louis, Missouri. Its construction and repair were financed initially by government sales of land, but in the 1830s this became the responsibility of the states through which it passed. The National Road played an important role in the expansion of the West.

National Security Council (NSC)
A body created by Congress in 1947 to advise the US President on the integration of domestic, foreign and military policies relating to national security. It was designed to achieve effective coordination between the military services and other government agencies and departments, and is composed of the President, Vice-President, Secretary of State and Secretary of Defence. The Chairman of the Joint Chiefs of Staff and the Director of Central Intelligence are advisers.

National Urban League
US civil rights organization. Founded in 1911 by professional blacks and progressive whites, it aimed to provide for rural blacks arriving in Northern cities the same services as those provided to white arrivals by settlement houses and charities. The definition of its aims demonstrates the influence of Booker T **Washington**: 'to promote, encourage, assist and engage in any and all kinds of work for improving the industrial, economic, social and spiritual condition among Negroes'.

Native Americans (American Indians)
The original inhabitants of the Western Hemisphere who arrived during the last Ice Age, estimated at 20 000 to 40 000 years ago. They came in several migrations over a land bridge connecting Alaska with Siberia, and spread gradually throughout the Americas. In what is now the USA, the Native Americans developed ways of life that suited the area in which they lived. Those of the Northwest Coast lived off the sea; those living on the buffalo-rich Great Plains were hunters and gatherers; those in the warm and abundant southeast were skilled farmers and fishermen. Columbus, mistakenly believing he had reached India, called the indigenous people he encountered 'Indians'. Friendships with the Native Americans were indispensable to the survival of the early European settlers, who were shown how to grow native crops and where to hunt and fish, saving them from almost certain starvation. The Europeans unwittingly brought diseases to which the native people had no immunity, wiping out thousands and nearly destroying whole tribes. In addition, as more Europeans came and spread further west, Native American resistance to the

encroachment of white settlers increased and the long conflict known as the **Indian Wars** began. The numerous tribes with their diverse languages lacked the cohesion to repel the influx of well-supplied, determined settlers. Since Native American land was increasingly in demand, most of the tribes east of the Mississippi River were pushed west. But as western land was opened to settlers, the Native Americans were forced onto reservations in hostile terrain and far from their original lands, sometimes close to traditional tribal enemies. With their affairs administered by the federal government, they lost control over their lives and were not granted US citizenship until 1924. In the USA today the Native American population is growing quickly (38% growth according to the 1990 census). Of the current population of almost 2 million, more than half live off reservations in metropolitan areas. Over 50 languages are now spoken among the more than 500 tribes. As a group, Native Americans are among the poorest in the nation and continue to contend with both the prejudice and romanticized images of the past. Throughout the second half of the 20c they have been pressing for increasing self-determination, striving to balance their economic and political survival against the preservation of their cultural and spiritual identities.

nativism

US anti-immigrant attitude, generally expressed by native-born white Protestants. From the early 19c, a major focus of anti-immigrant feeling was directed toward Irish Catholics who were accused by nativists of bringing the papacy into US politics. Nativist antagonism was also extended to other immigrant groups. Between 1854 and 1858, the nativist movement made significant political gains with the American Party, popularly known as the **Know-Nothings**. Nativism began to diminish in importance as the slavery issue became a dominant American concern. With the renewal of immigration in the late 19c and early 20c, nativist sentiment resurfaced and contributed largely to the passage of the Immigration Act of 1924, which eventually brought a sharp curtailment to immigration by establishing immigration quotas.

NATO (North Atlantic Treaty Organization)

An organization established by a treaty signed in 1949 by Belgium, Canada, Denmark, France, Iceland, Italy, Luxembourg, the Netherlands, Norway, Portugal, the UK and the USA; Greece and Turkey acceded in 1952, West Germany in 1955 and Spain in 1982. NATO is a permanent military alliance established to defend Western Europe against Soviet aggression. The treaty commits the members to treat an armed attack on one of them as an attack on all of them, and for all to assist the country attacked by such actions as are deemed necessary. The alliance forces are based on contributions from the member countries' armed services and operate under a multi-national command. The remit includes the deployment of nuclear, as well as conventional, weapons. Its institutions include a Council, an International Secretariat, the Supreme Headquarters Allied Powers, Europe (SHAPE), and various committees to formulate common policies. In the 1970s and 1980s, NATO policy of a first-strike nuclear attack to fend off a Soviet conventional attack became controversial in Western Europe, where many thought it increased the possibility of nuclear war. In 1966 France under Charles de **Gaulle** withdrew all its forces from NATO command, but it remains a member. After the 1989 changes in Eastern Europe, a NATO summit in London (July 1990) began the process of redefining NATO's military and political goals. ▷ **nuclear weapons**

Navajo (Navaho)

Athabascan-speaking Native Americans. They are thought to have migrated to the Southwest some time around AD1000. With a population numbering c.200 000, they are one of the largest Native American groups in the USA. In the 18c they carried out raids on Spanish settlers and Pueblo people in the area, but were themselves eventually defeated by US troops led by Kit **Carson** in 1863–4. They settled in 1868 on a reservation covering much of Arizona and some of New Mexico and Utah, measuring c.16 million acres. Tribal income is derived from the raising of sheep and horses, metalworking, weaving and some mining of gas, uranium and oil resources found on their reservation. The Navajo remain among the poorest of Native Americans.

Navigation Acts (1650–96)

Protective legislation in Britain, designed to increase England's share of overseas carrying trade. The laws stated that all imports to England had to be in English ships or in those of the country of origin. The laws were frequently contentious in the 18c, adding to the 13 American colonies' sense of grievance against the mother country. These Acts were not repealed until 1849. ▷ **American Revolution**

Neutrality Acts
A series of US acts passed in the 1930s which aimed to prevent the USA becoming involved in the escalating European conflict. The 1935 Act authorized a temporary embargo on arms shipments to all belligerents; the 1936 Act outlawed loans or credits to belligerents; and the 1937 Act forbade munitions shipments to either side in the Spanish Civil War. By the time of the attack on **Pearl Harbor**, the bans had been lifted and the neutral course had been abandoned.

New Deal (Canada)
The name given to the legislation influenced by US President **Roosevelt**'s New Deal, passed in 1935 by the Conservative administration of R B **Bennett**, after the failure of more orthodox measures to solve the problems of the Depression. It established a social insurance plan, maximum hours and minimum wages, a marketing board for natural products, and farm credit provisions. This programme and the fears of several Conservative supporters that the government would involve itself in economic planning and price-fixing led to a split in the party and the formation of the Reconstruction Party, which let in the Liberals under Mackenzie **King** with a landslide victory in the 1935 elections. Bennett's New Deal measures were declared unconstitutional in 1937, but they served as a basis for the **Liberal Party** programme after constitutional amendment. ▷ **New Deal (USA); Price Spreads Commission; Stevens, Harry H**

New Deal (USA)
The administration and policies of US President Franklin D **Roosevelt**, who pledged a 'new deal' for the country during the campaign of 1932. He embarked on active state economic involvement to combat the **Great Depression**, setting the tone in a hectic 'first hundred days'. Although some early legislation was invalidated by the Supreme Court, the New Deal left a lasting impact on US government, economy and society, not least by the effective creation of the modern institution of the presidency. Major specific initiatives included the National Recovery Act (1933), the Tennessee Valley Authority (1933), the Agricultural Adjustment Act (1933), the National Youth Administration (1935), the

National Labor Relations Act or Wagner Act (1935) and the Social Security Act (1935). The 'first New Deal' (1933–4), concerned primarily with restarting and stabilizing the economy, is sometimes distinguished from the 'second New Deal' (1935), aimed at social reform. Although Roosevelt was triumphantly re-elected in 1936 (losing only two states), his reform programme slowed considerably after his failure to reorganize the Supreme Court (1937), growing opposition to government spending and taxes, and the worsening situation in Europe, which increasingly directed Roosevelt's attention to foreign affairs. ▷ **NRA**

New Democratic Party (NDP)

Canadian political party. It was established in 1961 by the merger of the **CCF** and the **CLC**. Whilst it did not attract much support in the Atlantic provinces, it presented a much wider appeal to the urban electorate of British Columbia, Saskatchewan, Ontario and Manitoba. Under the leadership of T C (Tommy) Douglas the party won 19 seats in the federal elections of 1962, while in 1969 it was elected into government in Manitoba. In the early 1970s a group of Trotskyites, the 'Waffle' group, seized power until they were expelled from the party in 1972. Later that year the NDP managed to win 30 seats in the federal elections and was able to keep the Liberals in power, giving its support in return for policies of economic nationalism. By the 1980s the NDP had become more centrist because the Liberals had taken over its characteristic policies. In 1984, however, under the leadership of Ed Broadbent, the party was still able to muster 19 per cent of the vote and 30 seats in the legislature. The greatest contribution of the NDP to Canadian political life has been to present the country with an alternative to the major parties and exert a constant pressure from the left, which has ensured that social issues retained political importance.

New England Confederation (1643–84)

An agreement of the American colonies of Massachusetts, Plymouth, Connecticut, and New Haven aiming to establish a common government for the purposes of war and Native American relations. The confederation declined in importance after 1664.

New France

Technically this name was given to all the North American territories claimed by France between 1524 and 1803. Generally, however, it is used for the north-eastern colonies. In 1534 a cross was planted on the shores of the Gaspée by Jacques Cartier, who thus claimed the territory for the King of France. However, it was Quebec, founded in 1608 by **Champlain** as a base for exploration and fur-trading, which became the centre of the French colony. By 1663 the colony had become a royal province with a governor responsible for foreign relations and defence, an intendant to administer justice, and a bishop to impose spiritual discipline. It was therefore not given the opportunity to develop the early expressions of political responsibility and the sense of community which characterized the English colonies. It was, however, one of the early intendants, Jean Talon, who encouraged fishing, farming, lumbering, ship-building and the production of tar and potash, to ensure the colonies' economic development.

New Freedom
The political programme on which US President Woodrow **Wilson** was elected in 1912. It was directed against the acceptance of large-scale enterprise by his opponent, Theodore **Roosevelt**, and was intended to return the spirit of free enterprise to the marketplace, restoring an open society which would benefit individual entrepreneurs, immigrant minorities and women. The chief architect of Wilson's central argument that trusts and monopolies should be broken up by the federal government was Louis **Brandeis**, but the domestic record of Wilson's administration showed a very partial adherence to these principles. ▷ **New Nationalism**

New Frontier
The administration and policies of US President John F **Kennedy** (1961–3). The programme was characterized by a high international profile and a liberal domestic stance. ▷ **Peace Corps**

New Nationalism
The US political programme outlined by ex-President Theodore **Roosevelt** in a speech at Osawatomie, Kansas in Aug 1910, and on which he campaigned as the **Progressive Party**'s candidate in the election of 1912. Roosevelt advocated such policies as graduated income and inheritance taxes, compensation for employee accident, closer supervision of female and child labour and more effective corporate regulation. Greatly influenced by Herbert **Croly**'s *The Promise of American Life*, the programme was essentially a call for government intervention to achieve social justice,

and it later influenced such **New Deal** brain trusters as Raymond Moley. ▷ **New Freedom**

New Netherland
A Dutch colony in the Hudson River valley. The first settlement was Fort Orange (Albany), founded in 1617; Nieuw Amsterdam (New York City) followed in 1624. Conquered by the English and named New York in 1664, it was restored by treaty to the English in 1674 after a second brief period of Dutch rule. Initially established on feudal social lines, the colony prospered on the basis of the **fur trade**.

New Right
A wide-ranging ideological movement associated with the revival of conservatism in the 1970s and 1980s, particularly in the UK and USA. Its ideas are most prominently connected with classical liberal economic theory from the 19c. It is strongly in favour of state withdrawal from ownership, and intervention in the economy in favour of a free-enterprise system. There is also a strong moral conservatism — an emphasis on respect for authority, combined with a strong expression of patriotism and support for the idea of the family. Politically, the New Right adopts an aggressive style which places weight on pursuing convictions rather than on generating a consensus. In the USA in the 1980s it has been associated with the emergence of Christian fundamentalism (eg the **Moral Majority**).

New South Creed
A vision of the future projected for the post-**American Civil War** American South by Henry W Grady, editor of the *Atlanta Constitution*, in a speech of 1886. He argued for a new society, without **slavery** and no longer so reliant upon cotton, with a diversified and more industrial economy and with wealth and political power more evenly distributed.

New Spain (Nueva España)
The formal title of the Spanish viceroyalty covering the area of modern Mexico.

Nguyen Van Thieu (1923–   )

Vietnamese army officer and political leader. His military career began in the late 1940s and by 1963 he was Chief of Staff of the Armed Forces of the Republic of Vietnam (South Vietnam). In 1965 he became Head of State. Under a new, American-style presidential constitution, he was President from 1967 until the collapse of the Saigon regime in 1975. During those years, his relationship with the USA, and with American public opinion, was central to his survival. He was roundly condemned in the West for his authoritarian, commonly corrupt, methods; he, in turn, felt betrayed by the US withdrawal from Vietnam. With the communist victory in 1975, he went into exile, first in Taiwan and then in the UK.

Niagara Movement

US **civil rights** movement. Founded in 1905 by W E B **Du Bois** and others to resist the public acceptance of segregation advocated by Booker T **Washington**, and to agitate for 'every single right that belongs to a freeborn American, political and social'. The movement was superseded by the establishment of the **NAACP**.

Nimitz, Chester William (1885–1966)

US admiral. He trained at the US Naval Academy, served mainly in submarines, and by 1938 had become rear-admiral. Chief of the Bureau of Navigation during 1939–41, he then commanded the US Pacific Fleet, his conduct of naval operations contributing significantly to the defeat of Japan. He was made Fleet Admiral (1944) and Chief of Naval Operations (1945–7). ▷ **World War II**

Ninety-Two Resolutions (1834)

Canadian political reform demands. The list of complaints against the government of Upper Canada was drawn up by a committee of reformers led by William Lyon **Mackenzie**. The system of patronage, the dispensation of the **Clergy Reserves** and various economic policies were all attacked and coupled with the demand for an elective legislature. ▷ **Canada, Upper**

Nisei

The term used to describe US citizens of Japanese descent. Technically the term should be restricted to the second generation, the first being called *Issei* and the third *Sansei*. The first generation, mainly market-gardeners and farmers who had settled in Hawaii and California, were legally prohibited from applying for US citizenship. They numbered less than 25 000 at the beginning of the 20c, but their rapid increase led to President Theodore **Roosevelt** concluding a 'gentleman's agreement' with the Japanese government in 1907 to discourage further immigration. California and other states passed laws preventing them from owning or leasing real estate. After **Pearl Harbor**, President Franklin D **Roosevelt** ordered the *Issei* and the *Nisei*, even though the latter had been born with US citizenship, to be removed to concentration camps, and there was little protest from the rest of US society. In 1983 it was recognized by the federal government that these *Nisei* internees had been subjected to racial injustice and those still alive were awarded compensation of US$20 000 each.

Nixon, Richard M(ilhous) (1913–94)

US politician and 37th President. He became a lawyer, then served in the US Navy. A Republican, he was elected to the House of Representatives in 1946, where he played a prominent role in **HUAC**. He became Senator from California in 1950 and Vice-President under **Eisenhower** for two terms (1952–9). He lost the 1960 presidential election to John F **Kennedy** but won in 1968. As president he sought to bring an end to the Vietnam War, but did so only after the US invasion of Cambodia and Laos and the heaviest US bombing of North Vietnam of the entire conflict. He had diplomatic successes with China and the USSR. In his domestic policy he reversed many of the social programmes that had come out of the previous Democratic administrations. He resigned in 1974 under the threat of impeachment after several leading members of his staff had been found guilty of involvement in the **Watergate** affair, and because he was personally implicated in the cover-up. He was given a full pardon by President Gerald **Ford** and went on to write various books on international affairs. He died in New York City.

NLRB v Jones and Laughlin Steel (1937)

A US Supreme Court decision which sustained the **National Labor Relations Act** or Wagner Act. The action was prompted by a group of 60 eminent lawyers who believed that the National Labor Relations Board was unconstitutional. The decision demonstrated that, although President Franklin D **Roosevelt**'s attempt to pack the court had failed, its moderate members, including Chief Justice Charles Evans **Hughes**, were now aligned with the liberals, thus enabling them to outnumber the conservatives.

Nonpartisan League
An organization of farmers, founded in 1915 in North Dakota and spreading across the north wheat belt. Quasi-socialist, the league advocated public ownership of public utilities. It declined after 1920, in part because of opposition to involvement in **World War I**.

Noriega, Manuel (Antonio) (1939–)
Panamanian military leader. The ruling force behind the presidents of Panama in the period 1983–9, he had been recruited by the **CIA** in the late 1960s and supported by the US government until 1987. Alleging his involvement in drug trafficking, the US authorities ordered his arrest in 1989: 13 000 US troops invaded Panama to support the 12 000 already there. He surrendered in Jan 1990 after taking refuge for 10 days in the Vatican nunciature, and was taken to the USA for trial.

Normandy Campaign (1944)
A **World War II** campaign which began on **D-Day** (6 June 1944). Allied forces under the command of General **Eisenhower** began the liberation of Western Europe from Germany by landing on the Normandy coast between the Orne River and St Marcouf. Artificial harbours were constructed along a strip of beach so that armoured vehicles and heavy guns could be unloaded. Heavy fighting ensued for three weeks, before Allied troops captured Cherbourg (27 June). Tanks broke through the German defences, and Paris was liberated (25 Aug), followed by the liberation of Brussels (2 Sep), and the crossing of the German frontier (12 Sep).

North West Company
Canadian fur-trading association. Established in 1779, it set up a string of trading partnerships and achieved a remarkable record of exploration. The Montreal partners managed finance and marketing, meeting the 'wintering' partners once a year in Fort William to collect the furs and make policy decisions. The 'wintering' partners in turn organized the trappers and canoeists. In 1821,

however, the company was absorbed into the **Hudson's Bay Company** with which it had been conducting a bitter and often violent competition. ▷ **Fraser, Simon**

Northwest Ordinance of 1787
An Act of the American **Continental Congress** establishing procedures by which newly settled Western territories could become states on the basis of full political equality with the original states. It was one of several Northwest Ordinances passed in 1784–7.

North-West Rebellion (1885)
Canadian revolt. The **métis** of the Saskatchewan, like those of Red River, had suffered from the encroachments of English-speaking settlers without any governmental assurances or safeguards. Although they had an effective leader in Gabriel Dumont, they appealed to Louis **Riel**, who returned from the USA to lead them. When two Native American tribes also gave their support it began to look as if the North West was about to explode, but a large body of militia crushed the revolt. Dumont escaped but Riel was captured and later executed. The speed with which the militia were able to get from Ottawa to Winnipeg (six days instead of the two months taken in 1870 by the Wolseley expedition) showed the value of the **Canadian Pacific Railway**, encouraging the government to lend it the money essential for its completion. ▷ **Red River Rebellion**

NRA (National Recovery Administration)
A US government agency, established under the **New Deal** National Recovery Act (1933). Its aim was to develop fair standard codes in all sectors of industry in order to promote business recovery, reduce unemployment and improve working conditions. Companies which participated in the programme were awarded a 'Blue Eagle', the emblem of the agency. Despite initial success, it was declared unconstitutional and quashed by the Supreme Court in 1935 in Schechter Poultry Corporation v US.

Nuclear Non-Proliferation Treaty (NPT)
A treaty signed in 1968 by the USA, the USSR, the UK and an open-ended list of over 100 other countries. It sought to limit the spread of nuclear weapons, those possessing them agreeing not to transfer the capability to produce them, and those not possessing

them agreeing not to acquire the capability. Recent reductions in US and Russian nuclear stockpiles appear to have reinforced the Treaty, but a number of other states are thought to be close to producing their own nuclear arms.

nuclear weapons

Bomb, missile or other weapon of mass destruction deriving its destructive force from the energy released during nuclear fission or nuclear fusion. According to their size and the means of delivery, they may be classified as tactical short-range weapons (for use on the battlefield), theatre medium-range weapons (for use against deep military targets), or strategic long-range weapons (for use against enemy cities and command centres). ▷ **Nuclear Non-Proliferation Treaty**

nullification

A US political doctrine that a state has the power to render laws of the federal government void within its borders. It was tested by South Carolina during the 'Nullification Crisis' in 1832, over the issue of enforcing a federal tariff. That immediate issue was resolved by the **Jackson** administration's Force Bill, authorizing the president to use armed forces to enforce the laws of Congress. However, in larger terms the problem was not resolved until the **American Civil War**, and in some ways continued through the **civil rights** movement.

O

O'Connor, Sandra Day (1930–)

US lawyer and jurist. She studied at Stanford, and after practising law she entered Arizona politics as a Republican, becoming majority leader in the state Senate before moving to the state bench. In 1981 President **Reagan** named her to the US Supreme Court. She was confirmed, becoming the first woman in that position. ▷ **Republican Party**

October Crisis (1970)

Terrorist crisis in Quebec. After the arrest of Pierre Vallière and Charles Gagnon, the **Front de Libération de Québec** changed its tactics from bombing to kidnapping. One plan was foiled, but on 5 Oct the group kidnapped the British Trade Commissioner in Quebec, James Cross. A ransom of C$500 000 was demanded, along with the release of a number of 'political prisoners'. There was to be no police pursuit, transport out of the country was to be provided for the gang and the FLQ manifesto was to be broadcast on radio and television. The last two demands were accepted, and the Attorney-General of Quebec promised to support parole for a number of 'political prisoners'. Cross was not released, however, and on 10 Oct the Minister of Labour and Immigration, Pierre Laporte, was also kidnapped. Three days later students began a campaign of rallies and sit-ins, and the **Parti Québecois** began to put pressure on Premier Robert **Bourassa** to form an emergency coalition government. Instead, he brought in the army to back up the police and the **War Measures Act** was implemented to round up FLQ sympathizers. Although over 450 were arrested, only 20 were convicted in the 62 cases brought. Protest against the Act died down after Laporte's murder on 17 Oct. Cross was discovered and his release obtained after safe passage to Cuba was guaranteed to the kidnappers. Later that month the murderers of Laporte were apprehended and imprisoned.

Ohio Company
(1) Virginia-based speculators who acquired a crown grant of
200 000 acres (80 000 hectares) in 1749 in the area between the
Ohio River, Great Kanawha River and Allegheny Mountains. (2)
An organization of speculators in 1786 who used depreciated
currency and securities to acquire large amounts of Ohio land.
They were indirectly responsible for the passage of the **Ordinance
of 1787**, establishing a political basis for Westward expansion.

Olmecs
Members of a highly elaborate Mesoamerican culture on the
Mexican Gulf Coast, at its height 1200–600BC. The Olmecs influenced the rise and development of the other great civilizations of
Mesoamerica. They probably had the first large planned religious
and ceremonial centres, at San Lorenzo, La Venta and Tres Zapo-
tecs, where the resident elite and their families lived, served by
much larger populations dispersed throughout the lowland area.
The centres had temple mounds, monumental sculptures, massive
altars and sophisticated systems of drains and lagoons. They were
probably also the first people in the area to devise glyph writing
and the 260-day Mesoamerican calendar.

Onassis, Jacqueline Kennedy (1929–94)
US wife of President **Kennedy**. Born Jacqueline Lee Bouvier, she
married John F Kennedy in 1953, and as First Lady from 1960 she
became internationally renowned for her fashionable elegance.
Following Kennedy's assassination in 1963 she moved with their
two children to New York City (1964). In 1968 she married Greek
tycoon Aristotle Onassis (1906–75). After his death she returned
to New York City, where she worked as an editor in a publishing
house. She died in her New York home.

Open Door Note (1900)
US proposal for equal terms in the commercial access of foreign
nations to China. Issued by Secretary of State John **Hay**, its
objection to the tariffs imposed by the Great Powers in their
Chinese spheres of influence allowed in the competition of US
businessmen, and its recognition of Chinese independence, supplied a necessary precondition for the entry of an expeditionary
force to relieve the embassies under siege during the Boxer Rebellion.

Open Door Policy

US foreign policy towards China, formulated in response to the weakness of the later Qing Dynasty. Announced in Mar 1900 by Secretary of State John **Hay**, the Open Door policy sought to preserve Chinese integrity and US trade rights by opposing the development of spheres of influence dominated by Britain, Germany, Russia, France, Italy and Japan.

Orange Order (Canada)

The First Grand Lodge was established in Canada in 1830, and the order had grown to 2 000 lodges with 100 000 members by the 1980s. Its growth and activities have made it one of the most powerful pressure groups in Canadian politics. Not only did Orangemen reinforce the pro-British and Tory sentiments of the loyalists; they introduced the rigid hostilities nurtured in the old country, transferring their antagonism from Irish Catholics to the French-Canadian 'Papists'. In 1848 **Lafontaine** introduced a Secret Societies Bill to counteract their activities, but this only incited the Orangemen of Upper Canada to further demonstrations. During a visit by the Prince of Wales in 1860 they attempted, by various ruses, to force him to acknowledge a relationship between the order and the monarchy. This he managed to refuse, but John A **Macdonald** apologized to the order for him. The murder of the Orangeman Thomas **Scott** during the **Red River Rebellion** led indirectly to the campaign of D'Alton **McCarthy** and the **Manitoba Schools Act**. The murder of another Orangeman which occurred in Montreal during a provocative 12 July parade in 1877 also incensed the order, and Macdonald was able to use this anger to swing it behind the Conservatives to win the next election. In 1878 he included the Grand Master, Mackenzie **Bowell**, in his cabinet. ▷ **Canada, Upper**

Ordinance of 1787 ▷ Northwest Ordinance of 1787

Oregon Boundary Dispute

A disagreement between the British and US governments over the frontier between respective possessions on the west coast of North America. Britain claimed the north-west basin of the Columbia River to its mouth at Fort Vancouver, while the USA sought a boundary farther north. The Oregon Treaty (1846) settled the US–Canadian boundary on the 49th parallel, dipping south at

Juan de Fuca Strait to maintain British claims to Vancouver Island. Residual disputes over the disposition of the Gulf/San Juan Islands in the strait were settled by arbitration in 1872.

Oregon Trail
The main route for emigration to the far west of the USA during the 1840s. The trail began at Independence, Missouri, crossed the Rockies at South Pass in Wyoming, and terminated at the mouth of the Columbia River. Extending some 2 000 miles in length, it took approximately six months to travel it by wagon train.

Organic Acts
Statutes of the US Congress which laid down the relationship of Puerto Rico to the USA between 1900 and 1950. The First Organic Act of 1900 (the Foraker Act) effectively made Puerto Rico a US dependency in that supreme power was vested in the US governor and a nominated executive council. The Second Organic Act of 1916 (the Jones Act) conferred universal male suffrage and made Puerto Ricans citizens of the USA. The Public Law Act of 1950 allowed the new Commonwealth (a status devised by Muñoz Marín) to draft its own constitution.

Organization of American States (OAS)
A regional agency established in 1948 to coordinate the work of a variety of inter-American departments recognized within the terms of the United Nations Charter. The organization was formed to promote peace, economic cooperation and social advancement in the Western hemisphere. Its central organ, the General Secretariat, is housed in Washington DC, and consists of one representative from each member country. Thirty-one countries within the Americas are members. ▷ **Pan-American Union; UN**

Osceola (c.1804–38)
Seminole leader. He refused to accede to US government demands in 1835 that the Seminoles give up their lands in the Florida Everglades and move to the West. He fought for many months in the Everglades, but in 1837 he was tricked by a false peace overture to come out and have talks with General Thomas S Jesup. He was captured and died in prison in South Carolina.

Ostend Manifesto (1854)
A statement presented by the US ministers to Great Britain, France and Spain, effectively asserting US claims over the then Spanish colony of Cuba. It stated that if Spain refused to sell Cuba, then the USA was justified in taking it by force. Although repudiated by the US government, the manifesto gave notice of future US interest in Cuba and in the Caribbean.

Oswald, Lee Harvey (1939–63)
US alleged assassin of President John F **Kennedy**. A Marxist and former US marine, he lived for a time in the USSR (1959–62). On 24 Nov 1963, during a jail transfer two days after the assassination, he was killed in Dallas by nightclub owner Jack **Ruby**.

Otis, James (1725–83)
US politician. A leading Boston attorney, Otis was advocate general in 1760, when royal revenue officers demanded his assistance in obtaining from the Massachusetts superior court general search warrants allowing them to enter any man's house in quest of goods that violated the Sugar Act of 1733. Otis refused and argued powerfully before the court against taxation without representation and violation of the rights of colonists. In 1761, elected to the Massachusetts assembly, he became a radical opponent of British rule. In 1769 he was beaten in an altercation with revenue officers and received a head injury from which he never fully recovered.

Ottawa Conferences (1894, 1932)
British **Imperial Conferences**. The main topic in 1894 was the development of communications between the individual units of the British Empire. Underlying the conference was a realization that the nature of imperial relationships had altered and that a new way of dealing with them had to be found. A major evolution was evident by 1932 in the agreements at the Ottawa economic conference held between Britain and its dominions at the height of the world depression. The conference negotiated a limited amount of imperial preference following the adoption of a new protective tariff by the British government earlier that year.

P

Padlock Act (1937)
Canadian anti-communist legislation. Enacted by the **Duplessis Union Nationale** administration of Quebec, it authorized the closure of any premises which were suspected of producing communist propaganda. Since the term 'communist' was not properly defined, the government was able to hinder the growth of the **CCF** and also to use it against trade unions. The law was declared unconstitutional by the Supreme Court in 1957.

Paine, Thomas (1737–1809)
British-American political writer. In 1774 he sailed for Philadelphia, where his pamphlet *Common Sense* (1776) argued for complete independence from Britain. He served with the American Army, and was made Secretary to the Committee of Foreign Affairs. In 1787 he returned to England, where he wrote *The Rights of Man* (1791–2) in support of the French Revolution. Indicted for treason, he fled to Paris in 1792, where he was elected a Deputy to the National Convention (the assembly that ruled France from 1792 to 1795), but imprisoned for his proposal to offer the King asylum in the USA. At this time 1794–5 he wrote *The Age of Reason*, in favour of deism. Released in 1796, he returned to the USA in 1802.

Panama Canal
A canal bisecting the Isthmus of Panama and linking the Atlantic and Pacific Oceans. It is 51 miles (82 kilometres) long, and 490 feet (150 metres) wide in most places; built by the US Corps of Engineers (1904–14). In 1979, US control of the Panama Canal Zone (5 miles/8 kilometres of land flanking the canal on either side) passed to the Republic of Panama, which has guaranteed the neutrality of the waterway itself when control of the canal is passed to it in 2000.

Panama Congress (1826)

Attended by delegates from Mexico, Peru, Gran Colombia and the Central American Federation at the invitation of Simón Bolívar (who did not himself attend). The treaty of Spanish–American confederation agreed at the meeting had no practical effect, but the Congress remains a symbol of the quest for Latin American unity.

Pan-American Union

An organization founded in 1890 (and first called the International Bureau for American Republics) to foster political and economic cooperation among American states, and to draw North and South America closer together. Until **World War II** the Union concluded many agreements covering trade, migration and neutrality zones around their coasts, despite fears among many members of domination by the USA. In 1948 it became part of the wider Organization of American States (OAS), and now forms its permanent administrative and advisory machinery. It has four departments: economic and social affairs; international law; cultural affairs; and administrative services.

Papineau, Louis-Joseph (1786–1871)

French-Canadian politician. The speaker of Lower Canada's House of Assembly (1815–37), he opposed union with Upper Canada, and agitated for a greater degree of governmental independence from Britain. His leadership of the *Patriotes* during the **Rebellions of 1837** led to charges of treason. He escaped to Paris, but returned to Canada after a general amnesty was granted in 1844.

Paris, Pact of (27 Aug 1928) ▷ **Kellogg–Briand Pact**

Paris Peace Conference (1946–7)

Meetings of the five members of the Council of Foreign Ministers, representing the main **World War II** Allies (USA, Russia, UK, France and China), and delegates from 16 other nations involved against the **Axis Powers**. It drew up peace treaties with Bulgaria, Finland, Hungary, Romania and Italy. Despite repeated divisions, agreement was finally reached and the treaties signed in the spring of 1947.

Parkman, Francis (1823–93)
US historian. Educated at Harvard, he studied law, and became the authoritative writer on the rise and fall of the French dominion in America. Despite continuous ill-health in his middle years, he wrote many books, notably *England and France in North America* (1851–92).

Parks, Rosa Lee (1913–)
US civil rights protester. Her action as a black woman who refused to give up her seat to a white man on a bus in Montgomery, Alabama, led in 1955 to the **Montgomery Bus Boycott** by the black community. The boycott led to the Supreme Court decision in 1956 that declared bus segregation unconstitutional. Parks became an inspiration to other blacks and a symbol of the non-violent protest advocated by the civil rights movement. ▷ **civil rights movement**

Parti National
Canadian political party. Originally formed in 1871 by young liberals in Quebec who wished to assert their devotion to the Church, it was revived as an alliance of Liberals and rebel Conservatives who deeply resented the execution of Louis **Riel**. Under Honoré **Mercier**'s leadership, the party managed to oust Quebec's Conservative government in 1886, but scandal brought an early end to its administration in 1891.

Parti Québecois
Canadian political party, formed by **Lévesque** after the **Liberal Party** under **Lesage** was defeated in 1966, essentially for refusing to be more nationalistic. The party members (or *Péquistes*) gained support from all classes and from organized labour as well as from the business community. The major aim of the party has been to attain sovereignty-association for Quebec, that is, parity of status with the federal government. The pressure for this, however, has had to be balanced against the wish of the majority of Québecois to remain within Canada. As a result, the parliamentary party lost the support of its more radical *indépendentistes* in 1984.

Passchendaele, Battle of (31 July–10 Nov 1917)
The third battle of Ypres during **World War I**; a British offensive which was continued despite no hope of a breakthrough to the

217

Belgian ports, the original objective. It was notable for appallingly muddy conditions, minimal gains and British casualties of at least 300 000. In the final action, Canadians captured the village of Passchendaele, six miles north-east of Ypres.

Pastore, John Orlando (1907–)

US politician. After a career as a Democrat in Rhode Island state politics during the 1930s, he was elected Lieutenant Governor in 1944. When J Howard McGrath resigned in 1945, Pastore succeeded him as Governor. His re-elections in 1946 and 1948 made him the first Italo-American to be elected a state governor, and he was also the first to serve in the US Senate, in which he sat from 1950 to 1976. A commanding figure in state and national politics for a whole generation, his major interest was in nuclear power, its domestic energy potential and its international control. He played an influential role in the ratification of the Nuclear Test Ban Treaty (1963) and the Non-Proliferation Treaty (1969).

Paterson Strike (1913)

US labour conflict. A strike by 25 000 workers, mostly immigrants from Southern and Eastern Europe, in Paterson, New Jersey, against a decision by mill owners to increase productivity. The strike was backed by the **IWW**, and withstood considerable police violence. Inspired by John Reed and other socialists, the strikers held a pageant in Madison Square Gardens (New York City) to illustrate the events which had led to the strike. The proceeds amounted to only $150, and when the **AFL** persuaded the skilled workers to break the strike, it was quickly brought to an end.

Patrons of Husbandry ▷ Granger movement

Patton, George (Smith) (1885–1945)

US general. Known as 'Old Blood and Guts', Patton trained at the US Military Academy at West Point and became one of the most daring and flamboyant US combat commanders in **World War II**. An excellent strategist and proponent of mobile tank warfare, he played a key role in the Allied invasion of North Africa (1942–3), led the US 7th Army in its assault on Sicily (1943), commanded the 3rd Army in the invasion of France, and contained the German counteroffensive in the Ardennes (1944).

He was fatally injured in a motor accident near Mannheim, and died at Heidelberg. ▷ **Bulge, Battle of the; Normandy Campaign**

Paul, Alice (1885–1977)
US feminist. Involved with the British suffragette movement while living in England, on her return to the USA (1912) she became the leader of the **National American Woman Suffrage Association** (NAWSA) congressional committee and organized a march of several thousand women in Washington (1913). Although her tactics generated much publicity, they proved too militant for most members of NAWSA and she left the organization to found the National Women's Party. After the Nineteenth Amendment (1920) gave women the right to vote, she turned her efforts to working for other women's rights. ▷ **suffragettes**

Peace Corps
A corp of volunteers created during the Kennedy Administration in 1961 to assist and educate people in developing countries. By 1966, volunteers numbered more than 10 000 in 52 countries. The programme concentrates on education, health, agriculture and public works and emphasizes self-sufficiency. ▷ **Kennedy, John F**

Pearl Harbor
US naval base on the island of Oahu, Hawaii. On 7 Dec 1941 the bombing of the base by the Japanese, before any declaration of war, brought the USA into **World War II**. Nineteen US ships were sunk or disabled in the surprise attack, and over 2 000 lives were lost.

Pearson, Lester Bowles (1897–1972)
Canadian politician. Educated in Toronto and at Oxford, he was leader of the Canadian delegation to the **UN**, becoming President of the General Assembly in 1952–3. Secretary of State for External Affairs (1948–57), his efforts to resolve the Suez Crisis were rewarded with the Nobel peace prize in 1957. As prime minister (1963–8), he introduced a comprehensive pension plan, socialized medicine and sought solutions to the growing separatist feeling in Quebec. ▷ **Bilingualism and Biculturalism, Royal Commission on**

PEMEX (Petróleos Mexicanos)

One of the largest state-owned corporations in Latin America, and a virtual state within a state in Mexico, the oil company was created in 1938 by President Lázaro **Cárdenas**. He seized the assets of foreign (mainly British) multinationals as a result of the failure to implement the wage rates decreed by the 1917 Constitution's *junta de arbitraje y conciliación*, invoked by Cárdenas to rule on labour practices; the companies received compensation in Mexican bonds. PEMEX was charged with the management, regulation and production of oil found on Mexican soil. A logical outcome of the Criollo nationalism enshrined in the constitution, PEMEX was free from other ministries; only after the 1982 debt crisis was its autonomy curtailed.

Peninsular Campaign (1862)

In the **American Civil War**, an extended attempt by the Union army under General McClellan to take Richmond, Virginia (the Confederate capital), by moving up the peninsula between the James and York Rivers. Although Union troops won most of the battles, McClellan acted overcautiously, failed to take the offensive, and instead slowly moved his troops away from the capital. ▷ **Seven Days Battles**

Penn, William (1644–1718)

English Quaker leader and founder of Pennsylvania. Expelled from Oxford for his Puritan leanings, he joined the Quakers in 1666, was imprisoned for his writings (1668), and while in the Tower of London wrote the most popular of his books, *No Cross, No Crown*. In 1681 he obtained a grant of land in North America, which was called Pennsylvania in honour of his father. In 1682 he was granted land that later became Delaware. He referred to Pennsylvania as a 'Holy Experiment', where religious and political freedom could flourish.

People's Party ▷ Populist Party

Péquistes

Members of the **Parti Québecois**.

Pequot War (1637)

Colonial North American War between English settlers and the Pequot tribe of Connecticut. After the Pequots murdered an

English trader, the settlers retaliated with the aid of their allies,
the Mohegans and the Narrangansetts. They attacked the main
Pequot town on the Mystic River and slaughtered hundreds of
men, women and children, effectively destroying the tribe.

Perkins, Frances (1882–1965)

US politician. She was the first woman to hold cabinet rank, as
Secretary of Labor (1933–45) in President Franklin D **Roosevelt**'s
cabinet. This appointment recognized her reputation as a social
reformer, especially concerned with child labour and factory legislation. In 1945 she resigned from President Harry S **Truman**'s
cabinet, and became a member of the Civil Service Commission
(1946–52). Her memoir, *The Roosevelt I Knew* (1946), was the
first, and in many ways remains one of the best, recollections of
the **New Deal**.

Perry, Matthew Galbraith (1794–1858)

US naval officer. The brother of Oliver Hazard Perry (who
defeated the British at the Battle of Lake Erie in the War of 1812),
in 1837 he was appointed commander of the *Fulton*, one of the
first naval steamships. He was active in suppression of the slave
trade on the African coast in 1843, and in the **Mexican War**
(1846–8) he captured several towns and took part in the siege of
Veracruz. From 1852 to 1854 he led the naval expedition to Japan
that forced it to open diplomatic negotiations with the USA and
grant the first trading rights with Western powers.

Pershing, John Joseph ('Black Jack') (1860–1948)

US general. He trained at the US Military Academy at West
Point, and served in several **Indian Wars** (1886–91), in the Spanish-
American War (1898), in the Philippines (1899–1903), in the
Russo-Japanese War (1904–5) and in Mexico (1916). In 1917 he
commanded the American Expeditionary Forces in Europe, and
after the war became Chief of Staff (1921–4). His book *My Experi-
ences in the World War* (1931) won a Pulitzer Prize. ▷ **World War
I**

Phillips, Wendell (1811–84)

US abolitionist. He graduated from Harvard in 1831, and was
called to the bar in 1834. By 1837 he was the chief orator of the

anti-slavery party, closely associated with William Lloyd **Garrison**. He also championed the causes of prohibition, women's suffrage, organization of labour and currency reform. ▷ **abolitionism**

Pierce, Franklin (1804–69)

US politician and 14th President. He studied law and was admitted to the Bar in 1827. From 1829 to 1833 he was a Democratic member of the state legislature, was elected to the House of Representatives, and in 1837 to the US Senate. Returning to his private law practice in 1842, he volunteered for the **Mexican War** (1846–8), where he was made brigadier general. In 1852 he was nominated as a compromise candidate for the presidency against Winfield Scott, the Whig nominee, and elected. As President (1853–7), he favoured an expansionist policy succeeding in the purchase from Spain of a significant strip of land in the Southwest. On the issue of slavery, he had supported the **Compromise of 1850**, but then signed the **Kansas–Nebraska Act**, which kindled a flame that ultimately led to the **American Civil War**. Because of the unpopularity of this act, he was not renominated, and he retired from politics in 1857.

Pike, Zebulon (1779–1813)

US army officer and explorer. He led a party of explorers to the headwaters of the Mississippi River (1805–6) to try to establish its source. From 1806 to 1807 he explored the Arkansas and Red rivers, discovered the mountain peak which was later officially named Pikes Peak, and proceeded into New Mexico. He later produced a report on Santa Fe which was influential in encouraging expansion into Texas. He served as a brigadier general in the **War of 1812**, and was killed in the attack on York (Toronto) in Canada.

Pilgrim Fathers

The English religious dissenters who established Plymouth Colony in America in 1620, after crossing the Atlantic on the *Mayflower*. The men, women and children included Puritan separatists and non-separatists. Before disembarking the adult males aboard signed the **Mayflower Compact**. ▷ **Plymouth Colony**

Pinckney, Charles Cotesworth (1746–1825)

US statesman. Educated at Oxford, he became a lawyer. He was Washington's aide-de-camp at Brandywine and Germantown, but was taken prisoner at the surrender of **Charleston** (1780). He was a member of the convention that framed the US constitution (1787). His refusal to pay bribes extorted by French agents brought the **XYZ Affair** into the open. He was twice Federalist candidate for the presidency (1804 and 1808). ▷ **American Revolution**

Pinkerton, Allan (1819–84)

Scottish-born US detective. He was a Chartist who in 1842 settled at Dundee, Illinois, became a detective and deputy-sheriff, and in 1850 founded the Pinkerton National Detective Agency. He headed a federal intelligence network for General McClellan during the **American Civil War**, and his agency later took a leading part in breaking up the **Molly Maguires** and in policing other labour disputes.

Pitcher, Molly (c.1753–1832)

The popular name applied to Mary McCauley, a US heroine of the War of Independence. At the Battle of **Monmouth** (1778) in which her first husband was fighting, she carried water in a pitcher to the weary American soldiers. Legend also has it that when her husband collapsed from heat-exhaustion, she manned his cannon for the rest of the battle.

Pittsburgh Agreement (1918)

The agreement between Masaryk, the future President of Czechoslovakia, and Czech and Slovak immigrants to the USA, setting out the possible lines of a Czechoslovak constitution. As leader of the exiles struggling to win support from the Allied Powers in **World War I**, Masaryk wanted the immigrants' backing and promised the Slovaks that, to ensure the autonomy of Slovakia, it might be possible to create a federal state. When a unitary state emerged, the Slovaks in the USA felt betrayed and, particularly in the 1930s, worked hard to secure the separation of Slovakia that transpired in 1939 when **Hitler** occupied the Czech Lands and set up a puppet Slovakia.

Platt Amendment (1902)

Appendage to the Cuban independence constitution after the **Spanish-American War** (1898) which gave the USA the right to 'intervene for the preservation of Cuban independence'. Such interventions took place in 1906, 1912 and 1920 and, while the Platt Amendment was annulled in 1934, the USA's lease of the naval base at Guantanamo Bay was retained. The Reciprocal Trade Treaty of 1903 continued to allow the USA to dominate the Cuban economy, particularly under the **Batista** administration. The **Castro** revolution of 1959 can be seen as a response to that alien control while the US response (the **Bay of Pigs** invasion of 1961) was another manifestation of the rights claimed under the Platt Amendment.

Plessy v Ferguson (1896)

US Supreme Court decision that opened the way to racial segregation under the **US Constitution** by upholding the concept of 'separate but equal'. Homer Plessy was appealing against his conviction for refusing to leave a railroad car reserved for whites. The court ruled that if the facilities offered blacks were equal to those for whites, there was no infringement of the **Fourteenth Amendment**. Justice John M Harlan dissented with the prescient warning that the ruling was 'inconsistent with civil freedom' and would support prejudice. The decision came to underpin the whole structure of segregation in the Southern states during the first half of the 20c, eventually being overturned by **Brown v Board of Education of Topeka, Kansas** (1954).

PLO (Palestine Liberation Organization)

An organization that consists of several of the Palestinian groups opposed to Israel, led by Yasser Arafat. Founded in 1964, its charter denied the right of Israel to exist and called for Palestine to be liberated by armed conflict. In 1974 the Arab Summit in Rabat, Morocco, recognized the PLO as the sole legitimate representative of the Palestinian people. In 1982 its forces in Lebanon were attacked and expelled by Israel, with the support of the US Reagan administration; many US servicemen and diplomats in Lebanon were killed as a result. Secret talks in Norway (1991–3) between the Israeli Prime Minister Yitzhak Rabin and the PLO led to the agreement signed in Washington, DC (13 Sep 1993) by Rabin and Arafat on mutual recognition and limited self-rule in the Gaza Strip and West Bank town of Jericho.

Plunkitt, George Washington (1842–1924)

US politician. Tammany leader of the New York Fifteenth Assembly District, Sachem of the Tammany Society and chairman of the Election Committee of **Tammany Hall**, he was at various times an Assemblyman, State Senator, Police Magistrate, County Supervisor and Alderman. At one time he held four public offices and drew salaries from three of them simultaneously, a fact of which he was inordinately proud. He was immortalized in a series of 'Very Plain Talks on Very Practical Politics', recorded by the journalist William L Riordon, and published under the title *Plunkitt of Tammany Hall* in 1905. It was a cheerfully ingenuous defence of machine politics, and has become a minor classic of US political science. ▷ **political machine**

Plymouth Colony

The American colony established by the *Mayflower* Pilgrims in 1620, comprising the south-east corner of modern Massachusetts. It existed as a separate entity until 1686, when it was absorbed into the Dominion of New England. In 1691 it became part of Massachusetts Bay. ▷ **Carver, John; Pilgrim Fathers**

Pocahontas (1595–1617)

Native American princess, the daughter of a chief, Powhatan, who is said to have saved the life of Captain John Smith, leader of a group of colonists who settled in Chesapeake Bay in 1607. She was captured and taken to Jamestown in 1612, where she embraced Christianity, was baptized Rebecca, married an Englishman, John Rolfe (1585–1622), and went to England with him in 1616. She embarked for Virginia the following year, but died of smallpox off Gravesend in England, leaving one son. ▷ **Powhatan Confederacy**

political machine

A term used to describe the US urban political organization developed in the late 19c in response to the constitutional decentralization of local politics intersecting with the flood of immigration into Northern cities such as New York, Philadelphia and Boston at a time of very rapid physical growth. Hierarchically structured from the city level, down through the ward to the precinct, the machine depended on the ability of the 'boss' to respond to the individual needs of constituents who voted at his direction in return, thus allowing him to control nominations and to discipline office holders. Developed by both parties and sizable ethnic groups, political machines have been characterized by endemic corruption and inefficiency, and many contemporary observers regard them as a degradation of democratic politics.

Polk, James K(nox) (1795–1849)

US politician and 11th President. He was admitted to the Bar in 1820, served in the House of Representatives as a Democrat (1825–39), and was Governor of Tennessee (1839–41). Polk ran for President in 1844 as a 'dark horse' candidate who favoured the annexation of Texas. He became an activist President (1845–9) and a strong leader who set himself major objectives and achieved them. They included reducing the tariff, restoring the independent treasury system, settling the Oregon boundary dispute with Great Britain, and bringing Texas and California (which was under Mexican rule) into the Union. Texas was admitted to the Union in 1945. Unable to acquire California by peaceful negotiations, Polk ordered US troops to advance to the Rio Grande, precipitating war with Mexico. After the **Mexican War** (1846–8) the USA acquired California, New Mexico and most of the Southwest. ▷ **'Fifty-Four Forty or Fight'**

Pontiac's Conspiracy (1763)

An attempt by Native Americans of the Ohio and Great Lakes country to drive whites out of the area, led by Pontiac (c.1720–69), Chief of the Ottawa tribe, in retaliation against the English treatment of the Native Americans and the threat of expanding white settlements. The movement reached its peak with an unsuccessful siege of Detroit, and a final peace was signed in 1766. ▷ **Indian Wars**

Populist Party

US political party, founded in 1892 by farmers and labourers in the West who had become disenchanted with the economic and commercial policies imposed by the East. Running on a programme of economic and political reform, its first presidential candidate, James B Weaver, took more than 1 million votes in 1892, but at the next election (1896), the populists endorsed the Democratic nominee, William Jennings **Bryan**, and by the end of the century the party had disappeared as a political entity.

Potsdam Conference (17 July–2 Aug 1945)

The last of the great **World War II** strategic conferences, following the **Tehran Conference** and **Yalta Conference**. During this period Winston Churchill (and later Clement Attlee), **Stalin** and **Truman** met to discuss the post-war settlement in Europe. Soviet power in Eastern Europe was recognized *de facto*, and it was agreed that Poland's western frontier should run along the Oder–Neisse Line. The decision was also made to divide Germany into four occupation zones. The political differences which began to emerge between the USA and the USSR could be said to have marked the start of the **Cold War**.

Powderly, Terence V (1849–1924)

US labour leader. As Grand Master of the Knights of Labour (1878–93) he ended the secrecy of the order which had alienated the Catholic Church and won the great railroad strike against the Gould railroad. In general, however, he disliked using strikes as a weapon, and could not deal with the sheer bellicosity of employers. His failure to take a strong stand over the **Haymarket Square Riot** and the launch of the **AFL** led the Knights into decline. In 1893 he was deposed and by 1900 the Order had all but disappeared.

Powell, Adam Clayton (1908–72)

US clergyman and politician. Pastor of the Abyssinian Baptist Church in Harlem, he was a charismatic community leader. In 1941 he was elected as a Democrat to the City Council of New York and the following year he founded the People's Voice. Elected to the US House of Representatives in 1945, he was chairman of the House Committee on Education and Labor from 1951, though persistent absenteeism did inhibit his effectiveness. It was Powell who first used the phrase '**Black Power**' (at Howard University in 1966), and who acted as convenor of the first National Conference on Black Power. In 1967 he was expelled from the US House of Representatives for misusing public funds and for unbecoming conduct. Re-elected in 1968, he had the satisfaction of a Supreme Court ruling in favour of his appeal against expulsion, but he lost his seat in 1970.

Powhatan Confederacy

A group of Algonquian-speaking Native American tribes inhabiting the Tidewater region of Virginia at the time of the first white settlements. Named after Chief Powhatan, the group was initially receptive to the settlers, but grew suspicious of the newcomers, and in 1622 and 1644 launched massive attacks on them. They were defeated on both occasions. Scattered descendants of these tribes are still found in Virginia. ▷ **Indian Wars; Pocahontas**

Price Spreads Commission (1934)

Canadian governmental inquiry. Instituted by the Ministry of Trade and Commerce to investigate the retail trade, the Commission found that retailers, especially the large department and chain stores, made their employees work very long hours for very low wages. Premier R B **Bennett** went public with its findings, condemning employers for their exploitation. His radio addresses on 'the state of the times' upset many of his conservative adherents, but Bennett insisted on the reforms, such as the Wages and Hours Bill and Unemployment Insurance, which had been suggested by the commission. Employers who broke the new laws were to be punished as criminals, not civil offenders. It was the controversy over the commission that led Harry H **Stevens** to resign from the cabinet to lead the Reconstruction Party of disaffected conservatives in the 1935 election. ▷ **New Deal (Canada)**

primary

A preliminary election in US politics to determine which candidates for public office are to appear on the ballot for a general election. There are various forms of primary, the most common being the closed primary, in which any voter who has registered with a particular party can vote for that party's respective candidate.

PRI (Partido Revolucionario Institucional)

Mexican political party, previously known as the PRN (*Partido Revolucionario Nacional*, National Revolutionary Party) and the PRM (*Partido de la Revolución Mexicana*, Mexican Revolutionary Party). Founded by Plutarco **Calles** in 1929, in the wake of the Mexican Revolution (1910–20), as an instrument for change through the achievement of unified and dictatorial centralism, the party has dominated Mexican political life ever since. The PRN was a coalition of local military chiefs, officeholders and CROM, the largest labour organization, and owed its strength to Calles' steady erosion of the autonomy of the states. **Cárdenas**, Calles' successor, created the succeeding PRM by replacing regional chiefs with military, labour, peasant and popular groups: labour and peasant organizations were seen as an effective counterpoise to the military, while the resolution of conflict lay in the hands of the President. By the time the PRM became the PRI (in 1945, under Avila Camacho), the military sector had been disbanded, other interest groups had been included and the state organization strengthened. The party's political monopoly remained unchallenged until the late 1970s when opposition parties began to win congressional seats; the 1988 elections saw the PRI's first-ever loss of Senate seats, and in 1989 the PRI state governorship monopoly was broken for the first time.

Progressive Party (Canada)
The political party established in 1920 with the support of the farming community. It fought the 1921 federal election on a platform of lower tariffs and a reciprocity agreement with the USA. When it won 65 seats it became the second-largest group in the Commons, to the surprise of the country. Its leader, T A **Crerar**, chose not to make the party the official opposition and over the next few years Mackenzie **King** was able to cut away the farmers' support, so that by 1926 the party had all but disappeared.

Progressive Party (USA) (1912–16, 1924 and 1948)
US political parties. The name was used by three separate third-party political initiatives. The first, essentially a breakaway from the Republican Party, centred on former President Theodore **Roosevelt**, who was its presidential candidate in 1912. The second developed in 1924 from midwestern farmer and labour discontent. Its presidential candidate, Senator Robert **La Follette** of Wisconsin, won 4 million votes. In the 1948 election, Democrats opposed to President Harry S **Truman**'s cold war policy ran Henry A Wallace, who received only 1 million popular votes. ▷ **Bull Moose; New Nationalism; Republican Party**

progressivism
Reform movement in the US, addressing the social and economic problems resulting from the industrialization of the 19c. The movement, which had a broad political base, began with settlement houses set up in the new slums, such as Chicago's Hull House, established by Jane **Addams**. As the movement gained

229

support it targeted corruption in municipal government, the excessive power of the corporations (and particularly the railroads), electoral procedures, wages, pensions and protection for workers. With progressive governors such as Robert **La Follette** gaining power in Wisconsin, progressivism became a powerful force in state and ultimately in national politics. Little headway was made in the face of conservative Senate power, but several progressive measures were passed in the administration of Theodore **Roosevelt**, especially in the wake of public outrage following the revelations of the **muckrakers**. William **Taft** proved less amenable to implementing progressive measures, and in 1911 the progressive movement spawned the National Progressive Republican League in an unsuccessful attempt to prevent Taft's renomination. The progressives then formed a third party, the **Progressive Party**, putting forward Roosevelt as their presidential candidate. Although Woodrow **Wilson** won the election, he was sympathetic to many progressive aims. The movement subsided after **World War I**, although many of its proposals were later implemented in F D **Roosevelt**'s **New Deal**. ▷ **political machine**

Prohibition (1920–33)
An attempt to forbid the manufacture, transportation and sale of all alcoholic drinks in the USA, authorized by the 18th Amendment to the **US Constitution** (1919). Building on 19c temperance movements and the powerful lobbying of the Anti-Saloon League, Congress passed the national legislation as a wartime emergency measure. Its enforcement, through the Volstead Act, gave rise to one of the great political controversies of the 1920s, and led to various 'bootlegging' operations that created new opportunities for organized crime. It also gained celebrity for J Edgar **Hoover** and his 'G-Men'. It was repealed in 1933 by the 21st Amendment. ▷ **Capone, Al**

Pulaski, Kazimierz (Casimir) (1747–79)
Polish nobleman and soldier. One of the few who fought successfully against Russia, he was outlawed at the First Partition of Poland (1772). In 1777 he went to America, and for his conduct at Brandywine was given command of a brigade of cavalry. In 1778 he organized 'Pułaski's legion', and in May 1779 entered Charleston and held it until it was relieved. He was mortally wounded at the siege of Savannah.

Pueblo

Native Americans of south-west USA, living in settlements called *pueblos* in multi-storied, permanent houses made of clay. Culturally and linguistically diverse, they are divided into East and West Pueblo, the latter including the Hopi and Zuni. They are famed for their weaving, basketry, sand paintings and pottery, and have preserved much of their traditional culture intact.

Pullman Strike (1894)

A US labour conflict. During the depression of 1894 the Pullman Palace Car Company in Chicago cut workers' wages by 25–40 per cent, but maintained their high rents in the residential town founded by the company. The workers were members of the newly-formed American Railway Union, which retaliated by refusing to handle Pullman cars, and thereby interfering with the mail service. Despite pleas from Governor John Altgeld, President Grover **Cleveland** ordered federal troops to the site and after much violence, the strike was broken. The Attorney-General's court injunction, which forbade interference with the mail and interstate commerce, established the principle that a strike could violate the Sherman Anti-Trust Act. ▷ **Anti-Trust Acts; Debs, Eugene**

Q

Quakers ▷ Friends, Society of

Quayle, (J) Dan(forth) (1947–   )
US politician. Born in Indianapolis, Indiana, he was educated at DePauw and Indiana Universities, then served as a captain in the Indiana National Guard (1970–6). He worked as a lawyer, journalist, and public official, becoming a member of the House of Representatives (1977–81) and Senate (1981–8) representing the state of Indiana. He was elected Vice-President under George **Bush** in 1988. As Vice President he was a proponent of political conservatism and of a business community unhindered by federal regulation.

Quebec Act (1774)
British statute enacted to remedy the anomalous situation of Quebec within the empire. In 1769 the Board of Trade advised the extension of British institutions to the new colony and suggested that the French should participate in the government of the colony. Sir Guy **Carleton** took a different view of the problem, believing that the French seigniorial system should be maintained and that responsible government should be withheld. The Board of Trade report was suppressed and the Quebec Act, which reversed the established principle of colonial rule through British institutions, was passed. The governor was to rule with the assistance of a council which included the French seigniors; the seigniorial system of tenure continued and the position of the Catholic Church was maintained. The Act showed generosity to a conquered people but omitted to consider the expectations of either the **habitants** or the English-speaking settlers who were unhappy at the retention of the civil law embodied in the Custom of Paris and the absence of *habeas corpus*. The Act was superseded by the Constitutional Act of 1791.

Quebec, Battle of (13 Sep 1759)
A battle fought during the Seven Years War between British forces under General James **Wolfe** and French forces defending Quebec under the Marquis of **Montcalm**. It followed an audacious plan by Wolfe to transport British troops from the St Lawrence River up steep, wooded cliffs. British victory led to speedy capture of Quebec and the subsequent collapse of French power in Canada. Both Wolfe and Montcalm were killed in the battle.

Queen Anne's War (1702–13)
The second of the four intercolonial wars waged by Britain and France for control of colonial North America, known in Europe as the War of the **Spanish Succession**. Both sides made considerable use of Native American allies. Settled by the Treaty of Utrecht (1713), the war resulted in British control of Newfoundland, **Acadia** and Hudson's Bay. Britain also gained the Asiento, allowing trade with Spanish America.

Queenston Heights, Battle of (1812)
Military engagement in the **War of 1812**. A victory for the British regular army, it reassured Canadians who doubted Britain's commitment to their defence, while pro-Americans were forced to reconsider their loyalties. A monument was erected as a memorial to Isaac Brock, the commanding officer who charged somewhat injudiciously up the face of the Heights.

Quiet Revolution (1960–6)
Quebec reform programme. Pursued by Jean **Lesage**'s Liberal government of Quebec with the slogan, *Il faut que ça change* ('Things must change'), it sought to counteract the influence of the Catholic Church in civic spheres such as education and promoted state activism to 'decolonize' Quebec's economy from the influence of American and English-speaking institutions. It also began to participate in the federal/provincial shared-cost programmes, though previously shunned by **Duplessis** and the **Union Nationale**, to provide the range of social services available elsewhere in Canada. However, the resulting huge increases in the size of the provincial civil service and the tax burden gave the **Union Nationale** a platform for their return to power under Daniel Johnson. ▷ **Liberal Party**

R

Raleigh (Ralegh), Sir Walter (1552–1618)

English courtier, navigator and author. He became prime favourite of Queen Elizabeth I. He was knighted in 1584. From 1584 to 1589 he sent an expedition to North America to take unknown lands in the queen's name, and despatched an abortive settlement to Roanoke Island, North Carolina. He later made unsuccessful attempts to colonize Virginia, but successfully introduced tobacco and potatoes to Britain. His enemies turned James VI and I against him, and he was imprisoned (1603), his death sentence being commuted to life imprisonment. While in the Tower, he wrote his *History of the World* (1614), and several other works. Released in 1616, he made an expedition to the Orinoco in search of a goldmine, which was a failure. His death sentence was invoked, and he was executed.

Randolph, A Philip (1889–1979)

US labour organizer, socialist and civil rights activist. Initially a supporter of Marcus **Garvey**, he opposed the idea of economic separatism in his journal, *The Messenger*. In 1925 he organized the Brotherhood of Sleeping Car Porters, the first black union to gain major successes, such as recognition by the Pullman Company. In 1941 he organized a march on Washington to demand equal employment opportunities for blacks in the defence industries, and racial desegregation in the armed forces. The march was called off after President Franklin D **Roosevelt** established the **Fair Employment Practices Committee**, but the tactic was revived during the civil rights movement of the 1960s, when he became the director of the March on Washington for Jobs and Freedom (Aug 28, 1963).

Rankin, Jeannette (1880–1973)

US feminist and pacifist, the first female member of Congress. Educated at Montana University and the New York School of Philanthropy, she went on to work as a social worker in Seattle (1909), where she became involved in the fight for women's rights.

In 1914 she was appointed Legislative Secretary of the **National American Woman Suffrage Association**, and in 1916 entered the House of Representatives as a Republican, the first woman to do so. During her two terms there (1917–19 and 1941–3) she consistently voted against US participation in both world wars, promoted women's welfare and rights, and was instrumental in the adoption of the first bill granting married women independent citizenship. Continuing to campaign for women's issues throughout her career, she worked for the National Council for the Prevention of War from 1928 to 1939, and led the Jeannette Rankin March (1968) in which 5000 women gathered on Capitol Hill, Washington, to protest against the **Vietnam War**.

Reagan, Ronald (Wilson) (1911–)
US politician and 40th President. He began his career as a radio sports announcer, then went to Hollywood in 1937, where he acted in more than 50 films, and served as President of the Screen Actors Guild (1947–52 and 1959). Originally a Democrat and supporter of liberal causes, he became actively involved in politics as a union leader and increasingly anti-communist. He registered as a Republican in 1962. Governor of California for two terms (1967–75), he campaigned unsuccessfully for the Republican presidential nomination in 1968 and 1976. He was elected President in 1980, defeating Jimmy **Carter**, and, with George **Bush** as his running mate, won a second term in 1984. Reagan's popularity enabled him to make sweeping changes in social and economic policy, including cuts in social services, the deregulation of many industries, and a tax cut that mainly benefited the wealthy. His foreign policy was dominated by a strong anti-communist stand, which led to a massive increase in defence spending and the introduction of the Strategic Defence Initiative (**SDI**), or 'Star Wars'. During his second term, when his attitude toward the USSR became less confrontational, largely as a result of President Mikhail **Gorbachev**'s policy of *perestroika*, he reached a major accord on nuclear arms reduction. The **Iran–Contra Affair** (Irangate) tarnished the reputation of his administration in its last two years. Instead of the balanced budget Reagan had sought, 'Reaganomics' left behind a huge federal deficit.

Rebellions of 1837
(1) A rebellion in Quebec in Lower Canada generated by a stalemate between the legislative council and the appointed executive

council over control of provincial revenues. Led by **Papineau** and his *Parti Patriote*, it sought to dissolve the unsatisfactory imperial tie with Britain. It was crushed by British government troops after several brief confrontations. (2) Later in 1837, a rebellion in Ontario in Upper Canada, which opposed the oligarchical control exercised by the **Family Compact**, and the position of preferment enjoyed by the Church of England. Armed radicals led by **Mackenzie** marched on Toronto to seize the government, but were repulsed by pro-government troops and volunteers. Mackenzie and Papineau both fled to the USA. ▷ **Canada, Lower; Canada, Upper**

reciprocity

A movement begun in British North America during the 1840s for the bilateral reduction of tariffs between the British colonies and the USA; it resulted in the Reciprocity Treaty of 1854. The treaty negotiations represented an important step in the growth of Canadian political autonomy. Arrangements became a source of discord in Washington, however, and the treaty was dissolved by the USA in 1866. Attempts to renew reciprocity failed up to 1911, when the idea was finally shelved. ▷ **Blake, Edward; Canada, Dominion of; 'Commercial Union'; Merritt, William H**

Reconstruction

The period following the **American Civil War** when the South, reeling from the physical and economic devastation it had sustained, was moving toward recovery and the status of the former Confederate states and the process of integration of the freed slaves was yet to be determined. President Andrew Johnson favoured a conciliatory approach toward the region, but radical Republicans took a hard line against what they viewed as recalcitrant Southern legislators dedicated to maintaining the power of the old order and determined to limit blacks' rights by evading the spirit of the Thirteenth Amendment by passing restrictive **Black Codes**. The Republican-controlled Congress responded by passing four Reconstruction Acts, two Civil Rights Acts, and the Fourteenth and Fifteenth Amendments. Military law was established throughout the South. Eventually, however, Republican control of the area was weakened due in large part to corruption in the federal government, and Southern states were slowly readmitted to the Union. The **Ku Klux Klan**, founded in 1866, gained in power, and the era ended with the **Compromise of**

1877, when a bargain among politicians gave a disputed presidential election to the Republican candidate Rutherford B **Hayes** in return for 'home' (ie white) rule in the South. Once white rule was fully restored, a policy of racial segregation evolved to keep black people firmly subordinate.

Red River Rebellion (1869–70)

An uprising among the **métis**, caused by the failure of the Canadian government to treat their problems seriously after it had assumed sovereignty from the **Hudson's Bay Company**. Bitter resentment was generated by the government's square survey system, which brought into doubt the land titles of the *métis* whose boundaries were based on river-front lots. The settlement of Manitoba by waves of Anglo-Protestant immigrants from Canada and the USA also brought huge problems, including the destruction of the buffalo on which the *métis* depended. The *métis* organized a 'National Committee' with Louis **Riel** as its Secretary, prevented Lieutenant-Governor **McDougall** from entering the settlement, seized Upper Fort Garry and invited both English- and French-speaking inhabitants to discuss a 'List of Rights'. Some Canadians organized themselves to resist the committee, but Riel, now head of the Provisional Government, ordered their imprisonment. The committee issued the 'Declaration of the People of Rupert's Land and the North West'. Meanwhile the government decided to delay transfer of sovereignty from the Hudson's Bay Company and sent a delegation to meet with the committee and negotiate the territory's entrance into the confederation. When some of the imprisoned Canadians escaped and attempted to raise support among the Scots of the area, the *métis* captured them and also court-martialled Thomas Scott, an obstreperous Orangeman, whom they executed. News of an amnesty for all rebels arrived four days later. Riel freed the other prisoners and sent representatives to Ottawa. They reached agreement with the Canadian government and as a result the Manitoba Act was passed, granting the *métis* 1 400 000 acres and bilingual rights. However only verbal assurances of amnesty were given. When Ontario's Orangemen maintained pressure to punish Scott's executioners, the government sent in a military force and Riel fled to the USA.

Reforma, La

The name given to the period of Liberal rule in Mexico from 1855 to 1860 and its major reforming measures, which were generally associated with the governments of Benito **Juárez** and Sebastián Lerdo de Tejada. The reforms included the abolition of military and ecclesiastical *fueros*, the secularization of education and the constitution of 1857. These changes not only sparked off the War of the Reforma (1857–60) but legitimized gradual changes taking place in the Mexican countryside as *haciendas* encroached on collective lands and wage labourers emerged in more prosperous zones of the country. It created the legal basis for the dramatic transformations achieved during the presidency of Porfirio **Díaz** (the period known as the Porfiriato). ▷ **hacienda**

Regulator Movements

US colonial insurgencies which emerged in rural areas of South Carolina and North Carolina, just prior to independence. The South Carolina events took place in the mid-1760s, and the North Carolina movement followed a few years later, meeting military defeat in 1771. Both disputes pitched the slave-holding seacoast against small farmers of the interior, but otherwise the causes and outcomes were different. The ensuing bitterness spilled over into the **American Revolution**. The term 'regulator' was also used elsewhere in early America to describe popular insurrectionary movements.

Rehnquist, William H(ubbs) (1924–   )

US jurist. Educated at the Universities of Stanford and Harvard, he became a law clerk to Justice Robert H Jackson on the US Supreme Court before entering private practice. He served as Assistant Attorney-General from 1968 to 1971, became head of the Office of Legal Counsel of the Justice Department, and challenged many laws protecting the rights of defendants, such as Miranda v Arizona, giving him the reputation of a protector of law enforcement. In 1971, he was named Associate Justice of the Supreme Court by President Richard **Nixon**. He was chosen by President Ronald **Reagan** in 1986 to succeed Warren E **Burger** as Chief Justice of the Supreme Court, a controversial nomination due to his history of extremely conservative opinions. As Chief Justice, he has presided over a Supreme Court that has followed a conservative trend away from the more liberal Warren Court.

reparations

Payments imposed on the powers defeated in war to cover the costs incurred by the victors. For example, they were levied by the Allies on Germany at the end of **World War I**, though the final sum of £6000 million plus interest was not fixed until Apr 1921. The Dawes (1924) and Young (1929) Plans revised the payment schedule and reduced the scale of the payments, which were finally abandoned after 1932, because of the Depression.

Republican Party
US political party. It was formed in 1854 by Northern anti-slavery factions of the existing Whig and Democratic Parties who opposed the Fugitive Slave Act (1850) and the **Kansas–Nebraska Act** (1854). The party's presidential candidate, Abraham **Lincoln**, won the 1860 election, precipitating Secession and the **American Civil War**. With the exception of four terms, the Republicans continued to hold the presidency until the **Great Depression**, which set the stage for the election of Franklin Delano **Roosevelt** in 1932 and 20 years of Democratic Presidents. Although the Republicans had espoused isolationism before **World War II**, they won the 1952 presidential election with the popular war hero Dwight D **Eisenhower**. The next 40 years saw a series of split governments on the national level, with the Republicans often winning the presidency while the Democrats held majorities in Congress. The **Watergate** scandal, which led to the first resignation of an American president, Richard M **Nixon**, was a black mark for the party, but it regained the presidency with the election of Ronald **Reagan** in 1980 and held it for the next 12 years through George **Bush**'s one-term administration. The party has traditionally been identified with big business rather than with labour, and favoured states' rights, limited government regulation, free market economic policies, and (in the **Cold War** period that followed World War II) a strong military and firm anticommunistic stance. It has generally had the support of voters of high socioeconomic status and of white Anglo-Saxons rather than of ethnic minorities; however, Ronald Reagan managed to broaden the party's historical base, drawing in many so-called Reagan Democrats, who were disillusioned with the policies of Democratic President Jimmy **Carter**, and including right-wing conservatives and religious fundamentalist groups as well. ▷ **mugwump; National Republican Party; Progressive Party** (USA)

Responsible Government
A Canadian adaptation of British parliamentary practice. Developed by Robert **Baldwin**, the doctrine held that the

government of the Province of Canada should be exercised by a ministry chosen from the elected representatives of the people, and that it should be replaced if defeated in the elective legislature. Recommended in the Durham Report, it was several years before its practical implications were fully understood, and not until 1848 with the Baldwin–Lafontaine ministry in Canada and the Uniacke ministry in Nova Scotia did it come into operation.

Revels, Hiram Rhodes (1822–1901)

US politician and educator. Born in North Carolina, he was chaplain of a Union black regiment in the **American Civil War**, and later settled in Mississippi and served in the State Senate. Elected to the US Senate in 1869, he was the first black American to serve in that body. He founded a school for former slaves, and became President of Alcorn College, a newly formed state college for blacks.

Revere, Paul (1735–1818)

US patriot. He served as a lieutenant of artillery in the **French and Indian War**, then followed the trade of silversmith and copperplate printer. He was one of the party that destroyed the tea in Boston harbour, and was at the head of a secret society formed to watch the British. On 18 Apr 1775, the night before **Lexington and Concord**, Revere rode from Charleston to Lexington and Lincoln, rousing the **Minutemen** as he went. His ride was immortalized in a poem by Longfellow. ▷ **American Revolution; Boston Tea Party**

Rickover, Hyman George (1900–86)

Russian-born US naval engineering officer. He graduated from the US Naval Academy in 1922, and in 1929 received a master's degree in electrical engineering from Columbia University. He led the team that adapted nuclear reactors as a means of ship-propulsion and developed the world's first nuclear submarine, the USS *Nautilus*, launched in 1954.

Ridgway, Matthew B(unker) (1895–1993)

US general. Educated at the US Military Academy at West Point, he commanded the 82nd Airborne Division in Sicily (1943) and Normandy (1944). He commanded the 18th Airborne Corps in the North-West Europe campaign (1944–5) and the US 8th Army in **UN** operations in Korea (1950). He succeeded Douglas **Mac-arthur** in command of US and UN forces (1951), and was supreme allied commander Europe in succession to **Eisenhower** (1952–3), and Army Chief of Staff (1953). He received the Presidential Medal of Freedom in 1986.

Riel, Louis (1844–85)

Canadian politician. The leader of the **métis** during both the **Red River Rebellion** and **North-West Rebellion**, he fled to the USA when the federal government sent a military force into the Red River settlement in 1870, but he returned to live there quietly, although Ontario orangemen had offered a reward for his capture as the murderer of Thomas Scott. He was still regarded by French-speaking Canadians as a hero. When the USA threatened Manitoba with a **Fenian Raid** in 1871, he mustered a *métis* cavalry force in defence and received public (though anonymous) thanks from the governor. John A **Macdonald** provided him with funds in the hope that he might return to exile, but in 1873 he was elected to the House of Commons in Ottawa. After his re-election in 1874, a motion was introduced by Mackenzie **Bowell** demanding his expulsion from the House. He was finally granted amnesty in 1875 on condition of a further five years' exile. By this time he had suffered a nervous breakdown and was detained in a mental asylum in Quebec. In 1878 he had recovered sufficiently to leave for the USA where he became a schoolteacher. In 1884 Riel responded to the pleas of the *métis* in Saskatchewan and so became involved in his second rebellion. However, he provoked opposition by his religious manias, while his claims against the government for $35 000 also gave his motivation a mercenary cast. When he surrendered he was charged with treason, but he refused to let his defence counsel enter a plea of insanity. With a verdict of guilty the jury also recommended clemency, but after several reprieves and an assessment of his sanity, he was hanged. His body was interred in front of St Boniface Cathedral. French-Canadian outrage at his execution helped Honoré **Mercier** to gain power in 1886 and has continued to agitate their nationalist feelings ever since.

Rio de Janeiro Treaty (1947)

The Inter-American Treaty of Reciprocal Assistance, signed in Rio, which enshrines principles of hemispheric defence laid down during **World War II**, especially a US–Brazilian alliance. It provides for certain types of mutual assistance in the case of an armed attack on any American state from outside the region and for mutual consultation in the event of any aggression between them or warlike action affecting territories situated outside them. It was the first permanent collective defence treaty signed by the USA and has remained the cornerstone of its military commitment to Latin America and the institutional basis for its hegemony. It has been applied on 16 occasions since 1948, in all cases to long-standing inter-American disputes, and to incidents within the Caribbean and Central American regions. It was not, however, invoked during the Falklands/Malvinas conflict. Directed mainly against Cuba, Latin American diplomats have argued that it has disguised, but not modified, the extent of US hegemony in Latin America. Since the breakup of the USSR, its purpose has become more questionable.

Roanoke (North Carolina)

The site of Sir Walter **Raleigh**'s two attempts to found an English colony in North America. The first, in 1585, ended after trouble with the island's native population and the threat of an attack from Spanish forces. The second, an expedition of 117 men, women and children in 1587, had disappeared without trace by 1591 when a relief force found the town of 'Ralegh' deserted. The failures demonstrated that colonization was too expensive an enterprise for one individual to support, even with the monarch's blessing, and that settlements had to be defensible, Roanoke being an exposed island without a good harbour.

'Robber Barons'

US political epithet. First applied to railroad magnates like Jay **Gould** and Jim Fisk who exploited both national and local government, shareholders and the public in their ruthless operations, it was later extended to those like Cornelius **Vanderbilt**, Andrew Carnegie and John D **Rockefeller** who developed large-scale enterprises by coercive horizontal and vertical integration.

Robeson, Paul (1898–1976)

US singer, actor and civil rights activist. He achieved world fame through his Broadway, London and film appearances and his recording of *Ol' Man River*. During the 1930s and **World War II** he became increasingly active in civil rights and left-wing political causes, and outspoken in his sympathy for the USSR (for which he was eventually to receive a Stalin Peace Prize in 1952), all of which brought him into close association with the Communist Party. This he openly continued during the anti-communist campaigns of the post-war years, and the mis-reporting of his speech at the Paris World Peace conference in 1949 (in which he was said to have denounced the US government for a racial policy similar to that of **Hitler**), provoked accusations of treason. He was denied a passport between 1952 and 1954 and shadowed by the **FBI**. Living in Europe (England and then East Germany) between 1958 and 1963, his final years after returning to the USA were of increasing illness and withdrawal.

Robinson, Sir John Beverley (1791–1863)

Canadian politician. A prominent member of the **Family Compact**, he became Attorney-General in 1818 and later Chief Justice (1829). In his determination to protect the imperial connection and the elite status of the Compact, he insisted on classifying American settlers as aliens and depriving them of both their property and their political rights. In 1830 he became President of the Executive Council and during the rebellion of 1837 he was responsible for the execution of two rebels and the banishment of twenty-five.

Rockefeller, John D(avison) (1839–1937)

US industrialist and philanthropist. After high school he entered the business world, and showed a talent for organization. In 1875 he founded with his brother, William, the Standard Oil Company, securing control of the US oil trade. In the late 19c his power came under strong public criticism. He withdrew from active business in 1897, and devoted the rest of his life to philanthropy. He gave over US$500 million in aid of medical research, universities and churches, and established in 1913 the Rockefeller Foundation 'to promote the wellbeing of mankind'. ▷ **Republican Party**

Rockefeller, Nelson A(ldrich) (1908–79)

US politician. A grandson of John D **Rockefeller**, he served as US assistant Secretary of State (1944–5). He became Republican Governor of New York state (1958–73), sought the Republican presidential nomination in 1960, 1964 and 1968, and in 1974 became Vice-President (1974–7) under President **Ford**.

Rockingham, Charles Watson Wentworth, 2nd Marquess of
(1730–82)

British politician. As leader of a prominent Whig opposition group, he was called upon to form a ministry in 1765. He repealed the **Stamp Act**, affecting the American colonies, then court intrigues caused his resignation (1766). He opposed Britain's war against the colonists. He became Prime Minister again in 1782, the year he died. ▷ **American Revolution**

Roe v Wade (1973)

US Supreme Court decision legalizing abortion. It struck down state laws which prohibited abortion within the first three months of pregnancy on the grounds that the right to privacy, which included the right to have an abortion, was protected by due process.

Roosevelt, (Anna) Eleanor (1884–1962)

US humanitarian and diplomat. The niece of Theodore **Roosevelt** and wife of Franklin D **Roosevelt**, she became active in politics during her husband's illness from polio and proved herself invaluable to him as an adviser on social issues when he became President. In 1941 she became Assistant Director of the Office of Civilian Defence and after her husband's death in 1945 extended the scope of her activities, becoming a US delegate to the UN Assembly (1945–53, 1961), chairman of the UN Human Rights Commission (1946–51) and US representative to the General Assembly (1946–52).

Roosevelt Corollary (1904)

Amendment to the **Monroe Doctrine** enunciated by Theodore **Roosevelt** which stated that the USA had a duty to prevent political instability and financial mismanagement in the countries of its Caribbean 'backyard'. In its crudest form it was a justification for Roosevelt's 'big stick' and **Taft**'s 'dollar diplomacy' policies, and sanctioned US military intervention in Haiti (1915–34) and the Dominican Republic (1916–24). Such interference was theoretically reversed by F D **Roosevelt**'s 'good neighbour' policy of 1934 but this has not precluded further overt and covert interventions in Guatemala (1954), Cuba (1961), Dominican Republic (1965), Nicaragua (1979–87), Grenada (1983) and Panama (1989).

Roosevelt, Franklin D(elano) ('FDR') (1882–1945)

US politician and 32nd President, the fifth cousin of Theodore **Roosevelt**. He became a lawyer (1907), a New York State Senator (1910–13) and Assistant Secretary of the Navy (1913–20), and was Democratic candidate for the vice-presidency in 1920. Stricken with polio in 1921, he recovered partial use of his legs and went on to become Governor of New York (1929–33). During his first 'hundred days' as President (1933–45), he bombarded the economic crises with his **New Deal** for national recovery (1933), and became the only President to be re-elected three times. At the outbreak of **World War II** he strove to avoid US involvement and instead provided economic resources to the Allies in the form of a 'lend-lease' agreement, but Japan's attack on **Pearl Harbor** (1941) left him no choice and the US entered the war. He met with Churchill and **Stalin** at the **Tehran Conference** (1943) and **Yalta Conference** (1945) to formulate post-war plans, including the **UN**, but died three weeks before the German surrender. Throughout his presidency, his wife, Eleanor **Roosevelt**, was active in human rights and after his death became the US delegate to the **UN**.

Roosevelt, Theodore ('Teddy') (1858–1919)

US politician and 26th President. Educated at Harvard, he became a member of the New York legislature (1881–84). In 1898 he raised a volunteer cavalry of cowboys and college athletes known as the **Rough Riders** in the **Spanish-American War**. Upon his return he was elected Governor of New York State (1898–1900). A Republican, he was elected Vice-President in 1900, became President on **McKinley**'s assassination (15 Sep 1901), and was re-elected in 1904. During his presidency (1901–9), he strengthened the navy, initiated the construction of the Panama Canal and introduced a '**Square Deal**' policy for enforcing anti-trust laws. He received the Nobel Peace Prize in 1906 for his mediation during the Russo-Japanese War (1904–5). As organizer of the **Progressive Party** as well as its candidate for the presidency in 1912, he was defeated by **Wilson**. ▷ **Bull Moose; New Nationalism; Republican Party**

Root, Elihu (1845–1937)

US politician and international lawyer. Educated in New York, he became a lawyer, US Secretary of War (1899–1904) and Secretary of State (1905–9). He helped to establish civilian government in Puerto Rico, as well as governing policies for Cuba and the Philippines. A supporter of the League of Nations and the development of the World Court, he was awarded a Nobel Peace Prize in 1912 for his promotion of international arbitration.

Rosenberg Affair (1953)
US treason trial. Julius and Ethel Rosenberg were found guilty, like Klaus Fuchs in Britain, of passing atomic bomb secrets to the USSR. The worth of the information they had passed to the Russians was dubious and the sentence of death passed by Judge Irving Kaufman was more a measure of US fears of **communism** and the anger felt at betrayal than a judicial decision. The Rosenbergs' prison letters aroused great sympathy in Europe, and their execution compounded the fears aroused by McCarthyism. ▷ **McCarthy, Joseph**

'Rosie the Riveter'
US epithet. The generic name given to US women employed in defence production during **World War II**. By 1944, over 50 per cent of workers in aircraft manufacture and shipbuilding were women and the number of married women in work had increased from around 15 per cent to almost 25 per cent. Their level of performance, in jobs for which they had previously been considered unsuitable, was so high that attitudes towards women in work were permanently altered.

Ross, Betsy (Elizabeth) (1752–1836)
Upholsterer, who won a place in American folk history by making the first ever Stars and Stripes, the flag of the Union, in 1776. According to popular legend, George Washington, Robert Morris and General George Ross visited her workshop in Philadelphia with their design for the new flag, but Betsy rejected their six-pointed stars, insisting that stars with five points would look much better. She prevailed, and the flag was made according to her design.

Rossi, Angelo (1878–?)
US politician. Elected Mayor of San Francisco in 1931 he was the first Italian-American mayor of a major US city, preceding Fiorello **La Guardia**'s election in New York by two years. In his three terms of office during the Depression, Rossi was considered

competent if not brilliant and is remembered for his compassion towards the old and unemployed.

Rouges
French-Canadian political party. The reform party of **Canada East** which began to emerge from the late 1840s as the Institut Canadien acquired branches in the major towns of the province, and as the newspaper, *L'avenir*, spread ideas derived from American republicanism and French radicalism. Under **Papineau**, and after his retirement A A Dorion, the party grew to be the major opposition to the conservative bloc, seeking repeal of the 1840 Act of Union, universal education for all and a democratic suffrage. Although the rouges opposed confederation, they joined with the **Clear Grits** and cooperated thereafter with the **Liberal Party** in federal politics. Within Quebec their liberalism earned the opposition of the Catholic Church and the ultramontane **Castors**.

Rough Riders
The nickname created by the press for the First US Volunteer Cavalry Regiment, commanded during the **Spanish–American War** by Colonel Leonard Wood (1860–1927) and Lieutenant-Colonel Theodore **Roosevelt**. The fabled Rough Riders' 'charge' up San Juan Hill in Cuba (1 July 1898) was actually carried out on foot. Roosevelt emerged from the conflict a war hero.

Rowell–Sirois Commission (1940)
Canadian Royal Commission on national economic problems. Appointed by Mackenzie **King** in 1937, the commission was chaired by N W Rowell and, after his resignation in 1938, by J N Sirois. Its remit was to find a way by which the Dominion government, after R B **Bennett**'s New Deal had been declared unconstitutional, could administer federal aid without infringing provincial rights. The commission's report analysed regional economic inequalities in depth and recommended a fundamental revision in the balance of federal and provincial powers. In particular it suggested that the Dominion should take over responsibility for social services (the major area of provincial expenditure), while in return the provinces should cease to levy income taxes and succession duties. A federal-provincial conference called to discuss the report in 1941 was torpedoed by the hostility of Ontario, Quebec and British Columbia (while Alberta had already boycotted the Commission itself), but in 1946 new

revenue-sharing proposals were accepted by all the provinces except Ontario, which acceded in 1950, and Quebec, which made its own agreement in 1954.

Royal Canadian Mounted Police ▷ Mounties

Ruby, Jack (1911–64)

US assassin of Lee Harvey **Oswald**. He shot Oswald at close range two days after the assassination of President **Kennedy**. A nightclub owner, Ruby was reputedly also a small-town gangster with Mafia links, who claimed to be avenging Jacqueline Kennedy.

Rush, Benjamin (1746–1813)

American physician and political figure. A member of the Continental Congress, he was a signatory of the **Declaration of Independence**. In 1786 he set up the first free dispensary in the US. His method of treatment of yellow fever was controversial, but he did pioneering work with the mentally ill and was the author of *Medical Inquiries and Observations upon the Diseases of the Mind* (1812).

Rush–Bagot Convention (1817)

An agreement between the USA and Britain to demilitarize the Great Lakes by limiting the number, tonnage and armament of ships on each side. The convention ended the threat of a Great Lakes arms race, but complete disarmament on the US/Canada border did not follow until decades later. The parties involved were acting US Secretary of State Richard Rush and British Minister to the USA, Charles **Bagot**.

Rusk, (David) Dean (1909–)

US public servant. Educated at Davidson College and Oxford, he became Professor of Government at Mills College, California (1934), and after war service held several government posts. In 1961 he became Secretary of State under J F **Kennedy**, and played a major role in the **Cuban Missile Crisis** of 1962. He retained the post under the Lyndon B **Johnson** administration, retiring in 1969.

Ryan, Claude (1925–)

Canadian politician. Replacing Robert **Bourassa** as the Quebec **Liberal Party** leader after the defeat of 1976, he was largely responsible, with Jean **Chrêtien**, for the successful campaign against secession in **Lévesque**'s referendum of 1980. However, his own suggestions for a decentralized federation with a Federal Council serving as a provincially-based watchdog were not favourably received by anglophones and he resigned the Liberal leadership after defeat by the **Parti Québecois** in the elections of 1981. He has remained a Minister of the National Assembly, and following the Liberal victory in 1985, he was named minister of education in the Bourassa government.

Ryerson, Adolphus Egerton (1803–82)

Canadian educationalist and politician. A Methodist minister and editor of the widely read *Christian Guardian*, Ryerson wielded tremendous influence. He constantly attacked the privileges of the Anglican church, pressing for the secularization and sale of the **Clergy Reserves**, and for the proceeds to be used to support a compulsory school system. A reformer until a visit to England in 1833, he was absent during the rebellion of 1837, and condemned William Lyon **Mackenzie**'s radicalism and readiness to use force. He opposed **Responsible Government**, supporting Sir Charles **Metcalfe** in the struggle with Robert **Baldwin** and **Lafontaine**, who suspected that he had joined the **Tories**. In 1844 he was appointed chief superintendent of education in Canada West, a post he held until 1876 and in which he established the educational system of Ontario.

S

Sacajawea (c.1786–1812)
A Shoshone woman, also known as Bird Woman. She was sold into slavery to a French-Canadian trader, who took her with him in 1804 when he joined the US transcontinental expedition of Lewis and Clark. Her participation was vital to the success of the expedition, which established an American presence in the Pacific Northwest. ▷ **Lewis and Clark expedition**

Sacco and Vanzetti Affair (1921–7)
US political *cause célèbre*. Nicola Sacco and Bartolomeo Vanzetti were arrested in 1920, during the Red Scare, for a post office robbery and murder in South Braintree, Massachusetts. During the trial, the prosecutor was allowed to deliver inflammatory anti-communist speeches by the judge, who privately called the two defendants 'those anarchist bastards'. Their conviction and sentence to death therefore caused an uproar throughout the world. In response Governor Fuller of Massachusetts appointed a committee to examine the case. It found that, although the trial judge had been in grave breach of official decorum, justice had been done. The two men died in the electric chair in 1927. Debate on the case continues.

Sadat, Anwar el- (1918–81)
Egyptian politician. After becoming President in 1970, he temporarily assumed the post of Prime Minister (1973–4), after which he sought settlement of the conflict with Israel. He met Menachem **Begin**, the Israeli Premier, in Jerusalem (1977) and at Camp David (1978), in which year he and Begin were jointly awarded the Nobel Peace Prize. He was assassinated while still in office in Cairo by extremists. ▷ **Camp David Accords**

St Alban's Raid (1865)
A Confederate attack made from Canada, on the town of St Albans, Vermont, during the **American Civil War**. Such raids

heightened tension between Great Britain and the USA during the Civil War, and fears of retaliation were one of the factors leading Canadians to confederation.

Saint Laurent, Louis Stephen (1882–1973)
Canadian lawyer and politician. In 1914 he became Law Professor at Laval University and was appointed counsel to the **Rowell–Sirois Commission** between 1937 and 1940. In 1941 Mackenzie **King** appointed him Minister of Justice and, unlike other Quebec Liberals, he supported King on conscription in 1944, for which he was made Secretary of State for External Affairs in 1946. King's own choice as his successor, Saint Laurent became Prime Minister in 1948, and enacted such social programmes as the extension of the old-age pension scheme and hospital insurance. Under his leadership, the Liberals were re-elected in 1949 and again, with a huge majority, in 1953; but he was defeated by the Conservatives under **Diefenbaker** in 1958 after a campaign that focused on the Liberals' arrogance in power.

St Lawrence Seaway
A system of canals, locks and dredged waterways providing a navigable channel from the Gulf of St Lawrence to the head of Lake Superior. In 1954 the Canadian and US governments cooperated on a project to establish a shipping lane 27 feet (8 metres) deep along the St Lawrence River; this was completed in 1959. The Welland Ship Canal is generally considered to be part of the present-day seaway.

Salem Witch Trials (1692)
An outbreak of hysteria in colonial Massachusetts in which accusations were made that witchcraft was being practised. The situation quickly outran the control of the town authorities. Arrests were made on the unsupported testimony of young girls and 19 people were executed. Judge Samuel Sewall later publicly confessed that the trials had been in error and that he believed no witchcraft had been practised. The ramifications of the episode have been attributed to the breakdown of Puritan control, the tensions of economic and social change focused on conflict between Salem Village and Salem Town, and wider provincial fears (awakened by the recall of the charter) as to its future after the Glorious Revolution.

SALT (Strategic Arms Limitation Talks)

The name given to two rounds of talks held between the USA and USSR to limit their nuclear weapons arsenals and slow down the arms race. The first began in Helsinki in 1969, designed to place a numerical limit on intercontinental nuclear weapons. An agreement (SALT I) was reached in 1972. SALT II talks began that same year, and agreement was reached in 1979. There developed, however, a hardening of attitudes in the West towards the USSR, brought on in large part by the Soviet refusal to allow on-site verification. Once the USSR invaded Afghanistan, US Senate ratification of SALT II was doomed. Both countries, nevertheless, initially kept to the limitations established in the agreement. The arms situation was ultimately transformed by the **Reagan–Gorbachev** arms reduction accord, the revolutions of 1989 and the break-up of the USSR in 1991.

Sanger, Margaret Louise (1883–1966)

US social reformer and founder of the birth control movement. Educated at Claverack College, she became a trained nurse, and married William Sanger in 1902. Appalled by the tragedies she encountered as a nurse, in 1914 she published a radical feminist magazine, *The Woman Rebel*, with advice on contraception, and two years later founded the first American birth-control clinic, in Brooklyn, New York, for which she was imprisoned. After later completing a world tour, she founded the American Birth Control League in 1921. Divorced in 1920, she married J Noah H Slee in 1922.

Santa Anna, Antonio López de (1797–1876)

Mexican soldier and dictator. The son of a colonial official, he served in the Spanish army and supported **Iturbide** in the struggle for Mexican independence, although he was one of those who deposed him in 1823. Dubbed the 'Hero of Tampico' because of his role in defending his country against Spanish attempts at reconquest, he was President from 1833 to 1836. Following a revolt in Texas by US settlers and the state's declaration of independence from Mexico (1836), Santa Anna defeated Texan forces at the **Alamo**, but was routed at San Jacinto River, and imprisoned. Dictator in 1839 and 1841–5, he returned to power on two occasions (1846 and 1853) at the head of Conservative groups, from Mexico and Puebla, anxious to preserve their *fueros* from Liberal attack and to preserve central control over the republic.

An exile for many years, he was permitted to return to Mexico in 1872, and died in Mexico City. ▷ **Mexican War**

Santa Fe Trail

A trading route from west Missouri through Kansas and Colorado to Santa Fe in New Mexico. The trail was pioneered by William Becknell in 1821, the year of Mexico's independence from Spanish rule. It remained a commercially important route for over 50 years, but declined after the Santa Fe railway was opened in 1880.

Saratoga, Battle of (Oct 1777)

One of the most important engagements of the American Revolution. Actually fought near modern Schuylerville, New York, the battle brought the defeat of a large British army under John **Burgoyne** by American continental troops and militia under Horatio Gates. The outcome ended British plans to cut New England off from the rest of the states, and encouraged French intervention on the American side.

'Saw-off'

Canadian political manoeuvre. It was used by the Conservative Party during the late 19c in order to deplete the already impoverished Liberal Party's funds. After a particularly close election result, they would file a petition alleging irregularities under the Controverted Elections Act. Given the number of numerically small constituencies, there were many opportunities to use the device. Whether or not the petition was successful, the Liberal Party had to pay. If it was upheld then the election was void, and the expense of another election incurred. If the Liberals won, they still had to bear the legal costs.

Scalawags

US political epithet. A derogatory term for white Southerners who cooperated with occupying forces during the era of **Reconstruction** following the **American Civil War**. Many Scalawags had never favoured secession, and some were principled opponents of slavery.

Schechter Poultry Corporation v US (1935)

US Supreme Court decision striking down the National Recovery Administration. Nicknamed the 'sick chicken' case, it was one of the very rare unanimous decisions reached by Court. Chief Justice Charles Evans **Hughes** argued that the enabling act had permitted an unconstitutional delegation of legislative power to the code authorities and that the Schechter brothers' business was entirely conducted within the state of New York. It could not be regulated, therefore, by a federal agency which derived its powers from the interstate commerce clause of the **US Constitution**. The decision provoked President Franklin **Roosevelt**'s 'horse and buggy' retort, but the loss of the **NRA** proved to be more of a symbolic defeat than a material blow to the **New Deal**.

Schurz, Carl (1829–1906)

German-born US politician and journalist. He was forced to flee Germany after his involvement in the revolutionary movement of 1848–9, and settled in the United States in 1852. He promoted the emancipation of slaves, and in 1860 campaigned for the presidential nomination of Abraham Lincoln. He then served as US minister to Spain (1861–2) before joining the Union Army in which he became Brigadier general of volunteers (1862) and a commander of troops on several occasions including the Second Battle of Bull Run. From 1869 to 1975 he was US Senator from Missouri, and from 1877 to 1881 was secretary of the interior in the Republican government of President **Hayes**. He was editor of the New York *Evening Post* (1881–3), wrote biographies of Henry Clay (1887) and Abraham Lincoln (1889) and in the 1890s wrote for *Harper's Weekly*.

SCLC (Southern Christian Leadership Conference)

US **civil rights** organization formed in 1957 by Martin Luther **King** and other ministers to pursue racial integration, primarily in the South, through non-violent protest. As ministers they were natural leaders in their communities, able to explain their aims in terms of the Christian creed, and in a rhetoric which their people understood. An unsuccessful campaign in Albany, Georgia, in 1961 demonstrated the need for careful planning and preparation. In later campaigns the movement sought to develop a 'creative tension', inciting whites to overreact, attracting the media, and forcing the federal government to intervene. The success of this strategy was seen in Birmingham and Selma. However it did not succeed in Chicago where blacks lacked unity, the issues were far more complicated and white opposition was far more skilful. After the death of Martin Luther King, the organization lost much of its moral authority, though it still remained an important platform for leaders such as Ralph Abernathy and, later, Jesse **Jackson**.

Scott, Dred (?1795–1858)

US slave. He made legal and constitutional history as the nominal plaintiff in a test case that sought to obtain his freedom on the ground that he lived in the free state of Illinois: the celebrated **Dred Scott v Sanford** case (1848–57). The Supreme Court ruled against him, but he was soon emancipated, and became a hotel porter in St Louis, Missouri.

Scott, Thomas (c.1842–70)

Canadian Orangeman. He became a Protestant martyr when he was executed in 1870 during the **Red River Rebellion**. This disastrous incident was the root of later troubles which split the country, such as the execution of Louis **Riel**, the campaign of D'Alton **McCarthy**, and the **Manitoba Schools Act**.

SDI (Strategic Defense Initiative)

The proposal first made by President **Reagan** in 1983 (dubbed by the press 'Star Wars') that the USA should develop the technologies for a defensive layered 'shield' of weapons based primarily in space, able to shoot down incoming ballistic missiles. SDI has remained controversial because it seemed to overthrow the principle of 'mutual assured destruction' on which the idea of deterrence rested. Also the technologies it would need to perfect, such as directed energy, as well as being extremely difficult to achieve, might ultimately be used for offensive as well as defensive purposes.

Secession, Right of

The US constitutional doctrine that individual states enjoyed the right to leave (or secede from) the Federal Union. A development of the ideas of **nullification** and state sovereignty, it was espoused by the South before the **American Civil War**, and was discredited by that conflict.

Securities and Exchange Commission (SEC)

A body set up in 1934 in the USA during the **Great Depression** to regulate and control the issue of shares by corporations. It ensures that statements about the stocks being sold are accurate, and generally regulates the way US stock markets operate.

segregation

The cultural, political and typically geographical separation imposed by one racial or ethnic group over another. The term is most often applied to the subjugation of blacks by a politically dominant white elite, particularly through apartheid (literally 'separateness') in South Africa, and in the southern states of the USA c.1900–60. Segregation of blacks has been most apparent in housing, public facilities and transportation, and education. ▷ **civil rights; Jim Crow Laws**

Seminole

A Muskogean-speaking Native American group of south-east USA, descended from Creeks who settled in Florida in the late 18c, many intermarrying with runaway Negro slaves. One of the **Five Civilized Tribes**, they were drawn into war after aiding their fellow Creeks and fought against troops led by Andrew Jackson. They eventually surrendered to US forces in the 1820s and 1830s, and were moved to reservations in Oklahoma. ▷ **Native Americans**

Senate

One of the two chambers of the US Congress in which legislative power is vested. It consists of two Senators from each state (100 in all) chosen by the people to serve for six years; the terms of a third of the members expire every two years. It has powers of 'advice and consent' on presidential treaties and appointments. It is presided over by the US Vice-President, who has no part in its deliberations, but can cast the deciding vote if there is a tie. Legislation must pass both the House and the Senate before being signed by the President and becoming law. ▷ **Congress; House of Representatives**

Seneca Falls Women's Rights Convention (1848)

US feminist conference. It was organized by Elizabeth Cady **Stanton** and Lucretia **Mott**, who met after they had been denied seats

256

at the World Anti-Slavery Conference in London. Stanton and Mott protested against the contradiction of fighting for the rights of blacks when they themselves did not have the right to vote. The Convention adopted a Declaration of Sentiments modelled on the **Declaration of Independence**, maintaining that 'all men and women are created equal'. It not only claimed the vote for women but demanded equality in property, marriage and education. ▷ **slavery**

separation of powers

A political doctrine, associated with the 18c philosopher Montesquieu, which argues that, to avoid tyranny, the three branches of government (legislature, executive and judiciary) should be separated as far as possible, their relationships governed by checks and balances. The **US Constitution** is a practical example of an attempt at separation of powers. Parliamentary systems such as that of the UK do not have a complete separation, as the heads of the executive (ie government ministers) sit as members of the legislature. Nonetheless, most systems claim independence of the judiciary.

séparatisme

French-Canadian independence movement. It has played a significant role in Canadian politics since the 1960s. Some groups such as the **Front de Libération de Québec (FLQ)** were prepared to resort to the sort of violence which resulted in the **October Crisis**. One of the largest groups was the *Rassemblement Démocratique pour l'Indépendance* which was important in the defeat of **Lesage**, and became even stronger after the defeat of the **Parti Québécois** by the Liberals in 1985. Initially the federal government responded by attempting to remedy French-Canadian dissatisfactions through such initiatives as the Royal Commission on **Bilingualism and Biculturalism**. As Prime Minister, Pierre **Trudeau** reasserted the tradition of tolerant Canadianism for which **Laurier** had stood, in the hope that the province might be prevented from becoming racist and introverted. As a Québecois Liberal, his own success controverted the image of disadvantage that the separatist groups attempted to convey.

Sequoia (Sequoyah) (c.1770–1843)

Cherokee leader. He was a major figure behind the decision of the Cherokee to adopt as much as possible of white culture, while retaining their own identity, and personally invented an alphabet for their language. ▷ **Indian Wars**

Seven Days Battles (25 June–1 July 1862)
The final conflict in the Peninsular Campaign during the **American Civil War**, in which the Union drive to capture Richmond was halted.

Seward, William Henry (1801–72)
US politician. He won the governorship of New York State in 1838 and during the 1850s became a major spokesman for the anti-slavery movement and a leader of the **Republican Party**. His 'irrepressible conflict' speech was thought by many Democrats to be responsible for John **Brown**'s violence at **Harpers Ferry Raid**. He served as a very effective Secretary of State under Abraham **Lincoln**, taking an uncompromising attitude towards French support for Archduke **Maximilian** as Emperor of Mexico, which he saw as a breach of the **Monroe Doctrine**. Severely injured during the assassination of Lincoln, he recovered to remain Secretary of State in President Andrew **Johnson**'s cabinet. In 1867 he secured the purchase of Alaska from Russia, known as 'Seward's folly', by persuading a reluctant Congress of its vast mineral wealth.

sharecropping
A post-slavery system of tenant farming in the USA in which short-term tenants (usually black) worked land for landlords (usually white) for a percentage of the crop raised. As much a means of labour and racial control as of economic production, sharecropping provided the economic basis of post-slavery white supremacy, although it also provided a limited economic autonomy for tenants.

Shaw, Anna Howard (1847–1919)
English-born US minister and feminist. Her family migrated to the USA, and after a youth of considerable privation she studied at Albion College and Boston University. She became a Methodist minister, joined in the Women's Christian Temperance Union, and after striking up a friendship with Susan B **Anthony** became active in the women's suffrage movement. She became President of the **National American Woman Suffrage Association** in 1904, holding office until 1915.

Shawnee
Algonquian-speaking Native Americans who originally settled in Ohio, but who were pushed out of the area by the **Iroquois**. Defeated in 1794 by US forces at the Battle of Fallen Timbers, they were divided up into three sections and settled in Oklahoma. Their current population is c.2 200. ▷ **Algonquin; Native Americans; Greenville, Treaty of**

Shays, Daniel (c.1747–1825)
American revolutionary soldier. A farmer, who became a captain in the American army, after the War of Independence he returned to farming in Pelham, Massachusetts. However, like many of his fellows, he found himself subject to impossible economic demands. In 1786–7 he led a short-lived rural insurrection, known as Shays' Rebellion, against his state's policies on taxes and debt repayment. The rebellion was crushed by state troops, but it provided a major impetus to the drafting of the Federal Constitution at the **Constitutional Convention** of 1787.

Sherbrooke, Sir John Coape (1764–1830)
British general and Lieutenant-Governor of Nova Scotia (1811–16). His reputation was made during the Peninsular War and in the **War of 1812** he conducted a vigorous defence, which included the capture of Castine (Maine). He served as Governor-in-Chief at Quebec from 1816 until he suffered a stroke in 1818.

Sheridan, Philip Henry(1831–88)
US general. Educated at the US Military Academy at West Point, he commanded a Federal division at the beginning of the **American Civil War**, and took part in many of the campaigns. In 1864 he was given command of the Army of the Shenandoah, turning the valley into a barren waste, and defeating General Robert E **Lee**. He had a further victory at Five Forks in 1865, and was active in the final battles which led to Lee's surrender. He died at Nonquitt, Massachusetts, never having lost a battle.

Sherman, William Tecumseh (1820–91)
US general. Trained at the US Military Academy at West Point, he became a general in the Union Army during the **American Civil War**. His most famous campaign was in 1864, when he captured and burned Atlanta. He then commenced his famous 'March to

the Sea', in which his 60 000 men totally destroyed everything in their path en route to the coastal town of Savannah. His forces then moved north through the Carolinas causing even more devastation and gaining further victories which helped to bring forward the Confederate surrender. ▷ **Indian Wars; March through Georgia**

Shiloh, Battle of (6–7 Apr 1862)

An engagement in the **American Civil War** in Tennessee, near Corinth, Mississippi, between Union forces under General Ulysses S **Grant** and Confederate forces under Albert Sidney Johnston (1803–62). Losses were heavy on both sides, with 13 000 Union and 11 000 Confederate casualties.

Shultz, George P(ratt) (1920–)

US educator and public servant. He studied at Princeton and the Massachusetts Institute of Technology, then taught at MIT and Chicago, where he became Dean of the Graduate School of Business. He was named Secretary of Labor by President **Nixon** (1969), and went on to hold a number of high governmental posts before returning to private life in 1974. In 1982 President **Reagan** made him Secretary of State, a post he retained for the rest of the Reagan presidency.

Sifton, Sir Clifford (1861–1929)

Canadian politician. As Manitoba's provincial Attorney-General (1891–6) he vigorously defended the province's educational policy during the **Manitoba Schools Act**. After the problem was resolved, **Laurier** appointed him Minister of the Interior, and he established a very effective immigration policy which drew large numbers of Ukrainians and Doukhobors to the north-west. He broke with the Liberal government first in 1905, when he resigned over the restoration of separate schools in the north-west; and again when his defection over **reciprocity** helped the Conservatives to win the election of 1911. ▷ **Liberal Party**

Simcoe, Sir John Graves (1752–1806)

British colonial administrator. As Lieutenant-Governor of Upper Canada (1792–4), his intention was to re-create British social and political patterns in the colony, but his disagreements with both London and Canadian administrators caused his recall in 1796.

His most positive accomplishment was the use of the army in a huge road-building programme.

Sino-Japanese War (1937–45)
The war proper broke out in 1937 with the Japanese invasion of Tianjin (Tientsin) and Beijing, but this was only the ultimate phase of Japan's territorial designs on China. Manchuria had already been occupied (1931) and the puppet-state of Manzhuguo created in 1932. Nanjing was invaded in Dec 1937, and most of northern China was soon under Japanese control. From Dec 1941, US intervention became the major factor in the Pacific War, which ended with Japan's surrender in 1945. ▷ **World War II**

Sioux (Dakota)
A cluster of Siouan-speaking Native American groups belonging to the Plains culture. Having moved from further north into present-day north and south Dakota, they acquired horses, fought wars against other Native American groups, and hunted buffalo. They were later involved in clashes with advancing white settlers and prospectors, and were finally defeated at **Wounded Knee** (1890).

Sitting Bull (c.1834–90)
Native American warrior. The chief of the Dakota Sioux, he was a leader in the Sioux War of 1876–7. He is remembered especially for his role in the Battle of the **Little Bighorn**, following which he escaped to Canada, but surrendered in 1881. After touring with Buffalo Bill's Wild West Show, he returned to his people, and was present in 1890 when the army suppressed the 'ghost dance' messianic religious movement inspired by the Paiute Wovakq. Sitting Bull was killed during the army's action. ▷ **Native Americans; Cody, William F; Indian Wars**

slavery
A system of social inequality in which some people are treated as items of property belonging to other individuals or social groups. There have been different types and conditions of slavery throughout human history, and slavery has been present in societies that have otherwise been considered advanced. Slaves have often been captured peoples, considered part of the spoils of war. At one extreme, slaves have been worked to death, as in the Greek mining

camps of the 5c and 4c BC. At the other, slaves have been used less as chattels and more as servants, working in households, and to an extent even administering them and acting as tutors to young children. The institution of slavery was one of the major issues over which the **American Civil War** was fought.

Smalls, Robert (1839–1915)

US sailor and politician. A slave in Charleston, South Carolina, who with his brother shanghaied a Confederate paddle steamer, the *Planter*, and sailed it through Confederate guns to the Union fleet blockading the port. Later he enlisted as a pilot in the Union navy. Smalls was one of the 200 000 blacks who crossed to the Union lines and served as spies and guides in unfamiliar territory, as well as working as labourers. After the war his military service provided a springboard for a local political career in South Carolina, in the course of which he served in the US House of Representatives.

Smith, Alfred Emanuel (1873–1944)

US politician. He rose from newsboy to be Governor of New York State (1919–20 and 1923–8) with an impressive record of liberal reform. 'Al' Smith was beaten as Democratic candidate for the US presidency in 1928, and later became an opponent of President Franklin D **Roosevelt**'s **New Deal**.

Smith, Goldwin (1823–1910)

Canadian publicist. Regius Professor of Modern History at Oxford (1858–66), he settled permanently in Canada in 1871, and founded a chair of history at Toronto. He became one of the major figures in **Canada First**, and in *Canada and the Canadian Question* (1891) he argued for the union of Canada with the USA.

Smith, John (1580–1631)

English colonist and explorer. He fought in Transylvania and Hungary, where he was captured by the Turks, and sold as a slave. After escaping to Russia, he joined an expedition to colonize Virginia (1607) and helped found **Jamestown**. He was saved from death by **Pocahontas**. His energy and tact in dealing with the Native Americans led to his being elected president of the colony (1608–9). He wrote valuable accounts of his travels, and died in London.

Smith v Albright (1944)
US Supreme Court decision that abolished the Texas **Democratic Party**'s whites-only primary elections on the grounds that these were part of the electoral procedures covered by the 15th Amendment's suffrage guarantees.

SNCC (Student Non-Violent Coordinating Committee)
US **civil rights** organization. An offshoot of the **SCLC**, it was convened in 1960 at Raleigh, North Carolina. As a member of the Adult Advisory Committee, Martin Luther **King** was influential in its early years, especially in establishing the non-violent strategy seen in the initial campaign against segregated lunch counters. In the face of the physical brutality encountered in voter registration campaigns, it became increasingly difficult to maintain this non-violence, particularly as SNCC was becoming alienated by King's emotive religious fervour and his readiness to accept compromise, especially after the march from Selma to Montgomery. The integrationist gradualism and legal strategies of such organizations as the **NAACP** also came under attack as SNCC became receptive to the idea of **Black Power**. Its President, Stokely **Carmichael**, resigned to join the **Black Panthers**. His successor, H Rap Brown, was even more militant and SNCC came to believe that only through activity outside the established party system and without the assistance of whites could blacks achieve their full rights.

Social Credit Party
Canadian political party. The monetary theory known as social credit (regarded as nonsense by most economists) was developed by a British engineer, Major Clifford H Douglas, during the early 1930s. It held that government should issue payments (social credits) to everyone, in order to balance consumers' buying power with agricultural and manufacturing productivity. It attracted the attention of an Albertan radio-evangelist, William Aberhardt, who spread the doctrine to the depression-hit prairie farmers. In the provincial election of 1935, the Social Credit Party came to power. The federal government, however, disallowed its attempts to implement its policies, and in a short time the party became just another free enterprise neo-conservative political party. As such, it retained power and had cleared the province's debts by the mid-1950s. In 1952 it also defeated the Liberal–Conservative coalition in British Columbia, and throughout the 1950s it grew

in federal strength. By 1962 **Diefenbaker** required its support to maintain his fragile hold on power, but in 1979 it contributed to a Conservative defeat when Joe **Clark** refused to bargain for its support in a vote of confidence. By the 1980s, however, the party had all but disappeared. ▷ **Créditistes**

Social Gospel
An early 20c movement in the USA concerned with the application of Christian principles to the social and political order in the service of the Kingdom of God. Among its most prominent leaders were Washington Gladden (1836–1918), Walter Rauschenbusch (1861–1918) and Shailer Matthews (1863–1941).

Sons of Liberty
An organization in the **American Revolution** that provided popular leadership in the resistance movement against Britain. Composed mainly of merchants, lawyers, artisans and small traders, it operated as an organized inter-colonial group in 1765–6, opposing the Stamp Act. Thereafter, the men who had taken part continued to provide popular leadership, helping to organize the First Continental Congress in 1774. The term was also used to describe all Americans involved in the revolutionary movement.

Spanish-American War (1898)
The war in which Spain lost the final remnants — Cuba, Puerto Rico and the Philippines — of its empire to the USA. If the war signalled the emergence of the USA as an imperial power, it marked the eclipse of Spain as one. Although the material loss to Spain was substantial, the psychological blow was devastating. The end of the once vast empire confronted Spaniards not just with their declining power and status, but also their sheer backwardness. There emerged a generalized, if unfocused, demand for the 'regeneration' of a 'decadent' nation. The 'Disaster of 1898' thereby triggered off a protracted internal crisis which culminated in the fall of the monarchy in 1931.

spoils system
The practice in US politics of filling public offices on the basis of loyalty to the party in power. Such appointments were made beginning with the early presidencies but became widespread in Andrew **Jackson**'s administration. The term itself derives from

Senator William Marcy's defence of the system: 'to the victors belong the spoils'. The corruption and scandals in Ulysses S **Grant**'s administration led to the passage of civil service reforms and examination requirements, resulting in the establishment of a career structure in government bureaucracies. ▷ **Albany Regency; mugwump**

Square Deal
The popular name for the domestic policies of US President Theodore **Roosevelt**, especially the enforcement of the **Anti-trust Acts**. The term was coined by Roosevelt during a speaking tour in the summer of 1902.

Stalin, Joseph (Iosif Vissarionovich Dzhugashvili) (1879–1953)
Georgian Marxist revolutionary and virtual dictator of the USSR. In 1922 he became General-Secretary of the Party Central Committee, a post he held until his death, and also occupied other key positions which enabled him to build up enormous personal power in the party and government apparatus. In 1928 he launched the campaign for the collectivization of agriculture during which millions of peasants perished, and the first five-year plan for the forced industrialization of the economy. In 1939 he signed the Non-Aggression Pact with **Hitler** which bought the USSR two years respite from involvement in **World War II**. After the German invasion (1941), the USSR became a member of the Grand Alliance, and Stalin, as war leader, assumed the title of Generalissimus. He took part in the **Tehran Conference**, **Yalta Conference** and **Potsdam Conference** which with other factors resulted in Soviet military and political control over the liberated countries of postwar Eastern and central Europe. From 1945 until his death he resumed his repressive measures at home, and conducted foreign policies which contributed to the **Cold War** between the USSR and the West. He was posthumously denounced by Nikita Khrushchev at the 20th Party Congress (1956) for crimes against the party and for building a 'cult of personality'. Under Mikhail **Gorbachev** many of Stalin's victims were rehabilitated, and the whole phenomenon of 'Stalinism' officially condemned by the Soviet authorities.

Stamp Act (1765)
A British Act passed by the administration of George **Grenville**, which levied a direct tax on all papers required in discharging

265

official business in the American colonies. It was the first direct tax levied without the consent of the colonial assemblies, and it caused much discontent in the colonies, six of which petitioned against it. (The measure provoked the colonists' famous slogan, 'No taxation without representation'.) The Act was withdrawn by the **Rockingham** government in 1766. ▷ **American Revolution**

Standish, Myles (Miles) (c.1584–1656)
English colonist. After serving in the Netherlands, he sailed with the *Mayflower* in 1620, and became military head of the first American settlement at Plymouth, and treasurer of Massachusetts (1644–9). He was one of the founders of Duxbury, Massachusetts in 1631, where he lived until his death. He is the subject of Henry Wadsworth Longfellow's poem 'The Courtship of Miles Standish'.

Stanfield, Robert Lorne (1914–   )
Canadian politician. In 1967 he took over the leadership of the Conservative Party from John **Diefenbaker** after a bitter fight. He sought French-Canadian support by proposing to accept bilingualism and special conditions for Quebec, but in doing so he lost the support of many anglophone Conservatives. A successful Premier of Nova Scotia, he failed to project himself in national politics and in 1976 was replaced by Joe **Clark**.

Stanton, Elizabeth Cady (1815–1902)
US feminist. Educated at Troy (New York) Female Seminary, she involved herself in the anti-slavery and temperance movements, and in 1840 married the abolitionist Henry B Stanton. In 1848 she and Lucretia Mott organized the first women's rights convention in Seneca Falls, NY. She was personally responsible for the emergence of women's suffrage as a public issue, but she regarded women's rights as a much larger problem. ▷ **National American Woman Suffrage Association**

START (Strategic Arms Reduction Talks)
Discussions held between the USA and the USSR, beginning in 1982–3 after President Ronald **Reagan** came to power and resuming after Mikhail **Gorbachev** became General-Secretary in 1985. They were concerned with a reduction in the number of long-range missiles and their nuclear warheads and were complicated

partly by issues of mutual distrust and partly by the need to deal also with other types of weapons. Agreements were reached on the abolition of intermediate-range nuclear missiles in 1987 (the INF Treaty) and on conventional forces in Europe in 1990 (the CFE Treaty). The way was then open for President George **Bush** to agree the START I Treaty with President Gorbachev in July 1991 and the START II Treaty with President Boris Yeltsin in Jan 1993. Roughly speaking, the two powers agreed to cut their long-range nuclear capability by two-thirds within 10 years.

states' rights

A US constitutional doctrine based on the Tenth Amendment that the separate states enjoy areas of self-control which cannot be breached by the federal government. Debate has surrounded the interpretation of this Doctrine. At issue are the concepts of the implied power of the federal government and the extent or limitations of that power. The doctrine has been applied inconsistently and to support opposing points of view. It was adopted by white Southerners between **Reconstruction** and the **civil rights** movement, and amounted to a code term for white supremacy.

Steinem, Gloria (1934–)

US feminist and writer. A journalist and activist in the 1960s, she emerged as a leading figure in the women's movement. She co-founded *New York* magazine in 1968, was a co-founder of Women's Action Alliance in 1971, and was a founder of the feminist *Ms* magazine.

Stevens, Harry H (1878–1973)

Canadian politician. A member of **Meighen**'s Conservative administrations in 1921 and 1926, he was Minister of Trade and Commerce in **Bennett**'s government from 1930. In 1934 he became chairman of the **Price Spreads Commission**, and after the controversy surrounding its recommendations, he resigned to found the Reconstruction Party. He was its only successful candidate in the 1935 election, and returned to the Conservative Party in 1939.

Stevenson, Adlai Ewing (1900–65)

US politician. Educated at Princeton, he became a lawyer, took part in several European missions for the State Department

(1943–5), and was elected Governor of Illinois (1948) as a Democrat. He helped to found the UN (1946), ran twice against **Eisenhower** as a notably liberal presidential candidate (1952 and 1956), and was the US ambassador to the UN in 1961–5.

Stevens, Thaddeus (1792–1868)
US politician. After graduating from Dartmouth College, he began a law practice at Gettysburg, Pennsylvania. He was an outspoken opponent of slavery throughout his years in Congress (1849–53 and 1859–68). A radical Republican leader during reconstruction, he actively pressed for the impeachment of President Andrew **Jackson** (1868).

Stimson, Henry L (1867–1950)
US politician. Appointed a US District Attorney in New York by President Theodore **Roosevelt**, he made his reputation in antitrust actions. In 1911 he became Secretary of War in President **Taft**'s administration and modernized the army in which, as an artillery colonel, he fought in France in 1917. President Calvin **Coolidge** sent him to Nicaragua to negotiate an end to the civil war, and then to the Philippines as Governor-General. He became Secretary of State in President Herbert **Hoover**'s cabinet, and was the chief negotiator for the USA at the London Naval Conference (1930). At the 1932 Geneva Conference on arms limitation, he issued the 'Stimson Doctrine', condemning the Japanese occupation of Manchuria. Recalled as Secretary of War (1940) by President Franklin D **Roosevelt**, his experience made him a formidable influence on wartime policy, and (fearing that an invasion would be too costly in Allied lives) his advice was crucial in President Harry S **Truman**'s decision to use the atom bomb against Japan.

Stokes, Carl Burton (1927–)
US politician. A black Democrat, he defeated Seth Taft, the white grandson of President William **Taft**, to become (with Richard Hatcher, in Gary, Indiana) one of the first black mayors of a major northern industrial city, when he was elected in Cleveland, Ohio, in 1967.

Strachan, John (1778–1867)
Canadian bishop. Prominent in the **Family Compact**, he sought to maintain the ascendancy of the Anglican Church against the

challenge of the Methodists (whom he accused of being American in origin and loyalty). As President of the Board of Education, his policy of keeping education under the clergy's control caused resentment throughout Upper Canada. In 1839 he became first Bishop of Toronto and opposed the Reformers over such issues as the secularization of King's College in 1849 and the **Clergy Reserves** in 1854. ▷ **Canada, Upper**

Students for a Democratic Society (SDS)
A radical splinter group of the movement opposed to US involvement in Vietnam, founded at Columbia University, New York City, and advocating social disruption and violence. Although the movement spread to over 200 universities, it was subject to factionalism. Two of its members were given punitive sentences in the Chicago Conspiracy Trial of 1969. ▷ **Vietnam War**

Stuyvesant, Peter (1592–1672)
Dutch administrator. He became Governor of Curaçao, and from 1646 directed the New Netherland colony. He proved a vigorous but arbitrary ruler, a rigid sabbatarian and an opponent of political and religious freedom, but did much for the commercial prosperity of New Amsterdam until his reluctant surrender to the English in 1664.

suffragettes
Those women who identified with and were members of the late-19c movement to secure voting rights for women. The vote was 'won' after the end of **World War I** (1918), though it was limited to those women of 30 years of age or over. The 19th amendment to the US Constitution (1920) gave women the vote in state and federal elections.

Sugar Act (1764)
British statute that attempted for the first time to raise colonial revenue without reference to the colonial assemblies. Its main aim was to impose and collect customs duties and to prevent illegal trade. The colonials responded with protest, but not outright resistance, and the Act was sporadically enforced until the complete breakdown of British–American relations. ▷ **American Revolution; Boston Tea Party; Stamp Act; Townshend Acts**

superpowers

The description applied during the **Cold War** period to the USA and the USSR, the two nations with economic and military resources far exceeding those of other powers. With the collapse of the USSR in 1991, it is sometimes argued that there is only one superpower left. But arguments concerning gross national product and real or potential military strength suggest that China, Japan and the European Community might merit the description if still in use.

Supreme Court

The highest federal court established under the **US Constitution**, members of which are appointed by the President with the advice and consent of the Senate. In addition to its jurisdiction relating to appeals, the court exercises oversight of the Constitution through the power of judicial review of the acts of state and federal legislatures, and the executive. It was created in 1789 and has comprised nine members since 1869.

Swann v Charlotte-Mecklenburg Board of Education (1971)

US Supreme Court decision ruling that if educational integration could only be achieved by **busing** students out of their neighbourhoods, cities were legally required to follow that policy.

Sweatt v Painter (1950)

US Supreme Court decision that a black law school in Texas did not satisfy the 'separate but equal' conditions laid down in **Gaines v Canada**. One of the conditions which the college could not supply was familiarization with those with whom the students would need to interact in their professional lives, most of whom, of course, would be white. The decision had profound implications for the future of segregated professional education.

Sydenham (of Sydenham and Toronto), Charles Poulett Thomson, Baron (1799–1841)

British Liberal politician. He was President of the Board of Trade from 1834 to 1839, and promoted free trade and commercial reforms. As Governor-General of Canada (1839–41), he secured the union of Upper and Lower Canada (1840), was responsible for the introduction of municipal institutions in Upper Canada, and advanced public works. He also set up a structural basis for **responsible government** in Canada.

T

Taft, Robert Alphonso (1889–1953)
US politician. The son of President William **Taft**, he studied law at Yale and Harvard and in 1917 became counsellor to the American Food Administration in Europe under **Hoover**. A conservative Republican, he was elected to the Senate from Ohio in 1938, and co-sponsored the **Taft–Hartley Act** (1947) directed against the power of the trade unions and the 'closed shop'. A prominent isolationist, he was Republican leader from 1939 to 1953, failing three times (1940, 1948 and 1952) to secure the Republican nomination for the presidency.

Taft, William Howard (1857–1930)
US politician and 27th President. Educated at Yale, he became a lawyer, solicitor general (1890), the first civil Governor of the Philippines (1901) and then Secretary of War (1904–8) under President Theodore **Roosevelt**. As President (1909–13), he continued Roosevelt's aggressive foreign policy and his policies favouring conservation and regulation of big business, and achieved an excellent record of legislation. But he was handicapped by having followed the flamboyant and popular Roosevelt. While he was in fact a fairly progressive president, the public, in favour of reform as a result of Roosevelt's politics, perceived him as conservative, and he was not re-elected. From 1913 he was Professor of Law at Yale, and from 1921 Chief Justice of the US Supreme Court, where he made administrative improvements. He was the father of Robert Alphonso **Taft**, the US Senator and Republican leader. ▷ **Republican Party**

Taft–Hartley Act (1947)
US labour legislation. It outlawed 'unfair' labour practices such as the closed shop, and demanded that unions supply financial reports and curtail their political activities. It also gave the US government the power to postpone major strikes endangering national health or safety for a cooling-off period of 80 days. The

National Management Relations Act, its official name, was passed over President Truman's veto by the first Republican-controlled Congress in almost 20 years to limit the power of the **National Labor Relations Act** (the Wagner Act) of 1935, which the Republicans believed had shifted the balance between employers and workers far too much in favour of the unions.

Tammany Hall
US **political machine** of the Democratic Party in New York City and State. It was originally a club (the Society of Tammany) founded in 1789, and in the late 19c and early 20c became notorious for its political corruption. Its power declined in the 1932 election, and although revived for a short time, it has ceased to exist as a political power in New York politics.

Taney, Roger Brooke (1777–1864)
US jurist. He was admitted to the bar in 1799 and Andrew **Jackson** made him Attorney-General in 1831 and Secretary of the Treasury in 1833. The Senate, after rejecting his appointment as Chief Justice in 1835, confirmed it in 1836. His most famous decision was in the **Dred Scott v Sandford** case, when he ruled that the Missouri Compromise was unconstitutional and that slaves and their descendants had no rights as citizens. This precipitated the Civil War, and injured the reputation of the Court for years thereafter.

Tariff Policy (Canada)
After 1846 Britain's policy of free trade allowed the colonial governments to cease imposing duties on foreign imports. Canada, however, needing revenue for development, decided to raise tariffs from a general level of 10 per cent in 1846 to 20 per cent or 25 per cent by 1859. British manufacturers protested through the Duke of Newcastle to the Finance Minister, A T **Galt**, but he asserted Canada's economic independence. In the early years of confederation tariffs produced three-quarters of all federal government revenue, and by 1879 they had been raised to an average of 25 per cent through the **Macdonald** government's National Policy, despite the complaints of fishermen and farmers. In 1897 **Fielding** sought to solve their problems by introducing a two-tier system, which he also tried to embody in an agreement

with the USA in 1911. Later tariff agreements within the **Commonwealth of Nations** were negotiated through **Imperial Conferences**, and since **World War II** within the framework of the General Agreement on Tariffs and Trade (GATT). The Tokyo round, completed in 1979, envisaged an average of 9 per cent on dutiable goods (comprising 35 per cent of Canadian imports) by 1987. These tariff reductions, however, have been coupled with Canadian import restrictions on textiles, clothing and agricultural products.

Tariff Policy (USA)

Tariffs have always been a focus of political conflict in the USA because of its sectional differences both nationally and regionally. Although historically the **Democratic Party** has been associated with low tariffs and its successive opponents with high tariffs, party cohesion has always been much less important than constituency interest. After the winning of independence, the **Articles of Confederation** gave individual states the power to impose tariffs, which caused severe problems for those like New Jersey, without major ports of entry. The constitution of 1787 reserved tariffs to the federal government, and since then there has been constant pressure from manufacturers to keep them high in order to protect their goods from foreign competition. Henry **Clay**'s 'American System' of 1816 recognized this as a legitimate interest, though the Southern states' cotton economy made them dependent on exports and they were therefore afraid that high tariffs imposed on British imports would instigate retaliatory measures. The 1828 'Tariff of Abominations' was so high that South Carolina, in the **nullification** controversy, refused to allow its enforcement. The compromise tariffs that helped to settle this crisis set the precedent for the 1830s, 1840s and 1850s when the Democratic Party's dominance in Congress ensured that tariffs were kept low. The **Whig Party**'s argument for protection now came to include the wages of the US working man as well as the profits of the manufacturer, and when taken over by the **Republican Party** this became national policy for half a century from the **American Civil War**. These high tariffs insulated American manufacturing from foreign competition during a period of declining price levels in the late 19c. With rising prices after 1900 the differential advantages high tariffs gave 'monopolies' was a major reason for the downward revision of the Wilson administration's Underwood Tariff in 1913. However, when the Republicans were returned to power they introduced the highest tariffs in US history, the Fordney–McCumber Tariff of 1922 and the Smoot–Hawley Tariff of 1930. Both were counter-productive, preventing foreigners from earning the dollars necessary to buy US crops and worsening US agricultural surpluses, but a measure of international responsibility was returned to tariff policy by the 1934 Trade Agreements Act. During the **Cold War** such was US economic hegemony that tariff policy as a domestic political issue receded into insignificance, though it always remained an instrument of foreign policy through the grant of 'most favoured nation' trading status, and of encouragement to friendly powers. In 1962, for example, the Trade Expansion Act allowed President **Kennedy** to establish an Atlantic Partnership with Britain by giving him the power to decrease tariffs in return for trade concessions. During the 1970s and 1980s, in spite of internal pressures for reviving an aggressive tariff policy against such competitors as Japan, the international dimensions of tariff policy have remained salient with negotiations proceeding primarily through the General Agreement on Tariffs and Trade (GATT) talks. ▷ **US Constitution**

Taylor, Zachary (1784–1850)
US general, politician and 12th President. He joined the army in 1808 and fought in several campaigns against the Native Americans. In the **Mexican War** (1846–8) he captured Matamoros, and won a major victory at Buena Vista, though heavily outnumbered. He emerged from the war as a hero, and was given the Whig presidential nomination. The main issues of his presidency (1849–50) were the status of the new territories and the extension of slavery there, but he died only 16 months after taking office. He was succeeded by Millard **Fillmore**. ▷ **Whig Party**

Teamsters' Union (International Brotherhood of Teamsters, Chauffeurs, Warehousemen and Helpers of America)
The largest US labour union, with over 1.5 million members. Founded in 1903, it was expelled from the **AFL–CIO** in 1957 for corruption, but was reaffiliated in 1987.

Teapot Dome Scandal (1923)
US political scandal. One of several in the administration of President Warren G **Harding**, it involved the lease of naval oil reserves at Teapot Dome (Wyoming) and Elk Hills (California)

by the Secretary of the Interior, Albert B Fall. He allowed no competition to the bids of Harry F Sinclair (Mammoth Oil) and Edward Doheny (Pan-American Petroleum), who had both lent him considerable sums of money. A Senate investigation uncovered the scandal and Fall was eventually sentenced to prison for one year and fined US$100 000. Sinclair and Doheny were cleared of bribery charges, although Sinclair did serve nine months in jail for contempt of the Senate. In 1927 the Supreme Court found that neither of the leases was valid and the oilfields were returned to the government.

Tecumseh (1768–1813)

Native American chief of the Shawnee and a gifted orator. He joined his brother, 'The Prophet', in a rising against the whites, which was suppressed at the Battle of Tippecanoe in 1811. He then passed into British service, commanding the Native American allies in the **War of 1812**, and fell fighting at the Thames in Canada. ▷ **Native Americans; Indian Wars**

Tehran Conference (28 Nov–1 Dec 1943)

The first inter-allied conference of **World War II**, attended by **Stalin**, **Roosevelt** and Winston Churchill. The subjects discussed were the coordination of Allied landings in France with the Soviet offensive against Germany, Russian entry in the war against Japan, and the establishment of a post-war international organization. Failure to agree on the future government of Poland foreshadowed the start of the **Cold War**.

temperance movement

An organized response to the social disruption caused by the alcoholism so widespread in the 18c and 19c. Temperance societies were started first in the USA, then in Britain and Scandinavia. The original aim was to moderate drinking, but prohibition became the goal. Federal prohibition became a reality in the USA in 1919, but was impossible to enforce and was repealed in 1933.

territory

In US history, the political status of an area prior to the attainment of statehood. It was held in two stages: in the first, an 'unorganized territory' was ruled by a judge; in the second, an 'organized' territory could elect its own legislature and non-voting delegate to Congress. ▷ **Ordinance of 1787**

Tet Offensive (Jan–Feb 1968)

A campaign in the **Vietnam War**. On 30 Jan 1968, the Buddhist 'Tet' holiday, the Viet Cong launched an attack against US bases and more than 100 South Vietnamese towns (which had been considered safe from guerrilla attack), the targets including the US Embassy in Saigon and the city of Hue. There were heavy casualties, including large numbers of civilians. US public opinion was shocked by the scale of death and destruction, and support for the war declined rapidly. The offensive proved to be a turning-point in the war: on 31 Mar 1968, President Lyndon B **Johnson** announced an end to escalation and a new readiness to negotiate.

Thompson, Sir John Sparrow David (1844–94)

Canadian statesman. He entered the Nova Scotia Legislature in 1877 and was premier of Nova Scotia in 1882. As minister of justice for Canada in 1885, he defended the execution (by hanging) of Louis **Riel**. He was knighted in 1888 for his securing of a fisheries treaty with the United States. In 1892 he was elected premier of Canada, an office which he held until his death.

Tilley, Sir Samuel Leonard (1818–96)

Canadian politician. He was one of the few who supported confederation in New Brunswick and this lost him the 1865 election. John A **Macdonald** ensured that he was given massive aid, including direct grants to help him win the 1866 election, and he joined the federal government in 1867. When Macdonald fell in 1873, he became Lieutenant-Governor of New Brunswick, but on Macdonald's return to power he again entered government as Minister of Finance, bringing in the National Policy tariff. Ill health forced his retirement in 1885, although he remained as Lieutenant-Governor until 1893. ▷ **Tariff Policy (Canada)**

Toltecs

A people (or peoples) who controlled most of central Mexico between c.900 and 1150, and were the last such dominant culture prior to the **Aztecs**. Their capital was at Tula, 50 miles (80 kilometres) north of Mexico City. The most impressive Toltec ruins are at Chichen Itzá in Yucatán, where a branch of the culture survived beyond the fall of its central Mexican hegemony.

Tories (USA)

Also known as Loyalists, those who remained loyal to the crown during the **American Revolution**. After the **Declaration of Independence**, loyalty to the crown became treason, punishable by imprisonment and confiscation of property. It was estimated that one third of the colonial population were loyalists. Many chose to leave the country during or after the revolution and sufficient numbers enlisted in the British Army to make up several regiments.

Townshend Acts (1767)

British statutes imposing taxes on five categories of goods imported into the American colonies, after successful colonial resistance to the **Stamp Act** (1765). The Townshend Taxes likewise met resistance from the colonists, and four categories were repealed in 1770. The fifth, on tea, remained in effect until the **Boston Tea Party**. The Acts are named after British Chancellor of the Exchequer, Charles Townshend (1725–67), who sponsored them.
▷ **American Revolution**

Transcontinental Railroad

The first transcontinental system in the USA, formed when the Central Pacific and Union Pacific railroads were connected in 1869. The route surveys undertaken during the 1850s all had serious sectional implications and not until after the Republican victory in 1860 was the central route chosen. This had the advantage of being straight and using the lowest mountain passes; however, building was still delayed by Native American attacks and high costs. The two railroads joined at Promontory Point near Ogden, Utah, in 1869. Both had received huge land-grants in order to finance the project, but Leland Stanford and his associates of the Central Pacific used their economic power as much for their own private financial gain as for national economic objectives. Their evasion of taxes and their discriminatory freight charges were largely responsible for the establishment of the Interstate Commerce Commission (1887) and the move toward regulation by the Populist and Progressive reformers of the late 19c and early 20c.

transportation

Sentence of banishment from England for those convicted of certain offences, introduced in 1597. Increasingly large numbers of English convicts were shipped to North America in the 17c and 18c, but the practice was ended by the **American Revolution**. As a result, the British government turned their attention to Australia. 162 000 convicts (137 000 males and 25 000 females) were transported to Australia from 1788 to 1868, mainly to New South Wales (1788–1840), Van Diemen's Land (1803–52) and Western Australia (1850–68). Most of the convicts were young, poorly-educated urban-dwellers convicted of some form of theft. In the early years of settlement, convict labour was used on public works; subsequently the typical fate of most convicts was assignment to private service.

Trent Affair (1861)

An incident between the USA and Britain during the **American Civil War**, in which the USS *San Jacinto* forcibly removed two officials of the Confederate States from the British ship *Trent* while in international waters. The issue provoked considerable British anger until the Confederate officials were released by the American Secretary of State.

Tripartite Declaration (May 1950)

This represented an attempt by Britain, France and the USA to limit arms supplies to Israel and the Arab states in the wake of the emergence of the state of Israel, in the hope that this would ensure some stability for the area. Arms supplies were to be conditional on non-aggression, and the signatories to the Declaration undertook to take action both within and outside the framework of the **UN** in cases of frontier violation. Closer French relations with Israel subjected the Declaration to some strain, and with the Soviet arms deal with Gamal Abd al-Nasser's Egypt in 1955 it became a dead letter.

Trotter, William Monroe (1872–?)

US journalist and militant **civil rights** activist. With George Forbes, Trotter founded the *Boston Guardian* in 1901. Bitterly opposed to Booker T **Washington**, he was sent to jail after heckling at a public meeting in Boston in 1905. Trotter joined the **Niagara**

Movement of his friend W E B **Du Bois**, but his distrust of its white members made him refuse to join the **NAACP**.

Trudeau, Pierre (Elliott) (1919–)

Canadian politician. Educated at Montreal, Harvard, and London, he became a lawyer, helped to found the political magazine, *Cité Libre* (1950), and was Professor of Law at the University of Montreal (1961–5). Elected a Liberal MP in 1965, he became Minister of Justice (1967) and an outspoken critic of Québecois **séparatisme**. His term of office as Prime Minister (1968–79 and 1980–4) saw the **October Crisis** (1970) in Quebec, the introduction of the Official Languages Act, federalist victory during the Quebec Referendum (1980), and the introduction of the **Constitution Act of 1982**. He resigned as leader of the **Liberal Party** and from public life in 1984.

Truman, Harry S (1884–1972)

US politician and 33rd President. He fought in **World War I**, was a presiding judge in the Jackson County Court in Missouri (1926–34), was elected to the US Senate as a Democrat in 1934 and became chairman of a senate committee investigating defence spending. He became Vice-President (1944) and, on Franklin D **Roosevelt**'s death (Apr 1945), President. He was re-elected in 1948 in a surprise victory over Thomas E Dewey. As president (1945–53) he ordered the dropping of the first atomic bomb on Japan in Aug 1945, which led to Japan's surrender. Following **World War II**, he established a 'containment' policy against the USSR, developed the **Marshall Plan** to rebuild Europe and created **NATO** (1949). He authorized the sending of US troops to South Korea in 1950, and promoted the Four-Point Programme that gave military and economic aid to countries threatened by communist interference. He established the **CIA** (1947) and ordered the **Berlin Airlift** (1948–9). At home, he introduced his '**Fair Deal**' programme of economic reform. ▷ **Democratic Party**

Truth, Sojourner (c.1797–1883)

US abolitionist. Born into slavery in New York State, she escaped from her master in 1827 and settled in New York City, where she involved herself in the religious enthusiasms of the day until 1843, when she became a travelling preacher. She joined the abolitionist movement and became an effective anti-slavery speaker. She eventually settled in Battle Creek, Michigan but remained active after the Civil War in the causes of freed slaves and also of women's rights. ▷ **abolitionism**

Tubman, Harriet (c.1820–1913)
US abolitionist. She escaped from slavery in Maryland (1849), and from then until the **American Civil War** she was active on the slave escape route (the **Underground Railroad**), making a number of dangerous trips into the South. She acquired fame among abolitionists, and counselled John **Brown** before his attempt to launch a slave insurrection in 1859. During the Civil War she was a Northern spy and scout, but was denied a federal pension until 1897. ▷ **abolitionism**

Tupper, Charles (1821–1915)
Canadian politician and diplomat. As Nova Scotia's Premier (1864–7), his was the primary responsibility for persuading it to join the confederation; but Joseph **Howe**'s opposition had been so effective that he delayed until John A **Macdonald** persuaded the imperial government to apply direct pressure, and terms more favourable to Nova Scotia had been included. He entered Macdonald's administration in 1870 and again in 1878. In 1884 he became High Commissioner in London and in 1896 Secretary of State in Mackenzie Bowell's short-lived government. In the same year he himself became Premier for 10 weeks and committed the wavering Conservative Party to remedial legislation in the controversy over the **Manitoba Schools Act**. The bill was talked out, however, and after the Liberals won the election of 1896, he led the Conservative opposition until 1900.

Turner, Nat (1800–31)
US slave insurrectionary. He learned to read, and in 1831 made plans for a slave uprising. He succeeded in killing his master's family and some 50 other whites. But as many as 100 slaves were killed and the revolt quickly collapsed. Captured after six weeks in hiding, he was brought to trial and hanged at Jerusalem, Virginia.

Tuskegee Institute
US educational establishment, founded in 1881 by Lewis Adams, a former slave, and George Campbell, a former slaveowner and banker of Macon County, Alabama, in the belief that education was essential to black progress. Pressure on the state legislature

gained a charter for the 'Tuskegee Normal and Industrial Institute' (it became simply the Tuskegee Institute in 1937) and US$2 000 p.a. for teachers' salaries. The character and purpose of the institute was predominantly shaped by Booker T **Washington**, its first principal, and its emphasis lay on trades and craft skills. However, its graduates also staffed black schools throughout the South in the succeeding generations, and the criticism that Tuskegee muted rather than encouraged black aspirations ignores the extraordinary difficulties overcome in its establishment and maintenance of a real indigenous educational tradition.

TVA (acronym for Tennessee Valley Authority)

US experiment in regional economic planning. A symbol of the renewed sense of national purpose brought by the **New Deal**, the TVA built on proposals current in the 1920s to harness the Muscle Shoals of the Tennessee River for hydro-electric power. The Tennessee Valley watershed, an area of 41 000 square miles, was to be controlled by dams which would not only generate cheap power and produce fertilizers, but open up many rivers to navigation and provide many new jobs. The TVA was no less an experiment in government, run by federally appointed commissioners, who had to cooperate with the five Southern state governments it directly affected, and to encourage democratic participation in the local resettlements made necessary by the dams.

Tweed, William Marcy ('Boss Tweed') (1823–78)

US criminal and politician. He was a Democratic alderman in New York City (1852–6), sat in congress (1853–5), and was New York state Senator (1867–71). One of the most notorious 'bosses' of **Tammany Hall** (he gained control of it in 1868), he was made commissioner of public works for New York City in 1870 and, as head of the 'Tweed Ring', controlled its finances. His gigantic frauds were exposed in 1871, and in 1873 he was convicted and imprisoned. He was released in 1875 but was rearrested for a civil offence; after escaping to Cuba and Spain (1875–6), he was extradited in 1876 and died in a New York jail.

Tyler, John (1790–1862)

US politician and 10th President. He became a lawyer, member of the Virginia state legislature (1811–16), a US Congressman (1817–21), Governor of Virginia (1825–7), and then a US Senator

(1827–36). Elected Vice-President in 1840, he became President on the death of William Henry **Harrison** in 1841, only a month after his inauguration. He remained in office from 1841–5. His most important accomplishments were the annexation of Texas and the **Webster–Ashburton Treaty**. He later remained active in politics, adhering to the Confederate cause until his death.

U

U-2 Incident (1960)
On 1 May 1960 a US U-2 spy plane was brought down over Sverdlovsk in the USSR. After US denials, Premier Nikita **Khrushchev** produced the pilot, Francis Gary Powers, and his photographs of military installations. President **Eisenhower** justified the flights as essential for US national security. Khrushchev took advantage of the situation at the scheduled Paris Summit Meeting a few days later, when he withdrew Eisenhower's invitation to visit the USSR and demanded that he condemn the flights. The President's refusal allowed Khrushchev to walk out of the summit and to blame the USA for its failure.

UN (United Nations Organization)
An organization formed to maintain world peace and foster international cooperation, formally established on 24 Oct 1945 with 51 founder countries. The UN Charter, which was drafted during the war by the USA, UK and USSR, remains virtually unaltered despite the growth in membership and activities. There are six 'principal organs'. The General Assembly is the plenary body which controls much of the UN's work, supervises the subsidiary organs, sets priorities, and debates major issues of international affairs. The 15-member Security Council is dominated by the five permanent members (China, France, UK, USSR and USA) who each have the power of veto over any resolutions; the remaining 10 are elected for two-year periods. The primary role of the Council is to maintain international peace and security; its decisions, unlike those of the General Assembly, are binding on all other members. It is empowered to order mandatory sanctions, call for ceasefires and establish peacekeeping forces (these forces were awarded the Nobel Peace Prize in 1988). The use of the veto has prevented it from intervening in a number of disputes, such as Vietnam. The Secretariat, under the Secretary-General, employs some 16 000 at the UN's headquarters in New York City and 50 000 worldwide. The staff are answerable only to the UN, not national governments, and are engaged in considerable diplomatic work. The

Secretary-General is often a significant person in international diplomacy and is able to take independent initiatives. The International Court of Justice consists of 15 judges appointed by the Council and the Assembly. As only states can bring issues before it, its jurisdiction depends on the consent of the states who are a party to a dispute. It also offers advisory opinions to various organs of the UN. The Economic and Social Council is elected by the General Assembly; it supervises the work of various committees, commissions and expert bodies in the economic and social area, and co-ordinates the work of UN specialized agencies. The Trusteeship Council oversees the transition of Trust territories to self-government. In addition to the organs established under the Charter, there is a range of subsidiary agencies, many with their own constitutions and membership, and some pre-dating the UN. The main agencies are the Food and Agriculture Organization, the Intergovernmental Maritime Consultative Organization, the International Atomic Energy Authority, the International Bank for Reconstruction and Development ('World Bank'), the International Civil Aviation Organization, the International Development Association, the International Finance Corporation, the International Fund for Agricultural Development, the International Labour Organization, the International Monetary Fund, the United Nations Educational, Scientific and Cultural Organization, the Universal Postal Union, the International Telecommunication Union, the World Meteorological Organization, and the World Health Organization. The UN has presently 160 members. It is generally seen as a forum where states pursue their national interest, rather than as an institution of world government, but it is not without considerable impact.

Underground Railroad

A loose network of safe houses, hiding places and routes in the USA to aid fugitive American slaves to reach freedom in the North or Canada. Never formally organized, it was active as early as 1786, but was most widespread and active between 1830 and 1860. Estimates suggest that it may have assisted some 50 000 runaways.

Union Nationale

French-Canadian political party. It was formed by a coalition of the Conservatives and *Action Libérale Nationale* to fight the 1935 provincial elections in Quebec. Its failure to win led to an amalgamation under Maurice **Duplessis**. With the support of the rural and small-business sector, it won an easy victory in 1936 on a platform of political, social and economic reform. In practice, this turned out to be anti-radicalism and pro-corporatism. In 1939 it was defeated after the intervention of Quebec Liberals in the federal government, but it returned to power in 1944 after accusing them of betraying nationalist rights, and it was to emphasize nationalist leanings thereafter. Duplessis maintained a very personal control of the party until his death in 1959, following which the party lost the 1960 election. In 1966 it regained power under Daniel Johnson, but he died in 1968 and very soon the **Parti Québecois** had seized the nationalist mantle. The *Union Nationale* lost the 1970 election and its support declined precipitously.

United Automobile Workers (UAW)

US labour union. Originally formed by the AFL under the aegis of the **NRA**, an attempt to impose a president on the UAW led to a revolt in the spring of 1936, when the members elected their own leader, Homer Martin, and enrolled in the CIO. The UAW had to operate in an industry dominated by three aggressively anti-union companies, General Motors, Chrysler and Ford. However, by Dec 1936 the union had become strong enough to demand official recognition from General Motors. This was refused, despite the Wagner Act, so an official strike began in Jan 1937, the workers sitting in rather than walking out. The employers brought in the police, who used tear gas, but ineffectually. Michigan Governor Frank Murphy refused to use the state militia to remove the strikers and demanded negotiations between the employers and John L **Lewis**, President of the CIO. Backed also by President Franklin D **Roosevelt**, these discussions led to the UAW being recognized by General Motors, who also promised not to discriminate against union workers. Later that year, the same tactic was used to gain recognition from Chrysler. ▷ **AFL–CIO; National Labor Relations Act**

United Mine Workers of America (UMW)

US labour union, formed in 1890 by an amalgamation of mining unions within the AFL and the Knights of Labor. After unexpectedly successful strikes in 1897 and 1900, and the election in 1898 of a vigorous young president, John Mitchell, the union consolidated its position in 1902 with a strike in the anthracite fields. When it demanded recognition, an increase in wages and shorter hours, the coalfield operators responded aggressively and lost public sympathy when violence broke out. President Theodore **Roosevelt** saw the conflict as of national economic importance, and the intransigence of the operators led him to force arbitration. This established an important precedent for government intervention in the future. Under the leadership of John L **Lewis** (1920–60) the union became part of the CIO, which merged with the AFL in 1957. Its membership, which was as high as 500 000 in the 1930s, declined steeply in the latter half of the 20c, along with the decline of the labour movement itself. ▷ **AFL–CIO**

US Constitution

The US Constitution embodies the concepts on which the US system of government is based. The law of the land since 1789, it establishes a federal republic, balancing the power of the states and that of the federal government. In the federal government, power is divided among three independent branches: legislative, executive and judicial. The constitutional document comprises a short preamble followed by seven articles which include: the organization, powers and procedures of the legislative branch (Congress); the powers of the President and executive; the powers of the judiciary, including the Supreme Court; the rights of the states; and procedures for amending the Constitution. The articles are followed by 26 amendments, the first 10 of which are known as the **Bill of Rights** (although later amendments also deal with **civil rights** issues). The others cover such matters as the election, death or removal of the President, and eligibility to stand for election to Congress. Drafted at the **Constitutional Convention** of 1787 held in Philadelphia, the Constitution was adopted after it had been ratified by nine of the states. ▷ **Articles of Confederation**

US Steel Corporation

The first billion-dollar corporation, established in 1900 when J Pierpont **Morgan** bought out other operators such as Andrew Carnegie and John D Rockefeller. The company had an appalling record of labour relations and, when strikes did break out in 1904 and 1909, it was ready to use strike-breakers and injunctions as well as higher wages to exclude unions. In 1907 Morgan extended the corporation into the South, but only in 1911 was a suit lodged against US Steel under the Sherman Anti-Trust Act. In 1919 the

AFL made a sustained effort to unionize the corporation but it retaliated by attacking the labour leadership as dangerous radicals and the mills were not unionized until the 1930s. Because of its strategic economic importance, presidents have periodically intervened in the steel industry's labour disputes, but with mixed results. In 1946 this initiated a wage/price spiral, but in 1962 US Steel's unilateral price increase, after the first strike-free settlement since 1954, became a major test of the administration's anti-inflation policy. 'My father always told me that steel men were sons-of-bitches, but I never realized till now how right he was', said President John F **Kennedy**, who successfully secured a rescission of the increase. ▷ **Anti-Trust Acts; US v US Steel**

US v Butler (1936)
US Supreme Court decision which struck down the Agricultural Adjustment Act (AAA). The court ruled the processing tax unconstitutional because it penalised the processors for the benefit of farmers, but Justice Harlan Fiske Stone dissented, arguing from the preamble to the **US Constitution** that the tax was legal since its aim was to 'provide for the general welfare'. The Soil Conservation and Domestic Allotment Act re-established the agricultural programme which was made permanent in 1938.

US v US Steel (1920)
US Supreme Court decision enabling **US Steel**, the largest corporation in the nation, to maintain its monopolistic domination of the industry on the grounds that some competitors were still in business. It was a decision typical of those made in the 1920s under Chief Justice William Howard **Taft**.

US War of Independence ▷ **American Revolution**

V

Valley Forge

An area in Chester County, Pennsylvania, USA, which was the winter headquarters of George **Washington** in 1777–8. His troops are renowned for the endurance and loyalty they showed while stationed there during the severe winter. ▷ **American Revolution**

Van Buren, Martin (1782–1862)

US politician and 8th President. He became a lawyer, state Attorney-General (1816–19), Senator (1821), Governor of New York (1828), Secretary of State (1829–31) and Vice-President (1833–7). He was a supporter of Andrew **Jackson** and a member of the group which evolved into the **Democratic Party**. His presidency (1837–41) began during the financial panic of 1837 and in response to this, he introduced the Independent Treasury system. This crisis overshadowed his term in office and he was overwhelmingly defeated for re-election by the **Whig Party** in 1840. In 1848 he ran unsuccessfully for President as the candidate of the **Free-Soil Party**, which opposed the spread of slavery.

Vance, Cyrus R(oberts) (1917–)

US lawyer and public servant. He studied at Yale and served in the navy, before entering private law practice. He held a number of government posts, and served as Secretary of State under President **Carter**, resigning in 1980 over the handling of the **Iran Hostage Crisis**, when US diplomats were held in Teheran.

Vanderbilt, Cornelius (1794–1877)

US financier. At 16 he bought a boat, and ferried passengers and goods; by 40, he had become the owner of steamers running to Boston and up the Hudson River. In 1849, during the gold rush, he established a route to California, and during the Crimean War a line of steamships to Le Havre. At 70 he became a railroad financier. He endowed Vanderbilt University at Nashville, Tennessee.

Vaudreuil, Philippe de Rigaud, Marquis of (c.1643–1725)
French soldier and colonist. Vaudreuil resented the French government's aim of controlling the colony of Canada, while failing to support it adequately. The failure to resolve the differences between the French forces under the Marquis of **Montcalm** and the *Canadiennes* under Vaudreuil did much to weaken their defences against British invasion. After the defeat, he attained the best possible terms for the **habitants**, securing both their religious and their property rights.

vendus
A derogatory term for those French-Canadians who, like Sir George Étienne **Cartier**, were alleged to have 'sold out' to anglophone Canada.

Versailles, Treaty of (1919)
A peace treaty drawn up between Germany and the Allied powers at Paris. Of the 434 articles, the most controversial was article 231 assigning to Germany and her allies responsibility for causing **World War I**, and establishing liability for reparation payments. Germany lost all overseas colonies, and considerable territory to Poland in the East. The Rhineland was demilitarized and to be occupied by Allied troops for up to 15 years, and German armed forces were strictly limited. ▷ **Paris Peace Conference**

Vicksburg, Battle of (1863)
A major success for Union forces during the **American Civil War**, in which General Ulysses S **Grant** captured Vicksburg and thus the Mississippi River, splitting the Confederate forces in two. Pressured by an impatient President **Lincoln**, Grant circumvented the impregnable cliffs protecting the city, captured the nearby city of Jackson and only then laid seige to Vicksburg. With bombardment from Unionist gunboats on the Mississippi River that lasted for six weeks, he forced the Confederate General, Pemberton, to surrender. The victory proved Grant's abilities as a general and Lincoln placed him in command of all the Union's western forces. The cause of emancipation was also helped by the use of black units in the campaign.

Viet Cong or **Vietcong** ('Vietnamese communists')
The name commonly given in the 1960s to the communist forces that fought the South Vietnamese government during the **Vietnam War**.

Vietnam War (1964–75)
A war between communist North Vietnam and non-communist South Vietnam which broadened to include the USA. It was preceded by the Indo-China War (1946–54) between France and the Viet Minh, which ended with the defeat of the French at Dien Bien Phu. The Geneva Conference left North Vietnam under the rule of Ho Chi Minh, while the South was ruled first by the Emperor Bao Dai and then by Ngo Dinh Diem. Elections were planned to choose a single government for all of Vietnam, but when they failed to take place, fighting was renewed. From 1961, in an attempt to stop the spread of **communism**, the USA increased its aid to South Vietnam and the number of its 'military advisors'. In 1964 following a North Vietnamese attack on US ships, President Lyndon **Johnson** ordered retaliatory bombing of North Vietnam. Although the US Congress never declared war officially, it passed the **Gulf of Tonkin Resolution** which authorized US forces in South-East Asia to repel any armed attack and to prevent further aggression. US bombing of North Vietnam was continued, and in 1965 the USA stepped up its troop commitment substantially. By 1968 over 500 000 US soldiers were involved in the war. As the conflict dragged on, victory against the elusive communist guerrilla forces seemed unattainable. Opposition to the war within the USA badly divided the country, and pressure mounted to bring the conflict to an end. In 1968 peace negotiations were begun in Paris, and in 1973 a ceasefire agreement was signed. Hostilities did not end until two years later when North Vietnam's victory was completed with the capture of Saigon (renamed Ho Chi Minh City).

Villa, Pancho (Francisco) (1877–1923)
Mexican revolutionary. The son of a field labourer, he followed a variety of modest occupations until he joined **Madero**'s uprising against **Diáz** (1911) and the Mexican Revolution made him famous as a military commander. In a fierce struggle for control of the revolution, he and **Zapata** were defeated (1915) by Venustiano **Carranza**, with whom Villa had earlier allied himself against the dictatorship of General Victoriano Huerta. Both Villa and Zapata

withdrew to strongholds in north and central Mexico, from where they continued to direct guerrilla warfare. In 1916 Villa was responsible for the shooting of a number of US citizens in the town of Santa Isabel, as well as an attack on the city of Columbus, New Mexico, which precipitated the sending of a US punitive force by President Woodrow **Wilson**. The troops failed to capture Villa and he continued to oppose Carranza's regime until the latter's death (1920), when he laid down his arms and was pardoned. He was murdered at his hacienda in Chihuahua.

Virginia Company
A joint stock company established in 1606 to promote English settlement in North America. It was responsible for the founding of Virginia in 1607 and for its governance until 1624, when it was dissolved. Despite high investments, the company never returned a profit.

Virginia Resolutions ▷ Kentucky and Virginia Resolutions

Volstead, Andrew John (1860–1947)
US politician. A lawyer, he entered Congress for the Republicans in 1903 and is best remembered as the author of the 1919 Volstead Act, which prohibited the manufacture, transportation and sale of alcoholic beverages. The purpose of the legislation, which remained in force until 1933, was to placate the influential temperance movement, and to divert grain to food production in the wake of **World War I**. In fact, **Prohibition** proved impossible to enforce effectively, and did little other than to create enormous profits for bootleggers and speakeasies, and to provide Hollywood with the inspiration for countless gangster movies.

Voting Rights Act (1965)
US suffrage legislation. The law prohibited all means by which the segregationist Southern states had been able to prevent blacks from registering to vote. The Attorney-General was empowered to dispatch federal registrars anywhere that local officials were obstructing registration of blacks; the act was so effective that 250 000 new black voters had been able to register before the end of the year.

voyageurs
The canoeists of the New French and Canadian **fur trade**.

W

Wagner Act ▷ **National Labor Relations Act**

Wagner, Robert Ferdinand(1877–1953)
US Senator and legislator. Born in Germany, he moved to the USA in 1885. He became a lawyer in 1900, but turned to politics, becoming a Democratic member of the New York legislature (1904–19). He served as a justice of the New York Supreme Court from 1919 to 1926, and was then elected Senator (1927–49). He was much concerned to improve conditions for factory workers, and under the **New Deal** he introduced financial and social legislation such as the National Industrial Recovery Act (1933), the Social Security Act (1935) and the **National Labor Relations Act** or Wagner Act (1935). He also implemented the Wagner–Steagall Act (1937), which created an agency to facilitate purchase by the public of low-cost housing. ▷ **NRA**

Wall Street Crash
The collapse of the US stock market in Oct 1929. The Crash followed an artificial boom in the US economy (1927–9) fuelled by speculation. Panic-selling resulted in 13 million shares changing hands on 24 Oct, and 16 million on 29 Oct, causing widespread bankruptcy and a massive rise in unemployment. ▷ **Great Depression**

War Measures Act (1914)
Canadian statute. Enacted in the first weeks of **World War I**, it gave the federal government extraordinary powers. It could bypass the normal legislative process, suspend *habeas corpus* and deport without trial. It also included emergency economic regulations. Under the Act, immigrants from Germany and Austria-Hungary were forced to carry special identity cards and to register at regular intervals, while 8 300 aliens were interned in special camps. During **World War II** 6 414 orders were made under the War Measures Act, and it was still in force in 1945 when a defector

from the USSR, Igor Gouzenko, informed on a Soviet spy ring in Canada. The findings of a Royal Commission led to the arrest, under the Act, of the single communist MP, a prominent scientist and members of the civil and military service. In 1970 the Act was again invoked to deal with the **October Crisis** in Quebec.

War of 1812

The name given to the hostilities between the UK and the United States between 1812 and 1814. Its deepest causes went back to some unfulfilled provisions of the Peace of 1783, which secured American independence. However, war was eventually provoked by the persistent refusal of Britain to recognize American neutral and maritime rights. After 1793, in the course of the Anglo-French war, American trade was incessantly disrupted and American ships continually subjected to boarding and their crews to impressment. The most notorious of these incidents, the surrender of the USS *Chesapeake* to HMS *Leopard* in 1807, provoked commercial retaliation with President Thomas **Jefferson**'s embargo policy. The failure of both this and the subsequent Non-Intercourse Act to alter British policies eventually left the USA no other option but to declare war, if independence was to mean anything at all. Ironically, war began as British policy was changed with the suspension of the Orders in Council, while the most decisive military engagement, the American victory at the Battle of New Orleans, occurred after peace had been made at the Treaty of **Ghent** (Dec 1814). Apart from this defeat, the British were militarily more effective, victorious with their Native American allies against American attempts to gain Canadian land, and even burning down the Capitol and the White House in Washington. The peace treaty marked a change in the attitude of Britain towards the USA, allowing a mutually beneficial commercial relationship to develop and for the USA marking the achievement of substantive, as well as formal, independence.

War of Independence, US ▷ American Revolution

War Powers Act (1973)

US legislation requiring that Congress be consulted before the President dispatch US forces into battle, and that Congress approve any continuance of war beyond 60 days. Public confidence in the executive branch had been greatly diminished after the **Vietnam War** and **Watergate** and, like the Freedom of Information Act, this act aimed to limit its power.

Warren, Earl (1891–1974)
US jurist. He attended the University of California law school and was admitted to the bar. An active Republican, he became Governor of California (1943–53) and made an unsuccessful run for the vice-presidency in 1948. He became Chief Justice of the US Supreme Court in 1953. The Warren Court (1953–69) was active and influential, notably in the areas of civil rights and individual liberties. It was responsible for the landmark decision in **Brown v Board of Education of Topeka, Kansas** (1954), which outlawed school segregation, and for Miranda v Arizona (1966), which ruled that criminal suspects be informed of their rights before being questioned by the police. Warren was chairman of the federal commission (the Warren Commission) that investigated the assassination of President John F **Kennedy**.

Washington Armaments Conference (1921)
Three major treaties were negotiated at this conference held under the auspices of the US. The Treaty of Non-Aggression between US, Japan, Britain and France replaced the problematic Anglo-Japanese Alliance. A naval treaty between these powers and Italy agreed to limit new warships in proportion to the current strength of their navies. And a nine-power agreement divided the world into naval spheres of interest: British from the North Sea to Singapore, American in the Western Hemisphere and Japanese in the Western Pacific. These powers, together with the Netherlands, Belgium and Portugal, also committed themselves to the **Open Door Policy** in China.

Washington, Booker T(aliaferro) (1856–1915)
US black leader and educationist. He was born a slave in Franklin County, Virginia. After emancipation (1865), he was educated at Hampton Institute, Virginia, and Washington DC, then became a teacher, writer and speaker on black problems and the importance of education and vocational training. In 1881 he was appointed principal of the newly-opened Tuskegee Institute, Alabama, and built it into a major centre of black education. The foremost black leader in the late 19c, he encouraged blacks to focus on economic equality rather than fight for social or political equality. He was strongly criticized by W E B **Du Bois**, and his

policies were repudiated by the 20c **civil rights** movement. He is the author of *Up From Slavery* (1901).

Washington, George (1732–99)

US general and 1st President of the USA. He had an informal education, worked as a surveyor, and first fought in the campaigns of the **French and Indian War** (1754–8). He then managed the family estate at Mount Vernon, Virginia, becoming active in politics as a member of the Virginia House of Burgesses (1758–74). He then represented Virginia in the first (1774) and second (1775) Continental Congresses. In 1775 he was given command of the American forces, where he displayed great powers as a strategist and leader of men. Following reverses in the New York area, he retreated through New Jersey, inflicting notable defeats on the enemy at Trenton (1776) and Princeton (1777). He suffered defeats at Brandywine and Germantown, but held his army together through the severe winter of 1777–8 at **Valley Forge**. After the alliance with France (1778), he forced the surrender of **Cornwallis** at Yorktown in 1781, marking the end of the war. He then retired to Mount Vernon, and sought to secure a strong government by constitutional means. In 1787 he presided over the Constitutional Convention, and became the first President, an office he held from 1789 to 1797. He tried to remain neutral as political differences increased between the Federalists and Jeffersonians, and refused to continue for a third term in office. He retired to Mount Vernon and died two years later. ▷ **American Revolution**

Washington, Treaty of (1871)

Treaty between the USA and Great Britain (whose delegation included the Canadian Prime Minister, John A **Macdonald**). The USA demanded compensation for the damage inflicted during the **American Civil War** by Confederate raiders using arms manufactured in Britain, together with arbitration of the boundary south of Vancouver Island and the possession of the strategic island of San Juan. Canada hoped to negotiate a trade agreement in return for the admission of US fishermen to her inshore waters. Macdonald was well aware that Britain, above all, wished to establish good relations with the USA and he was determined that Canadian interests should not suffer. While the USA secured compensation and a favourable settlement of the boundary question, Macdonald ensured that Canada gained free navigation of the rivers of Alaska (crucial for the **Hudson's Bay Company**) in exchange for free US use of the St Lawrence. Fishing and trade agreements were also negotiated between Canada and the USA which formed the basis for a consultative arrangement to resolve problems before they became international crises involving the British.

Watergate (1972–4)

US political scandal. It led to the first resignation of a President in US history (Richard **Nixon**, in office 1968–74). The actual 'Watergate' is a hotel and office complex in Washington, DC, where the **Democratic Party** had its headquarters. During the presidential campaign of 1972, a team of burglars was caught inside Democratic headquarters, and their connections were traced to the White House and to the Committee to Re-elect the President. Investigations by the *Washington Post*, a grand jury and two special prosecutors revealed that high officials who were very close to Nixon were implicated, and that Nixon himself was aware of illegal measures to cover up that implication. A number of officials were eventually imprisoned. Nixon himself left office when it became clear that he was likely to be impeached and removed. ▷ **Iran–Contra Affair**

Webster, Daniel (1782–1852)

US lawyer and statesman. He was called to the Bar in 1805, and served in the US House of Representatives (1813–17). Settling in Boston as an advocate in 1816, he distinguished himself before the US Supreme Court in the Dartmouth College case (1818) and **McCulloch v Maryland** (1819), and as an orator became famous by his oration on the bicentenary of the landing of the **Pilgrim Fathers**. He returned to Congress (Dec 1823) as a Massachusetts Representative, and in 1827 he became a Senator. Having previously favoured free trade, in 1828 he defended the new protective tariff. His career was marked by a deep reverence for established institutions and for the principle of nationality. When the **Whig Party** triumphed in 1840, Webster was called into Benjamin **Harrison**'s cabinet as Secretary of State (1841–3). Under President **Tyler**, he negotiated the **Webster–Ashburton Treaty** (1842) with Britain, but resigned in May 1843. In 1844 he refused his party's nomination for President and supported Henry **Clay**. He opposed the **Mexican War**. In 1850 he voiced his abhorrence of slavery, and unwilling to break up the Union to abolish it, supported compromise measures. Under President **Fillmore**, he was recalled as Secretary of State (1850–2) to settle differences with England. He was one of the greatest of US orators.

Webster–Ashburton Treaty (1842)

An agreement between Britain and the USA which established the boundary between north-east USA and Canada. Among specific issues were disputed territory between Maine and New Brunswick and at the north end of Lake Champlain, navigation rights on the St John's River, and control of the Mesabi iron deposits. The treaty also established provisions for later joint action between the USA and Britain.

Weed, Thurlow (1797–1882)

US politician. A journalist who began his political career as a lobbyist for the *Rochester Telegraph*, he supported John Quincy **Adams** in the 1824 presidential election. Weed himself was elected to the state assembly, where he initially aligned himself with the **Anti-Masonic Party**. However, it was as a leader of the **Whig Party** in the state of New York that he exercised his greatest influence, contributing to the election of William **Seward** as Governor of New York (1838) and William Henry **Harrison** as President (1840). His support also proved vital for the presidential nominations of Henry **Clay** and Zachary **Taylor** in 1844 and 1848. In 1854, Weed joined the newly formed **Republican Party** and, when he failed to get the presidential nomination for his friend, Seward, backed Abraham **Lincoln**. After Lincoln's death, his influence declined.

Westminster, Statute of (1931)

Legislation which clarified that Dominions in the British Empire were autonomous communities and effectively independent, though owing common allegiance to the crown. The statute closely followed the formulation made by Arthur Balfour in the 1920s about the relationship of the Dominions to Britain and it also established a free association of members in the **Commonwealth of Nations**.

Westminster, Treaty of (1674)

Anglo-Dutch agreement that gave final recognition to English control of New York. Originally founded as the New Netherlands, the province was conquered by the English in 1664 and again, after another brief period of Dutch control, 10 years later.

Whig Party
One of two major US political parties during the decades prior to the **American Civil War**. The name was adopted in 1834 to signify opposition to President Andrew **Jackson** (1829–37). The Whigs stood for greater governmental intervention in the economy than did the Democrats, who followed Jackson, but both parties agreed on the necessity of keeping the slavery issue out of politics. The Whigs collapsed in 1854, precisely because the slavery issue could no longer be contained. Daniel **Webster** and Henry **Clay** were prominent members of the party.

Whiskey Rebellion (1794)
An insurrection of farmers in western Pennsylvania and Virginia against the excise tax imposed by the federal government on whiskey, which they made in large quantities from their crops of grain. The rebellion was suppressed by government forces led by Henry Lee and Alexander **Hamilton**.

Whiskey Ring (1875)
A conspiracy of distillers and tax officials during the administration of President Ulysses S **Grant** to defraud the government of taxes due on liquor: 238 people were indicted, including Grant's private secretary.

Whitney, Eli (1765–1825)
US inventor. Educated at Yale, he became a teacher, but then came to reside on a cotton plantation and devised the cotton-gin (patented in 1793). In 1798 he got a government contract for the manufacture of firearms, and made a fortune in this business, developing a new system of mass production.

Wilderness, Battle of (1864)
An indecisive conflict in the **American Civil War** between the Union army under General Ulysses S **Grant** and the Confederate army under General Robert E **Lee**, fought in the Wilderness area of Virginia. Both sides sustained heavy losses in a month of relentless fighting.

Wilkins, Roy (1901–81)
US civil rights leader. He began working for the NAACP in 1931, and became its executive director (1965–77). Throughout his career he fought to end segregation, rejecting the concept of separate development for blacks and opposing the black nationalism of both Marcus **Garvey** and the **Black Power** movement. Because of his insistence on using constitutional means to effect change, he fell out of favour in the 1960s with the more militant civil rights leaders.

Willard, Frances Elizabeth Caroline (1839–98)
US temperance campaigner. She studied at the Northwestern Female College, Evanston, Illinois, and became professor of aesthetics there. In 1874 she became secretary of the Women's Christian Temperance Union, and edited the Chicago *Daily Post*. She helped to found the international Council of Women.

Williams, Roger (c.1604–83)
English colonist, founder of Rhode Island. A member of the Anglican church, his espousal of Puritan beliefs led him to emigrate in 1630 to the Massachusetts Bay colony. He refused to participate in the church in Boston, believing it had not separated from the English church, and moved to Salem where, after challenging the authority of the Puritan magistrates over matters of personal conscience, he was persecuted and eventually banished. He took refuge with the Native Americans, then purchased land from them on which he founded the city of Providence in 1636. His colony was a model of democracy and religious freedom; he went to England in 1643 and 1651 to procure a charter for it and served as its President (1654–7).

Wilmot Proviso (1846)
A motion introduced in US Congress by David Wilmot (Democrat, Pennsylvania) to forbid the expansion of slavery into territory acquired during the Mexican War. It passed the House of Representatives but not the Senate, where the South and the North had equal strength. The debate was a major step in the politicization of the slavery issue.

Wilson, (Thomas) Woodrow (1856–1924)
US politician and 28th President. He practised law in Atlanta, later became a university professor and, in 1902, President of

Princeton University. He served as Democratic Governor of New Jersey (1911–13), and was elected President in 1912, running against Theodore **Roosevelt** and William Taft, and served two terms (1913–21). His 'New Freedom' program, establishing equality and opportunity for all men, created the Federal Reserve Board and the Clayton Anti-Trust Act (1914), which accorded many rights to labour unions. Wilson tried to keep the USA out of **World War I** but was compelled to enter the war in Apr 1917 to make the world 'safe for democracy'. He laid out his peace plan proposal in the **Fourteen Points**, and actively championed the idea of forming a **League of Nations**, which was part of the Treaty of **Versailles**. When the Senate rejected the treaty, his idealistic vision of world peace was shattered. In 1919 he was awarded the Nobel Peace Prize, but thereafter his health declined severely, and he never recovered.

Winnipeg General Strike (1919)

One of the most significant Canadian strikes, it began when the employers in the building and metal trades refused to negotiate a collective bargaining procedure or to raise wages. After two weeks, the Winnipeg Trades and Labour Council voted to strike in sympathy. Fearing, like business leaders, that unionization would damage industrial profitability, the federal government immediately intervened. Despite the strikers' non-violence, specials were brought in to replace the city police force. A peaceful march was broken up, one spectator killed and 30 injured. The strike came to an end; its leaders jailed for sedition and the premier's promise of a Royal Commission. It did, however, politicize the issues, and in Manitoba's provincial elections of 1920 four of the jailed strike leaders were elected as socialists. The following year J S **Woodsworth** became the first socialist member of the federal House of Commons, as a representative from Winnipeg. ▷ **Meighen, Arthur**

Winthrop, John (1588–1649)

English colonist. Educated at Cambridge, England, he became a lawyer, and in 1629 the first Governor of the Bay Company. He crossed the Atlantic to settle what would become Massachusetts and Massachusetts colony, and was re-elected Governor 12 times. His political and religious conservatism greatly influenced the political institutions that were formed in the Northern states of America.

Wolfe, James (1727–59)
British general. Commissioned in 1741, he fought against the Jacobites in Scotland (1745–6) and was sent to Canada during the Seven Years War (1756–63). In 1758 he was prominent in the capture of Louisbourg in Nova Scotia; the following year he commanded at the famous capture of **Quebec**, where he was killed.

Woodsworth, James Shaver (1874–1942)
Canadian social worker, Methodist minister and politician. Having emerged as the country's conscience following the **Winnipeg General Strike** and the federal elections of 1921, his social work in the cities showed him that his church's complicity with capitalist society compromised any capacity for reform. He then turned to politics, but in 1917 lost his job in provincial government for criticizing conscription. He also resigned his ministry as a protest against the Church's support for the war. Arrested for sedition (as an editor of the Winnipeg strikers' bulletin), although not convicted, the resulting publicity helped to spread his reputation as a spokesman for the disadvantaged. Well-informed also on the problems of the prairie farmers, he was a founder and President of the **CCF**. In 1926 he and A A Heaps were able to take advantage of the government's tiny majority: while **Meighen** refused to negotiate with them, Mackenzie **King** promised to introduce an Old Age Pensions Act and rescind the 1919 amendments to the Immigration Act and the Criminal Code. Woodsworth argued that both parties were corrupt and that it was his duty to use his parliamentary position to promote the cause of socialism. Although it took 10 years to repeal the 1919 amendments, the Old Age Pensions Act was passed in 1927. Winning his last election in 1940, Woodsworth was the one MP who voted against Canada's involvement in **World War II**, and his speech of conscience was heard in respectful silence.

Works Projects Administration (WPA) (1935–43)
A US federal agency established under President Franklin D **Roosevelt** to combat unemployment during the **Great Depression**. Originally called the Works Progress Administration, it built transportation facilities, parks and buildings. Some 8 500 000 people were employed during its history, including artists and writers as well as manual workers. ▷ **New Deal**

World War I (1914–18)

A war whose origins lay in the increasingly aggressive foreign policies as pursued by Austria-Hungary, Russia and, most significantly, Germany. The assassination of the heir to the Habsburg throne, Francis Ferdinand, at Sarajevo in Bosnia (28 June 1914), triggered the war which soon involved most European states. The USA remained neutral, even after the sinking of the *Lusitania* (1915). After three years of campaigning the Allies organized a large offensive for the Western Front in 1916, but were forestalled by the Germans, who attacked France at Verdun (Feb–July). To relieve the situation, the Battle of the Somme was launched, but proved indecisive. The Germans then unleashed unrestricted submarine warfare (Jan 1917) to cripple Britain economically before the USA could come to her aid. The USA declared war on Germany (2 Apr 1917) when British food stocks were perilously low, and the German submarine menace was finally overcome by the use of convoys. The American Expeditionary Force began to arrive in France in June 1917, commanded by General **Pershing**. By mid-1917, the Russian armies were defeated, revolution broke out in St Petersburg and Moscow, and Lenin's government sued for peace. In the spring of 1918, the Germans launched a major attack in the west, but after several months of success were driven back, with the USA providing an increasing number of much-needed troops. By Sep, the German Army was in full retreat, and signified its intention to sue for peace on the basis of President **Wilson**'s **Fourteen Points**. By Nov, when the armistice was signed, the Allies had recaptured western Belgium and nearly all French territory. Military victories in Palestine and Mesopotamia resulted in a Turkish armistice (31 Oct 1918); Italian victories and a northward advance by Franco-British forces finished Austria-Hungary (and Bulgaria). Estimated combatant war losses were: British Empire, just under 1 million: France, nearly 1.4 million; Italy, nearly $\frac{1}{2}$ million; Russia, 1.7 million; USA, 115000; Germany, 1.8 million; Austria-Hungary, 1.2 million, and Turkey 325000. About double these numbers were wounded. ▷ **Paris Peace Conference; Passchendaele, Battle of; reparations; Versailles, Treaty of**

World War II (1939–45)

A war whose origins lay in three different conflicts which merged after 1941: **Hitler**'s desire for European expansion and perhaps even world domination; Japan's struggle against China; and a resulting conflict between Japanese ambitions and US interests in the Pacific. After the German invasion of rump Bohemia-Moravia (Mar 1939), Britain and France pledged support to Poland. Poland was invaded (1 Sep), and Britain and France declared war on Germany (3 Sep), but they could not prevent Poland from being overrun in four weeks. For six months there was a period of 'phoney war', when little fighting took place, but the Germans then occupied Norway and Denmark (Apr 1940), and Belgium and Holland were invaded (10 May), followed immediately by the invasion of France. A combination of German tank warfare and air power brought about the surrender of Holland in four days, Belgium in three weeks, and France in seven weeks. Italy declared war on France and Britain in the final stages of this campaign. There followed the Battle of Britain, in which Germany tried to win air supremacy over Britain, but failed. As a result, German attempts to force Britain to come to terms came to nothing, not least because of Winston Churchill's uncompromising stance and the Congress vote for Lend-Lease aid. Germany launched submarine (U-boat) attacks against British supply routes, but also invaded Greece and Yugoslavia (Apr 1941). British military efforts were concentrated against Italy in the Mediterranean and North Africa. In June 1941, in line with Hitler's longheld hostility to the USSR, and in his quest for *Lebensraum*, Germany invaded her ally Russia along a 2 000 mile front, and German armies advanced in three formations: to the outskirts of Leningrad in the north, towards Moscow in the centre, and to the Volga River in the south. In the Far East, Japan's desire for expansion, combined with a US threat of economic sanctions against her, led to her surprise attack on **Pearl Harbor** and other US and British bases (7 Dec 1941), and the USA declared war against Japan the next day. In reply Japan's allies, Germany and Italy, declared war on the USA (11 Dec). Within four months, Japan controlled South-East Asia and Burma. Not until June 1942 did naval victories in the Coral Sea and at Midway stem the advance, and Japanese troops defended their positions grimly. The tide began to turn in the West with **Montgomery**'s victory over **Rommel** at Alamein. This was followed by the invasion of Algeria by US troops, who joined the British and the Free French force of General de **Gaulle**. The Axis forces were defeated in North Africa by May 1943. On the Eastern Front, the Germans were being defeated by the harsh winter and the reverses at Stalingrad (1942–3) and Kursk (May 1943). Leningrad was under siege for nearly $2\frac{1}{2}$ years, but the

Germans were driven out of the USSR in 1944. On 6 June (**D-Day**) of that year the Allies invaded Normandy from England and Paris was liberated (25 Aug). Despite German use of flying bombs and rockets against Allied bases, the Allies, led by Montgomery and Omar N Bradley, advanced into Germany and linked with the Russians on the River Elbe. The Germans surrendered unconditionally at Rheims (7 May 1945). Bitter fighting continued in the Pacific until Aug, when, with Japan on the retreat, the USA dropped two atomic bombs on Hiroshima and Nagasaki (6 and 9 Aug). Japan then surrendered on 14 Aug. Casualty figures are not easy to obtain accurately, but approximately 3 million Russians were killed in action, 3 million died as prisoners of war, 8 million people died in occupied Russia, and about 3 million in unoccupied Russia. Germany suffered $3\frac{1}{4}$ million military casualties, around 6 million total casualties, and lost a million prisoners of war. Japan suffered just over 2 million military casualties and just over $\frac{1}{4}$ million civilian deaths. France lost a total of $\frac{1}{2}$ million dead, and Britain and her Commonwealth just over 600 000. The USA suffered just over 300 000 casualties. It is also estimated that in the course of the German occupation of a large part of Europe, about 6 million Jews were murdered in extermination and labour camps, along with a million or more other victims. ▷ **Atlantic Charter; Bulge, Battle of the; Casablanca Conference; Lend-Lease Agreement; Normandy Campaign; Paris Peace Conference; Potsdam Conference; Yalta Conference**

Wounded Knee (29 Dec 1890)

The site in South Dakota of the final defeat of the **Sioux**. The 'battle' was in fact a massacre of men, women and children by US troops, finally suppressing the Ghost Dance cult inspired by the visions of the Paiute religious leader Wovoka. In 1973, members of the American Indian Movement occupied the site to protest at the conditions of Native Americans. Two people were killed in the ensuing seige by **FBI** agents and federal marshals. ▷ **Indian Wars**

X

XYZ Affair (1797)
A diplomatic incident between the USA and France. It arose when French agents, identified as 'X', 'Y' and 'Z', solicited a bribe from US agents sent to negotiate an end to maritime hostilities.

Y

Yalta Conference (4–11 Feb 1945)

A meeting at Yalta, in the Crimea, during **World War II**, between Winston Churchill, **Stalin** and **Roosevelt**. Among matters agreed were the disarmament and partition of Germany, the Russo-Polish frontier, the establishment of the **UN** and the composition of the Polish government. In a secret protocol it was also agreed that Russia would declare war on Japan after the war with Germany ended.

Yankee

The nickname for an inhabitant of New England, or Northerner in general (especially during and since the **American Civil War**). It is also a general term for people of the USA, especially among non-Americans. The source is obscure, but it may derive from the Dutch *Janke* (a derivation of *Jan*), used as a nickname by early settlers.

Yorktown Campaign (30 Aug–19 Oct 1781)

The final campaign of the **American Revolution**, in which the British Army under General **Cornwallis** was trapped at Yorktown in Virginia, by troops under George **Washington** and a French fleet under Admiral de Grasse (1722–88). The defeat destroyed the political will on the English side to continue the war. It brought the fall of Lord North, Prime Minister since 1770, and opened the way for peace negotiations.

Young, Andrew properly **Andrew Jackson Young, Jr** (1932–   )

US clergyman, civil rights leader and politician. He graduated in divinity from the Hartford Theological Seminary in 1955, and as a pastor in various black churches in the US South, became involved in the **civil rights** movement. As a staff member of the **SCLC** (Southern Christian Leadership Conference) until 1970, he worked with Martin Luther **King**, Jr, and Ralph **Abernathy**. He was first elected to Congress in 1972, and following the election of President **Carter** in 1976, he served as US ambassador to the **UN** (1977–9). He was mayor of Atlanta from 1982 to 1989.

Young, Whitney M, Jr (1921–71)

US civil rights leader. Born in Kentucky, he was a graduate in social work from the University of Minnesota. Executive director of the National Urban League from 1961 until his death, some of his social welfare proposals were incorporated into President **Johnson**'s anti-poverty programmes.

Z

Zapata, Emiliano (1879–1919)

Mexican revolutionary. The son of a mestizo peasant, he became a sharecropper and local peasant leader. After the onset of the Mexican Revolution, he occupied estates by force and mounted a programme for the return of land in the areas he controlled to the Native Americans. He initially supported Francisco **Madero** and, with a small force of men, was largely responsible for toppling the dictatorship of Porfirio **Díaz**. Along with Pancho **Villa**, he subsequently fought the **Carranza** government. Meanwhile, he continued to implement agrarian reforms in the southern area under his control, creating impartial commissions responsible for land distribution and setting up the Rural Loan Bank. He was eventually lured to his death at the Chinameca hacienda in Morelos.

Zapotecs

A Precolumbian Mesoamerican civilization of southern Mexico (300BC–AD300), influenced by Olmec culture. It was centred on Monte Alban, a ceremonial site located on a high ridge in the Valley of Oaxaca.

Zouaves

A body of troops in the French army, first raised from Algerian tribes in 1830, who dressed in flamboyant Moorish costume. During the **American Civil War**, several 'Zouave' style volunteer regiments were raised on the US side.